T0312146

The Museum as a Space of Social Care

This book examines the practice of community engagement in museums through the notion of care. It focuses on building an understanding of the logic of care that underpins this practice, with a view to outlining new roles for museums within community health and social care.

This book engages with the recent growing focus on community participation in museum activities, notably in the area of health and wellbeing. It explores this theme through an analysis of the practices of community engagement workers at Tyne & Wear Archives & Museums in the UK. It examines how this work is operationalised and valued in the museum, and the institutional barriers to this practice. It presents the practices of care that shape community-led exhibitions, and community engagement projects involving health and social care partners and their clients. Drawing on the ethics of care and geographies of care literatures, this text provides readers with novel perspectives for transforming the museum into a space of social care.

This book will appeal to museum studies scholars and professionals, geographers, organisational studies scholars, as well as students interested in the social role of museums.

Nuala Morse is a Lecturer in Museum Studies at the University of Leicester. Drawing on theories from social geography and museum studies, her research focuses on the 'social work' of culture professionals and the links between museum participation and health, wellbeing and recovery.

Critical Studies in Heritage, Emotion and Affect
In Memory of Professor Steve Watson (1958–2016)

Series Editors: Divya P. Tolia-Kelly, *University of Sussex* and
Emma Waterton, *Western Sydney University*

This book series, edited by Divya P Tolia-Kelly and Emma Waterton, is dedicated to Professor Steve Watson. Steve was a pioneer in heritage studies and was inspirational in both our personal academic trajectories. We, as three editors of the series, started this journey together, but alas we lost his magnificent scholarship and valued counsel too soon.

The series brings together a variety of new approaches to heritage as a significant affective cultural experience. Collectively, the volumes in the series provide orientation and a voice for scholars who are making distinctive progress in a field that draws from a range of disciplines, including geography, history, cultural studies, archaeology, heritage studies, public history, tourism studies, sociology and anthropology – as evidenced in the disciplinary origins of contributors to current heritage debates. The series publishes a mix of speculative and research-informed monographs and edited collections that will shape the agenda for heritage research and debate. The series engages with the concept and practice of Heritage as co-constituted through emotion and affect. The series privileges the cultural politics of emotion and affect as key categories of heritage experience. These are the registers through which the authors in the series engage with theory, methods and innovations in scholarship in the sphere of heritage studies.

Heritage in the Home
Domestic Prehabitation and Inheritance
Caron Lipman

Affective Architectures
More-Than-Representational Geographies of Heritage
Edited by Jacque Micieli-Voutsinas and Angela M. Person

The Museum as a Space of Social Care
Nuala Morse

For more information about this series, please visit: www.routledge.com/ Critical-Studies-in-Heritage-Emotion-and-Affect/book-series/CSHEA

The Museum as a Space of Social Care

Nuala Morse

Routledge
Taylor & Francis Group

LONDON AND NEW YORK

First published 2021
by Routledge
2 Park Square, Milton Park, Abingdon, Oxon OX14 4RN

and by Routledge
52 Vanderbilt Avenue, New York, NY 10017

Routledge is an imprint of the Taylor & Francis Group, an informa business

British Library Cataloguing-in-Publication Data
A catalogue record for this book is available from the British Library

Library of Congress Cataloging-in-Publication Data
A catalog record has been requested for this book

ISBN: 978-1-138-20767-7 (hbk)
ISBN: 978-1-315-46140-3 (ebk)

Typeset in Times New Roman
by codeMantra

This book is for community engagement workers in museums worldwide.

Contents

Figures

Preface

This book is about care in the museum. Talking about care in the museum is entirely ordinary – care for collections is central to museum work. But this book is not about objects. Rather, it is about care for people, care for communities, care for place and care for ideas. In this sense, care is a new way to approach museum work. This book is the first-considered exploration of what 'care thinking' might bring to scholarship and practice in museums, galleries and heritage sites more widely. Care in the museum is located and described through the practice of community engagement workers at Tyne & Wear Archives & Museums (TWAM), a large local authority museum in North East England. I approach care thinking as a geographer and museum studies scholar, and this book is an interdisciplinary project, drawing on theoretical approaches taken from a wide variety of disciplines including cultural geography, museum studies, feminist ethics and sociological studies of practice. From this local work and these interdisciplinary perspectives, I present the idea of the museum as a space of social care, which is introduced as a new theory, practice and ethics for museums, with implications well beyond the immediate sites of my empirical research.

The original intention for my research was to write about community engagement. This was led in part by frustration at the lack of meaningful discussion of practice from the perspectives of those museum practitioners involved in this work. Over many years, I had been involved with colleagues in this area of work, but we found that our work was often misunderstood, underestimated and undervalued. My original research sought to write up practice in order to write up its value. TWAM was the chosen case study, as a museum service with a long-standing commitment to this work, led by the Outreach team. I came to write about care quite quickly, although I had not planned to. Care was unmistakable in the work of my colleagues during engagement sessions and how they engaged with participants. Care was also the wider context: museum professionals at TWAM were working more often and more closely with health and social care partners and their clients to develop their outreach provision. Through this book, I develop care thinking in both these senses: care as relational and affective work and care as a unique form of 'museum' care – distinct from, but also allied to, formal care.

Close studies of everyday professional practice are still uncommon in a museum context, and this book marks itself out as perhaps the first to study community engagement work in detail, in a bid to uncover the logics that inform this practice. Inspired by the work of Annemarie Mol in science and technology studies, it describes the logic of care in museums' community engagement practice. In doing so, I present a different approach to the majority of those studying community engagement and participatory practices in museums who have followed a critical tradition to explore ongoing issues of power, knowledge and politics. These issues are still important in my own discussion of community engagement, but care thinking enables me to consider these matters in other ways. Methodologically, the project draws on approaches from practice theory and organisational studies but always with a clear attention to how the institutional life of museum workers is saturated with emotions and affective forms of labour. The process of researching the museum was inspired by Sharon Macdonald's work at the Science Museum, as I went 'behind the scenes' and embedded myself at TWAM to explore how the museum is made through everyday practice. While I also draw on the ethnographic tradition, this project is very different in presentation. What appears here are partial and selective moments from what I observed and activities that I took part in. My intention was to develop a manner of writing the museum that captured a sense of its work-worlds. I narrate these through short moments from practice to analyse care, participation and power relations. The reader might also notice the relative absence of a community voice and puzzle over this in a book about community engagement. This is another deliberate choice, linked to my focus on those professionals 'doing' community engagement work. I have sought to write in an accessible and practice-oriented manner to make clear the wider implication of care for museum practice. I write as an academic first, and practitioner second, so my key concern in the final write up that forms this book is to present the underlying logics of practice into a theoretical intervention.

Community engagement is an area of contemporary museum work that has relevance internationally, and a significant amount of discourse has emerged from the UK context, where it takes particular form linked to ideas of inclusion, tolerance and social justice. In recent years, there has been much new work on the role of museums as agents of social change drawing on examples of practice in UK museums (including TWAM). This is influencing international dialogue about the public function of museums. This book adds to this important scholarship. It also responds to innovative practice and research that is breaking new ground about the roles for museums in contributing to the health and wellbeing of communities, again in a British context. The project of the museum as a space of social care emerges from this specific national context; however, its possibilities and potential are much wider.

This book is foremost about care in the museum, but along the way, it brings together many more considerations and fundamental questionings: about the wider social role of the museum; about the politics of participation in museums; about the professionalisation of museum work; about bureaucratic structures and their effects on museum practice; about the benefits of cultural participation on health and wellbeing; about the impact of austerity on museums, health and communities. Each of these considerations touch upon areas that animate different interests in researching the museum in the twenty-first century, as an institution and as an idea. My hope is that readers will draw much more from my singular case study to bring to these wider debates.

Although a sole-authored project, this book would not have been possible without the support of others, and especially the teams at TWAM. The Outreach team became a second home during this work, and in many ways, it still is. It was here that I first started thinking about care. I am grateful to everyone who gave their time and allowed me to follow their work over the years and made me feel so welcome. The team is the inspiration for this book, and I hope that I have done justice to their work in my attempts to articulate their care-ful practice of community engagement, and in my efforts to forge meaningful connections between theoretical debates and everyday practice. I owe so much from this book to Zoë Brown who has led the team over many years and ignited my enthusiasm for this research. I remain deeply grateful to all the members of the Outreach team and its associates, Michael McHugh, Suzanne Prak-Sandilands, Kath Boodhai, Joanne Charlton, Sophie Robinson, Anita Moffit, Kylea Little and Robert Latham. In more ways than one, this book is for them.

I am also grateful to the museum service more widely. The director Iain Watson has been hugely supportive of this work, providing access to the information, staff and sites that form the research for this book. I am extremely grateful to everyone at TWAM who gave their time for this research over the years, from museum staff to health and social care workers and community project participants. Much of this research was made possible first through funding from the Economic and Social Research Council, and I am grateful for their support.

I am forever thankful for the advice and support of my academic and museum supervisors across the different periods of work that informed this book: Rachel Pain and Mike Crang at Durham University, Hazel Edwards and Morag Macpherson (then at TWAM), Helen Chatterjee at UCL. Colleagues in the School of Museum Studies provided comments on the manuscripts, and I am thankful for all their astute advice: Richard Sandell, Suzanne MacLeod, Amy Barnes and Simon Knell. Other academics and colleagues have provided inspiration and encouragement when it was most needed, and I am particularly grateful to Helen Graham, Ealasaid Munro, Hannah Turner, Piotr Bienkowski, Rhiannon Mason and all my Leicester colleagues. My thanks also to the series editors, Emma Waterton and Divya Tolia-Kelly, and with fond memories of Steve Watson. Finally, I owe a great deal of thanks to George Adamson for proof work and much more.

Nuala Morse, April 2020

Abbreviations

ACE	Arts Council England
BAME	Black and Asian Minority Ethnic groups
DCMS	Department for Culture, Media and Sport
HLF	Heritage Lottery Fund
ICOM	International Council for Museums
MLA	Museums, Libraries and Archives
MA	Museums Association
NEET	Not in Education, Employment or Training
SEU	Social Exclusion Unit
TWAM	Tyne & Wear Archives & Museums

1 Introduction

Discussions of care in the museum are plentiful. Care for objects is the very foundation of museum work. Care requires intimate knowledge of individual objects, their materials and their vulnerabilities. Prevention of harm or damage, keeping objects safe, is the basis of this care. Objects are treasured and gently handled, displayed or carefully stored away. In all these ways, care practices make the museum. But while care for collections is part of the well-described operational and technical field of museum studies, care for people is less well defined. In fact, it has hardly featured at all, despite a recent focus on relational work.[1] In scholarly discussion and practice, this is often described in terms of audience engagement, community collaboration and participation. What would it mean to talk of this work in terms of care? What does care look like in the museum? These are the two questions that I explore in this book.

Outside of museums, the language of care is most commonly associated with the world of health provision or the intimacy of parenting. Within feminist ethics, care is positioned as a fundamental activity and a way of being together (Barnes, 2006; Held, 2006; Tronto, 1993, 2013). Care is important because it is part of everyday life: we have all received care during our lives, and at times, we have been called upon to care for others. As an activity, caring is about how we demonstrate concern for the needs of another, and how we take responsibility for meeting those needs. In this book, I explore care from a number of perspectives including geography and the field of care ethics to establish how we might talk about care in museum work. My starting point is a deep examination of community engagement practice – that is, the work of museum professionals that is directed at engaging vulnerable or otherwise marginalised groups and individuals who tend not to visit museums. My specific focus is on the work of museums with groups accessing social care services and healthcare, mental health services and other support organisations. As I will go on to show, care is unmistakable in the practices of museum professionals across this range of engagement settings. Care describes the ways in which practitioners use museum resources to support participants to cope with and flourish in challenging circumstances they face, due to either ill-health or social exclusion. Building on this, I make the case for 'care thinking' and its application to other areas of museum work and the wider field of museum studies. This book is the first-considered exploration of care for the museum – as 'thinking', as practice and as ethics.

The central aim of this book is to propose a view of the museum as a space of social care, where practices and relations of care are central. In this view, the work of the museum is purposefully re-oriented through ideas of care: care for things, care for stories, care for the issue, care for people, care for the community, care for staff, care for the present and the past and care for the future. Such an orientation to care opens up new ways of thinking about museum work, its aims and purposes and the skills and commitments required in practice. The museum as a space of social care also describes a new form of the museum within a wider landscape of community support organisations for people in need of care, either formal care or broadly defined. The universality of care I argue provides an approach with broad appeal and application across countries and contexts. Indeed, we all need care. At the same time, there is an urgency to this argument at a time when the habit of caring for others is largely devalued. We are faced with a loneliness epidemic and crises in social care and mental health support affecting millions worldwide, while care for our places and our environment is often discarded. As a space of social care, the museum can play a meaningful role in addressing these issues in partnership and collaboration. The hope is that this book will inform and stimulate new ways of thinking and working through care in international museum settings and support those striving towards more caring institutions. To guide these ambitions, the book draws out the wider implications of care thinking for different aspects of contemporary museum work and how the discipline itself approaches questions of practice and ethics in the museum. The museum as a space of social care is presented as a theory and practice-based concept with significant potential to strengthen the social role of the museum and reinvigorate the museum's capacity to create value for society in the twenty-first century.

To unravel what care looks like in the museum, I begin by exploring the practices of care and affective cultural work of community engagement workers in the museum. The practices that are described in this book include work with mental health charities, dementia care units, addiction recovery services, stroke survivor support groups and a community exhibition. One aim of the book is to articulate this professional area of museum work in terms of care and care practices. My discussion is primarily based on a long-term ethnographic research project that took place between 2011 and 2013 with Tyne & Wear Archives & Museums (TWAM), a large local authority museum service in the North East of England, follow-on research in 2016–2018 and my own involvement through research and practice in this broader area of museum work in the last eight years. The project of the museum as a space of social care emerges from these varied contexts.

My original focus on care was part of an empirical research project to describe the distinct quality of the community engagement work that I observed during my time at TWAM. Community engagement is a central facet of contemporary museum practice that is increasingly used as a strategy to democratise and pluralise museums and position them as social agents (Golding and Modest, 2013; McSweeney and Kavanagh, 2016; Sandell, 2002b; Sandell and Nightingale, 2012; Simon, 2010). In its broadest sense, it refers to how museums work with their diverse communities, and it is central to what we might term the 'participatory turn' in the museum. As a key domain of contemporary museum work, it is perhaps surprising that little serious attention has been paid to the professional practices of community engagement. The majority of scholarship has focused its attention either on the experience of participants within community engagement projects or on the wider political and institutional ramifications of this work. This book sets itself apart by attending to the experience, perspectives and everyday practice of those museum professionals 'doing' community engagement work, in an effort to understand the museum from the inside out. To explore the museum from the inside, I go 'behind the scenes' of the museum (Macdonald, 2002) into the work-worlds of community engagement workers. I follow these practitioners in the museum and out in the community in order to understand the work that they do. Through a close examination of practice, my aim was to understand something of the logic that shapes this practice: the emotional stances and rational objectives of this work. Over the course of this book, I describe this as *the logic of care*, inspired by Annemarie Mol (2010).[2] Mol developed the term through her careful ethnographic observations of practice in the clinic and the doctor's surgery in order to examine how people with diabetes care for themselves and are cared for by others. The 'logic of care' describes the inner workings of practice, how patients, doctors and nurses all negotiate ways of working towards 'good care'. As a logic, it describes the rationality of practice, as well as a 'style', a manner with plenty of creativity, perseverance and adaptability. In order to understand 'good care', we need to look closely at practice. Caring is an activity that is known only from within practice. Exploring care and its logics 'invites the exploration of what is appropriate or logical to do in some site or situation, and what is not' (Mol, 2010: 9–10). As such, it is not necessarily obvious to those who practice within it; it requires description to make explicit what motivates practice in each situation, and how they come together into a 'local, fragile yet pertinent coherence' (Mol, 2010: 10). Based on this logic in practice, Mol suggests that an ethics of care can be developed to determine good caring practices for people with diabetes. The museum is very different to the clinic, but as I will go on to discuss in this book, it is increasingly becoming a space of care in which service users, patients, support workers, care professionals and museum practitioners come together in community engagement sessions. In discussing the logic of care in the museum, I focus on two different dimensions and scales: the intimate relations, emotional registers, museum materialities and affective labour of care within community engagement sessions; and the wider geographies of care extended by museum community engagement schemes through their strategic partnerships with health and social care organisations in their localities. Across these different emphases, I place caring at the centre of community engagement work. Moving across these two scales, the book articulates the museum as a space of social care. The concept of 'social care' serves to connect the discrete affective practices of community engagement workers to the wider social role of the museum, and link it specifically to a growing area of practice around museums' contribution to health and wellbeing (Chatterjee and Noble, 2013). To make clear the wider potential of care for museums, in the final part of the book, I establish a theory of care for the museum.

The book is about revealing care in the museum, and it also has two other intentions. It begins with a doubt and a paradox. My sense of doubt is about the current framings of participation and community engagement in the museum literature. While participation is central to contemporary museum practice, policy and scholarship, debate appears to be caught in a bind. The critical scholarship reveals the hidden power inequalities that shape museum participation as a form of governance (Golding and Modest, 2013; Lynch, 2011a; Lynch and Alberti, 2010; Onciul et al., 2017; Smith and Waterton, 2009; Waterton and Watson, 2011). Despite the well-meaning intentions of staff to share power and hand over control, the museum continues to exercise invisible power, and so the experience of participants is reduced to 'empowerment-lite', leaving everyone, the museum included, 'generally dissatisfied' (Lynch, 2011b, 2014). Another aspect of this critique is a practice of engagement focused on 'doing for' rather than 'doing with', in a way that is further disempowering for participants (Lynch, 2011b). Notwithstanding these criticisms of current forms of participatory/community engagement practice, there has been a general trend in the critical scholarship to redeem participation – the museum just needs more and better forms of participation. In other words, the scholarship is currently caught in a critical impasse (Graham, 2012). I am not writing directly against the critical discourse, but I do seek to move beyond this impasse. To do so, I will suggest the logic of care as an alternative conceptual path to addressing these debates and as a way out of the impasse.

Introducing a new logic presupposes that another logic is already dominant within current discourse. A further intellectual contribution of this book is to put forward the argument that the current understandings of participation are based on a *logic of contribution*, with particular unintended consequences that limit discussions of participatory practice and community engagement in the museum. In the logic of contribution, community engagement is focused on the contribution that people make to the museum, whether an object, a story or a form of interpretation, and discourse is concerned with the ideas of participant choice and control within the process. Choice and control are important in community engagement, but I will also suggest there is also a lot more going on. Others have argued for the need to focus on the process over the outcomes of participatory work (Mygind et al., 2015). I argue we need to go further to engage with both process and outcomes at a more fundamental level. I suggest another logic is needed to better account for participatory practice (and community engagement) in the museum – this is where the logic of care comes in. The logic of care addresses issues of choice and control, but it does so through another set of optics. I discuss these in detail through the empirical case from practice throughout the book.

The paradox I want to discuss is found in my very earliest conversations with community engagement workers at TWAM, when they told me that *despite* the prevalence of community engagement in the official language of the museum, they felt their institution was resistant to their work. This feeling is echoed in the literature (Bienkowski, 2016; Lynch, 2011b). In my case, I was struck here by how often staff spoke about the challenges of doing community engagement work as coming from within their organisation. Community engagement workers clearly stated that they felt their practice was not understood, recognised or valued within the museum. Thus, this book uncovers how this work is perceived, managed and valued within the institutional frame of the museum and across different organisational departments, and it discusses the operational and institutional barriers to this work. There are links here to wider international debates and discussions within both academia and the museum sector. In the UK, where this study is set, a publication called *Whose Cake Is It Anyway?* (2011b), written by Bernadette Lynch on behalf of the Paul Hamlyn Foundation, discusses the findings of a collaborative investigation with 12 museums and their community partners into the achievements of participation and public engagement in museums and galleries. It concludes that

> [d]espite presenting numerous examples of ground-breaking, innovative practice, the funding invested in public engagement and participation in the UK's museums and galleries has not significantly succeeded in shifting the work from the margins to the core of many of these organisations (Lynch, 2011b: 5).

The report highlights a number of barriers to this work in relation to a reliance on short-term external funding, projects driven by museum agendas and an institutional view of engagement work as external to the 'core'. The report is significant in revealing the institutional power that shapes and constrains participation. TWAM was a partner in this original research, and several of these concerns are followed through in this book, but I also wanted to push these further. The experience of those working on the frontline of engagement projects as described in this book suggests more complex and fundamental ways in which institutions are resistant, despite the prevalence of participatory discourse in museums. To explore this, I am influenced by the feminist scholar Sara Ahmed (2012) and her work with diversity practitioners in universities, which begins with a similar paradox and examines the work that diversity practitioners must do in order to change their institutions. In this book, I describe how community engagement workers attempt to negotiate, resist and revise their institutional settings. These revisions are the basis from which to carve out the possibilities for the museum as a space of social care.[3]

Locating care in the museum

The theoretical project at the heart of this book is interdisciplinary, though it is most pertinent to the fields of museum studies and geography. I have already described two key interdisciplinary influences in the works of Annemarie Mol and Sara Ahmed. Another objective of this book is to bring together museum practice and theory with matters of concern in the discipline of geography, in particular geographers' engagement with notions of care. The book can be situated in what is often termed the 'geographies of care' (Bowlby, 2012; Lawson, 2007; Milligan et al., 2007; Power and Hall, 2018). This work is unified by concerns over the spaces, scales, relations, emotions and politics of care, focusing primarily on healthcare and welfare, but also beyond. Geographers have explored a range of ordinary yet unusual sites that act as spaces of care in the city, from drop-in centres (Cloke et al., 2005; Conradson, 2003; Darling, 2011; Johnsen et al., 2006) to allotments, community garden and parks (Knigge, 2009; Laws, 2009; Milligan et al., 2004), art sessions (Hall, 2013; Parr, 2008) and cafés (Warner et al., 2013). This book develops the idea of the museum as a space of care (following previous work in Morse and Munro, 2015), with attention given to the practices of care of museum professionals taking place both inside and outside the museum.

Another area of research that has influenced ideas in this book is the recent turn to emotions and affect in museum and heritage studies (Crang and Tolia-Kelly, 2010; Crouch, 2015; Smith et al., 2018; Tolia-Kelly et al., 2016; Waterton, 2014). Central to this work is a shift away from textual readings of heritage, 'towards engaging with experience, the sensory realm and affective materialities and atmospheres of the heritage landscape' (Tolia-Kelly et al., 2016: 1). It also connects with work that engages with the politics of emotions (ibid.). The book sits alongside this body of work by exploring these ideas in relation to the professional lives of museum staff and the felt qualities of community engagement sessions. Emotions are essential to understanding caring relations with others, so they have particular relevance for community engagement workers who engage with the feelings of participants as a matter of routine. This, in turn, affects them. In this book, I write about the intentional and improvised practices that come together to form the logic of care: how community engagement workers decide what is logical and appropriate to do in the emotionally charged sessions that take place in the museum. The final body of literature that influences thinking in this book and which I come to towards the end is the field of care ethics (Barnes, 2006; Held, 2006; Tronto, 1993, 2013). Care ethics provides a new way to conceptualise the relationships between museums and their communities across a variety of scales: from the relations that take shape in museum engagement projects to the wider social role of museums and how they connect with communities near and far. Within an ethics of care perspective, ideas of care extend beyond the daily activities of care to describe a wider set of attitudes at the centre of a serious moral philosophy. In the final part of the book, I use care ethics to develop the broader framework of the museum as a space of social care and to outline the significance of care to the broader project of museum ethics (Marstine, 2011; Marstine et al., 2011) and socially engaged museum practice (Janes and Sandell, 2019; Sandell, 2002b; Sandell et al., 2010; Sandell and Nightingale, 2012).

Community engagement practice in museums

Within museum studies, as yet, there is no fully developed body of literature for community engagement practice. There are important academic readers and edited collections on communities (Crooke, 2008; Karp et al., 1992; Peers and Brown, 2003; Watson, 2007), socially engaged practice (Sandell, 2002b; Sandell and Nightingale, 2012), and collaboration and participation (Golding and Modest, 2013; Onciul et al., 2017) including reflections written by experienced practitioners (McSweeney and Kavanagh, 2016). However, research about the actual *practice* of community engagement is far less well developed. In comparison, practitioners of museum education, a relatively recent area of museum work that was professionalised in the 1950s, have conceived of their work as a distinctive practice and sought to theorise it as such (Hein, 1998, 2006). Community engagement as a *professional practice* is rarely treated as an area of study in its own right. To a certain extent, this reflects a wider trend. Very little is written about practice in museum studies more generally, which 'lacks the kind of wide-ranging and detailed empirical studies of professional practice in museums that are found in practice-based enquiry in hospitals, schools and other professional setting' (McCarthy, 2016: 30). This book aims to respond to this gap. Conal McCarthy suggests this lack of writing around practice could be related to the lack of a unified sense of professional identity in museums. Indeed, this is mirrored in the scant amount of work on the nature of museum work as a profession as well as the limited attention given to the organisational settings in which it takes place (Morse et al., 2018). Attending to practice in the museum also brings us to a long-standing discussion about the relationship between theory and practice in museum studies. Following Anthony Shelton's (2013) project of critical museology, I locate the research that comprises this book at the 'productive overlap' between theory and practice (McCarthy, 2015: xxxv), as 'opposed to a mode of critique which stands outside looking inwards' (Mason, 2006: 29). My research thus provides an analysis of the current practice of community engagement from the ground up, in the case of a large local authority museum, from which I build an empirical picture of the contemporary museum.

As I will go on to explore in the book, the idea of 'community engagement' (in the UK certainly) occupies an ambivalent position within museum practice and the professional project of museum work. It is used to refer to a set of specific activities or a broad approach and ethos. There is no single term to define this specialised role in the museum. It is sometimes performed by staff across different teams (curatorial, collection-focused, learning or project-based), though more often it is the focused remit of dedicated roles. Posts are variably defined as outreach officer, community engagement co-ordinator or community engagement curator, amongst others. At TWAM, community engagement is undertaken by the (Assistant) Outreach Officers in the Outreach team, which I often refer to more generally as 'community engagement workers' throughout the book. The community engagement practice I describe is drawn from my observations at TWAM, where it takes on a particular local inflexion. At the same time, however, there are common threads across community engagement programmes across the UK and beyond. When talking about community engagement, I am referring specifically to work with external groups and localities, typically including people who do not or cannot visit museums. I do not mean audience engagement or the more generic public engagement. Community engagement refers to a more active and outward-facing type of museum work with a socially engaged ethos. Participants in community engagement projects are usually identified through established community groups, voluntary organisations or via health and social care services, and are typically considered vulnerable or otherwise socially excluded. In the examples I will go on to discuss, projects have included work with mental health charities, addiction services, care homes, the probation service, young people at risk of exclusion, refugee and asylum seeker groups and hospitals, amongst others. There is no standard template for community engagement, as it is a relational and responsive practice, and it is therefore tailored to the groups' interests and their needs. However, there are certain common features (Morse and Munro, 2015: 9): community engagement programmes usually follow a regular pattern, with small groups of people coming together weekly, fortnightly or monthly, either in the museum or in community spaces, often alternating between the two. Sessions are facilitated by museum professionals (and sometimes freelance artists) around a specific theme, collection, archive or exhibition, usually chosen in discussion with the group. Sessions can include exhibition visits and behind the scenes tours; object handling and object research; oral histories; contemporary collecting; and creative activities, including arts and crafts, photography or creative writing. Most projects have a creative outcome of some sort. Some programmes will result in a small display or a large co-curated exhibition, while other programmes may be more focused on building relationships between the museum and those communities that currently do not or cannot visit the museum.

We might favourably consider community engagement as a 'new' type of work in the museum that has developed over the last 30 years or so, with increasing recognition across the sector, but little theorisation. There was a sense throughout my empirical research of a professional group in the process of defining itself and its work at a practical level (for example, by writing strategic plans), as well as on a more fundamental level, in the process of articulating a sense of their professional selves. As such, community engagement is an emergent area of museum practice and an occupation 'in the making' that is explored in this book. To be clear, however, this book is not a 'how to' for community engagement. I am mindful when discussing professional practice that while professional bodies often talk of 'best practice' in order to produce guidelines and standards for museum workers, they rarely capture the complexity of museum cultures and relational work. The recent prominence of participation work across the museum and heritage sector has been accompanied by a proliferation of frameworks, toolkits, checklists and training packs.[4] These have tended to focus on practical information, including how to decide on the methods most suitable for the level of engagement required (from online surveys to consultation events, public meetings and community panels), or they have focused on how to measure social impact by providing guidance on evaluation methods and data-driven metrics. While these publications offer many important principles for developing work with communities, they are limited as instructional documents. While seeming to present concrete practicalities, in fact, they primarily operate at an abstract level. For example, the idea that collaboration should be underpinned by 'mutual benefit' is often cited as an essential criterion; however, the process of identifying benefits is not often discussed. It is assumed to proceed in linear, step-by-step stages when, in fact, collaborative work is often something that develops over time, through many interactions and conversations, and is often temporary and contestable, and requires work to initiate and sustain. Equally, lists of principles such as 'reciprocity' and 'respect' are important, but the emotional and administrative work through which 'respect' is something felt by those involved needs to be illuminated. Academic literature also tends towards these too-quick abstractions without really engaging with what happens in practice. Instead, then, of defining 'best' practice in relation to community engagement, the book examines what makes 'good' practice by attending to the affective registers, practical skills and working logics of this area of museum work.

When I write about practice I am interested in understanding *what people do* and *what people say they do*, following the directions set out in the field of sociology and the framework of practice theory in museums (Bourdieu, 1977; McCarthy, 2016; Schatzki, 1996, 2001). Practices are constellations of 'doings' and 'sayings' performed by groups of people, and since practice is not easily translatable into words (Hastrup, 1995), it must be uncovered through analysis of language, stories and activities, and the narrative of how practice develops over time. Sharon Macdonald explores this in her study of the Science Museum (2002) as she describes the various ways in which some practice is simply 'done' or 'got on with', appearing to unfold under its own momentum. Mol's proposal to examine caring logics is also aimed at uncovering practice as it takes place. Another important feature of practice theory is the notion that activities are located in non-propositional bodily abilities – that is, maintaining practice requires activity, skill development and a shared understanding of embodied knowledge or know-how (Schatzki, 2002: 3). The analytical purchase of a practice orientation is to bring clarity to the practice of community engagement (and participation more generally) in the museum and open it up to further critical interrogation. The conceptual questions that guided my analysis are: what consists the singularity of engagement work as a specific domain of museum practice? What are its distinctive qualities, dispositions, emotional registers, skills and the 'know-how' required for this work? What logic frames these activities and what makes this work 'work' for its participants? The book proposes a new theoretical framework for understanding these grounded practices through ideas of care and the logic of care in the museum to inspire expanding practice.

The social role of the museum

This book can be read alongside literature on the social role of museums and galleries. Since the 1980s (at least), a coming together of critical scholarship, identity politics, activist movements, the establishment of social history, the emergence of new digital media and complex socio-economic contexts have altered fundamental ideas about the roles that museums should play, now and in the future. This work has focused on the museum's relationship with its varied communities and in understanding new functions for the museum in the service of society. The idea that museums have a social role beyond or as part of their distinct cultural role as an institution that collects, preserves and educates about art and artefacts is becoming a broadly accepted way of framing the public function of the contemporary museum in practice and policy (Sandell, 2002b), though, in some quarters, this remains a contested idea. Ideas about the social role of the museum vary across continents, with particular genealogies in Europe, the US, Australia or Latin America (see Brown and Mairesse, 2018). The more explicit notion that museums are social institutions with a responsibility to act as 'agents of social change' is an idea that finds voice in collected works based on international empirical research about the role of museums in countering social inequality and promoting social justice and human rights (Sandell, 2002b, 2007, 2016; Sandell et al., 2010; Sandell and Nightingale, 2012); in work on the 'socially responsible' role of museums in addressing contested issues and the environmental challenges of our time (Cameron and Kelly, 2010; Janes, 2009; Janes and Conaty, 2005; Janes and Sandell, 2019; Message, 2013, 2017); their role in providing community support (Gurian, 2006); and museums' roles as agents of wellbeing (Chatterjee and Noble, 2013). The trend is reflected in the practice of a growing number of museums, galleries and heritage organisations internationally that are confidently articulating their social role within these terms and are expanding their partnerships with a range of civil society associations, welfare agencies, third sector and community organisations through programmes aimed at addressing contemporary issues such as health, inequality and social justice. The recent interest in the social role of the museum has led to a notable re-organisation of museum work towards participatory practices and a renewed interest in museum ethics as a social practice (Marstine, 2011). In this book, I want to start from a position that reaffirms the social role of the museum in order to consider how it is constituted through the practice of community engagement museum professionals on the ground, and how we might envision the museum as a space of social care.

This book is also a response, or perhaps a follow-on, to the idea of the 'social work' of the museum, developed by Lois E Silverman and published in her 2010 book of the same name. 'Social work' is a useful umbrella term to encompass socially engaged (Sandell, 2002a) and socially purposeful (Dodd, 2015) practices in museums. At the centre of Silverman's research is an attempt to connect the museum experience fundamentally with social life. The 'social work' happens when museums, objects and people come together. Museums are, at their core, spaces of meaning-making (Hooper-Greenhill, 1992, 2000). When we come to the museum, we bring with us prior knowledge and a whole range of emotions and memories that influence the ways in which we encounter the museum's message and the meanings we construct in these moments (Falk and Dierking, 1992). This is further influenced by companions (partners, friends, family members) who take part in the visit and the many other people we might encounter in the museum – staff and strangers. Museum meaning-making is also shaped in the relationships between people and objects. The very 'thingness' of objects provokes a range of immediate reactions – emotional, sensory and visceral – as well as cognitive (Dudley, 2012). Through these responses, personal connections and meanings are created and senses of identity and belonging are formed (e.g. Dicks, 2000; Hooper-Greenhill, 1994; Kaplan, 1994; Smith, 2006). These dimensions of the museum experience are captured in TWAM's mission statement:

> To help people determine their place in the world and define their identities, so enhancing their self-respect and their respect for others.

The social work perspective focuses on the potential of museums to support human flourishing; and in particular, supporting people to cope and thrive in circumstance ranging from personal challenges to systemic social exclusion and injustices. Indeed, underpinning much the wider literature on the social role of the museum is an ideological position advocating for the inclusion of those groups that are oppressed, marginalised, vulnerable or otherwise excluded. Silverman's research draws on historical examples and trends in international practice to highlight the work of museums that are working with people whose lives are directly affected by social and health inequalities, economic deprivation and other forms of disadvantage. In the UK context, where my book is set, this work has been shaped in relation to recent government agendas concerning social inclusion from the late 1990s. This has included social policy directives that have positioned the museum sector as playing a key role in tackling social exclusion through partnerships with other social agencies to contribute to areas such as rehabilitation, employment and health promotion (Newman and McLean, 2004; Sandell, 2002a; Tlili et al., 2007). Drawing on empirical research from this period, scholars describe how engaging with museums can lead to a range of positive outcomes at three interrelated levels, wherein individual benefits (such as self-esteem, creativity and sense of belonging) can lead to greater engagement in society, which can then transfer onto community settings and societal contexts (Sandell, 2003). At a community level, museums can support community renewal and the wellbeing of community life through inclusion, cohesion and social membership (Dodd and Sandell, 2001). At a wider level, through the representation of inclusive communities through their collections and display, museums have the potential to challenge stereotypes and prejudices and promote tolerance (Sandell, 2007; Sandell et al., 2010; Sandell and Nightingale, 2012).

In *The Social Work of Museums*, Silverman proposes that the social role of museums and their practice of public engagement, outreach and exhibitions can be integrated into the theoretical perspectives and professional practices of formal social work. This is my point of departure. While the idea of social work captures a sense of the practices that I explore across this book in the work of the museum with social care services and healthcare patients, the museum professionals I spoke with made it very clear:

> We are not social workers. We have a lot of skills that community development workers and social workers have but that's not what we are employed to do. It's very important that we are not seen by participants as being able to offer those skills.[5]

It is therefore essential to define this area of museum work as distinct from social work (as a profession) in order to draw out the boundaries of this practice and develop another language. This book proposes care (as a distinct, museum-like form of care) and practices of care as alternatives.

Museums, health and wellbeing

In recent years, there have been a growing number of collaborations between museums and the health and social care sector and a considerable increase in programmes targeting the health and wellbeing of museum audiences through outreach, public engagement programmes or exhibitions. Helen

Chatterjee and Guy Noble (2013) identify this as a new field of study and practice in museology, which they call 'Museums in Health', echoing the longer tradition of the Arts in Health movement from which it draws many parallels. In recognition of this growth in the UK, the National Alliance for Museums, Health and Wellbeing was launched in 2016 to provide sector-wide advice and training.[6] An initial mapping report by the Alliance recorded 600 'museums in health' activities across 261 museums including object handling, creative cultural activities and guided museum visits, with activities aimed at older adults, people living with dementia and people with mental health issues. Examples of this work in the UK include large institutions to much smaller-scale museums and heritage sites. For instance, the Victoria & Albert Museum of Childhood, London, has a long-standing partnership with hospital schools in the Greater London Area (Morse and Bloore, 2018). In Manchester, the Whitworth Art Gallery and Manchester Museum have developed a number of partnerships with local NHS hospitals, including weekly activities with stroke rehabilitation patients and artist residencies on medical wards (Not So Grim Up North Research Team, 2018). The Whitworth also uses the park in which the gallery sits for a green wellbeing programme for mental health service users, where participants connect with nature and respond to nature themes in the art gallery's collection through the 'Natural Cultural Health Service' (Thomson et al., 2020). At the Fitzwilliam Museum in Cambridge, older adults from a sheltered housing scheme regularly come to dance in the gallery, while in the Manchester Art Gallery, audiences can take part in mindfulness tours. A number of programmes in the UK have been inspired by the international programme *Meet Me* initiated by the Museum of Modern Art, New York, which offers supported guided tours for small groups of people with dementia and their care partners. These are but a few examples. Social meet-up and regular activities for older adults, stroke survivors, mental health service users and people with long-term conditions are appearing across museums internationally, especially in Canada, USA, Belgium, Australia, Japan and New Zealand.

In the UK, this work is driven by recent changes in the health policy landscape, including a shift towards care in the community, and towards prevention and wellbeing, with parts of care provision now devolved to local authorities. This has opened up further opportunities for museums to play an active role in public health interventions, integrating arts and cultural activities into a range of services, including mental health and wellbeing, services for older people and place-based commissioning (Camic and Chatterjee, 2013; Chatterjee, 2015). The UK is now seeing the beginning of a movement towards arts- and culture-led approaches to health focused on social prescription. 'Social prescribing' is defined as a formal framework enabling primary care services to refer patients to a range of local non-clinical services to address social, emotional or practical needs (Brandling and House, 2009). A new National Academy for Social Prescribing (NASP) was launched by Health and Social Care Secretary in October 2019 to further develop training and awareness of this approach. The concept of 'museums on prescription' is now gaining traction,[7] as a recent All-Party Parliamentary Group on Arts for Health and Wellbeing has given new visibility to the connections between health and culture. It gives the arts, and museums, a central role 'to assist in addressing a number of difficult and pressing policy challenges', including 'strengthening preventative strategies to maintain health for all; helping frail and older people stay healthy and independent; enabling patients to take a more active role in their own health and care; improving recovery from illness; enhancing mental healthcare; improving social care; mitigating social isolation and loneliness, strengthening local services and promoting more cohesive communities' (2017: 5).

There is now a range of evidence that points to the positive impacts of engaging with museums in areas such as cancer support, mental health, addiction recovery, social isolation and dementia.[8] There are common themes across these studies that establish the impact of museum engagement in terms of significant positive impact on psychological wellbeing, positive emotions such as hope, joy and optimism, increased self-esteem, sense of identity and community, and enriched social connections (Camic and Chatterjee, 2013; Chatterjee, 2015). Through this field of research, a picture is emerging of the distinct qualities of museums as spaces where therapeutic work can take place, in particular highlighting the unique emotional and wellbeing benefits of engaging with art and artefacts and of object handling. First, scholars have suggested that objects can trigger ideas, memories and emotional responses in ways that other sources of information cannot (Chatterjee and Noble, 2013; Dudley, 2010; Kavanagh, 2000). This underpins museum programmes that have used objects in reminiscence and creative activities (Camic et al., 2015; Eekelaar et al., 2012; Phillips, 2008). Second, is the capacity for objects to act as vehicles for people to open up about themselves and their feelings. For instance, in a hospital context, museum objects have been shown to act as vehicles for discussing difficult topics such as distress, death, loss and mourning, working through these emotions in a therapeutic manner through forms of personal healing, finding comfort through object interactions and in the objects themselves (Ander et al., 2013; Chatterjee et al., 2009; Dodd and Jones, 2014). Another unique element of object engagement is the impact of 'emotional touch', with contribution from both psychoanalytic and neurological perspectives suggesting sensory information gathered by touch is directly linked to emotional states, feelings and memories (Chatterjee, 2008; Froggett and Trustram, 2014; Pye, 2008; Solway et al., 2015). A further unique therapeutic quality of the museum is its spaces: the point about museums is that they are not medicalised, compulsory or judgmental (Camic and Chatterjee, 2013; Wood, 2009). Instead, they can be spaces of escape, contemplation and reverie. More generally, the unique role of museums in meaning-making has also been presented as the distinctive contribution that they can make to wellbeing. By creating personal connections with objects, art and artefacts, people can express themselves in powerful ways, make sense of their identity and find their emotional place in the world (Dodd and Jones, 2014; Froggett et al., 2011; Wood, 2009).

In the UK, at the time of writing, the Museums Association (MA) plays a central role in advocating for museums as agents of wellbeing and as vehicles for social change. In its 2013 manifesto, *Museums Changes Lives*, the MA outlined three contributions that museums can make, supported by evidence-based research:

- Museums enhance health and wellbeing.
- Museums create better places to live and work.
- Museums inspire engagement, debates and critical reflection.

Collectively, these contributions present a new direction for museums where the power of objects and museum settings are harnessed in the support of the care of people, and cultural practice is reoriented towards therapeutic and wellbeing aims. While much of the recent research in this area has focused (and rightly so) on the impact for participants, this book differentiates itself by focusing on the museum professionals who are delivering these types of activities. From this perspective, I will define the museum as a space of social care, using this conceptual framework to understand this new direction of museum practice.

Tyne & Wear Archive & Museums

The museum as a space of social care emerges from a close engagement with practice at TWAM (throughout this book, more generally referred to as 'the museum'). This museum service is located in North East England, with venues mostly in urban centres. The service manages nine museums and galleries,[9] with collections of local and international significance in archives, art, science and technology, archaeology, military and social history, fashion and natural sciences. It is governed by a joint committee, which includes representatives from the four local councils. The average number of visitors to the different sites is 1.4 million per year, and the museum employs around 280 staff. TWAM provides an interesting case study as a museum service with multiple venues and collection types; the arguments I draw out are therefore applicable across different types of museum or art galleries, irrespective of their collections. TWAM is also noteworthy as a museum service with a long tradition of community engagement work that has influenced practice across the UK museum sector and internationally, driven in part (though not exclusively) by a dedicated Outreach team. The commitment to community engagement is captured in work from the early 1990s under its then director David Fleming,[10] developing substantially in scale from the late 1990s to early 2000s in the context of governmental social inclusion policies. This period saw the development of innovative practice and collaborative approaches to exhibitions and expanded the partnerships between TWAM and a wide range of community groups, civil society associations, health and social care organisations and welfare agencies. In recent years, the work of the Outreach team has refocused around health and wellbeing through partnerships with health and social care partners in North East England. One aspect of the practices that I describe in this book takes place in the context of the museum service's recently launched 'Adult Health and Wellbeing' programme, which includes the Wellbeing Programme (supporting people living with mental ill health), the Recovery Programme (supporting people in recovery from addiction and those involved in the criminal justice system) and the Platinum Programme (for older adults, including work with care homes and hospitals). An additional programme, the Network, is another focus of the practices for this book. This is centred around community collaborations, exhibitions and heritage events, both inside and outside of Discovery Museum, Newcastle, one of the largest TWAM venues.

The contexts in which these practices have taken shape is significant to my discussion of care. The practices that I describe have operated over a period of continuing austerity and public sector cuts following the 2008 economic crash and a period of dis-investment in culture following changes in government. Coupled with changes to health and social care policy, these contexts have influenced the development of practice in the Outreach team. The long-term commitment to engaged practice and the conditions under which it has emerged and now operates makes TWAM an important case study for an analysis of museum-based community engagement in the UK. In one way, the stories of practice in this book are highly specific and local. However, this does not mean that their significance is only local. Care is specific to its contexts; it needs to be understood in relation to its 'local, fragile yet pertinent coherence' (Mol, 2010: 10). To understand care in the museum, we must be specific, and the case of TWAM enables this empirical discussion of care in/as practice. However, throughout the book, I also make clear the wider significance of care for museum practice and research beyond the sites of my research.

In order to examine the logic of care in community engagement using TWAM as a case study, I embedded myself over 18 months in the life of TWAM. During my time in the museum, I gathered a range of resources, collected through ethnographic fieldwork, organisational documents, interviews and informal discussions with a range of museum staff.[11] These enabled me to consider the different interpretations of community engagement that circulate within a single institution, to which I add my own interpretations. For the most part, however, I spent time with the Outreach team, where I became both a participant and an observer in a variety of programmes and exhibitions. In order to articulate a logic in practice, I immersed myself in the daily practices of these workers. Following Mol (2010: 10), 'if logics are embedded in practices, articulating them demands that we go out into the world and immerse ourselves in those practices (...) if one immerses oneself long enough in a case, one may get a sense of what is acceptable, desirable, or called for in a particular setting'. I spent much of my time in programmes with mental health service-users, people living with dementia, people accessing substance misuse services, stroke survivors, and with different support workers and care professionals. I then returned to my site some years later as part of another research project to further consider this work.[12] Although the book is based on an ethnographic method, it is not written up with the lengthy details and 'thick descriptions' that we (rightly) associate with ethnography. Instead, I sometimes choose to privilege discursive analysis of what people say and other times short descriptions of events to which I add my own interpretations and offer new perspectives. Over the different chapters of this book, the description of practice is presented through the voices of practitioners; other times, I work through snapshots of practice in narrative form, deliberate moments I have chosen that are particularly revealing of the logic of care that I seek to describe.

Structure of the book

The book is organised in four parts. It begins by placing my discussion in its theoretical contexts. Part I discusses the participatory turn in museums. Chapter 2 outlines a number of different origins and discourse for community engagement work. It highlights the ambivalent nature of community engagement, as a term that exists within the complementary and contradictory tendencies that make up the political form of the contemporary museum. The chapter then outlines 'the problem of community engagement', whereby scholarship is stuck in a critical impasse: a cycle of critique is followed by optimism for an improved form of participatory practice, and then further critique (following Graham, 2012). I suggest that this cycle persists because it is informed by a view of participation as a form of contribution. I describe this as *the logic of contribution* in current participatory practice and theory in museum studies. The empirical research that forms this book is then developed along two lines of enquiry. My first concern is with the institutional life of community engagement workers (Part II), and my second is focused on their emotional life (Part III). Both are founded in a practice-based approach and derive from grounded, qualitative perspectives of museum practice. I borrow the phrase 'institutional life' from Sara Ahmed (2012) to describe community engagement workers' experience of the institutions they inhabit. This returns us to the paradox that I described earlier: despite an institutional commitment to community engagement, museum professionals experience resistance from their institutions. Chapter 3 begins by considering how the language of community engagement is constructed across varied museum departments and teams. Predictably, differences in meaning appear, and I consider why and where these matter, in terms of how they frame the value of this work within the institution. I also begin to address the paradox presented around this work: if an institution says it is committed to community engagement, how should we look at the barriers that community engagement workers face when undertaking it? Here, I develop Sara Ahmed's (2012) idea of commitment as a 'non-performative' speech act, when committing to something sometimes comes to stand in for taking action. Chapter 4 considers how community engagement is managed and operationalised with the museum, attending to the different bureaucratic structures that get in the way of this work, in particular, the growth of an 'audit culture' (Strathern, 2000) and organisational silos. I then consider a number of areas of tension where community engagement workers are faced with what they described as 'black lines' – moments when they encounter institutional resistance to their work. These tensions gather around ideas of knowledge and expertise; the notion of quality in the museum; the need to manage participant expectations in community projects; and ideas of choice and control in community engagement. Each area presents a tension wherein the very idea of what a museum is, and what it does, is tussled over. In the final part of this chapter, I consider some of the 'institutional work' (Lawrence et al., 2009) of community engagement practitioners as they move around these black lines and negotiate their institutional settings.

My second concern with the emotional life of community engagement practitioners (Part III) focuses on the work that they do with participants, within community engagement sessions and exhibition projects. I articulate this work by describing its skills and dispositions and the felt quality of practice. As I will demonstrate, emotions saturate these events, and there are clear affective dimensions to this practice that have effects on both practitioners and participants. Within this section, I outline *the logic of care* in practice. Chapter 5 focuses on museum projects in collaboration with a range of support organisations for people facing mental health challenges, people living with dementia and those recovering from stroke or addiction. Through snapshots of practice, I explore the caring practices of museum professionals in engagement sessions and the different museum materialities of these engagements. Drawing from the wider literature on care from feminist scholarship and geography, the chapter presents 'the museumness of care', a practice with distinct relational, affective and material dimensions. Chapter 6 describes another aspect of community engagement: community-focused exhibition work. This aspect of community engagement work closely intersects with another area of museum practice, that of curatorial work. The chapter focuses on a long-term project led by the Outreach team in the West End of Newcastle. It describes how this practice developed through 'networks of engagement' in the West End that temporarily assembled people, organisations, interests and emotions, connecting the museum into its locality and extending geographies of care into the community. It then looks at an exhibition, *West End Stories.* Focusing on the practices, events and relationships that led to this final display, the chapter reflects on issues of authorship, collaboration and agency in community-focused curatorial work. The chapter re-imagines curatorial work through the logic of care discussed in the previous chapter, extending the work of taking care of objects to taking care of stories, memories, people, communities and place.

The different parts are brought together in a final chapter that provides a conceptual framework for thinking of museums as spaces of social care (Part IV). Chapter 7 examines the wider significance of care as a transformative way of viewing the museum and its social relations. This chapter draws together themes from the book in four substantial parts. First, it details a *logic of care* for museums as an alternative to the current dominant logic of contribution that underpins participatory work. I then outline the implications of care thinking across the museum, focusing on three key areas of museum work: management, front-of-house and curatorial work. The chapter then discusses how feminist care ethics, and geographers' engagement with this work, can be applied to the wider project of museum ethics. From here, I put forward the concept of the museum as a space of social care and its potential across international context. This outlines a new role for the museum within landscapes of formal care and beyond, linking to the growing area of practice in health and wellbeing, and to wider concerns of museum practice. The chapter proposes social care as a wider orientation in the museum that holds the capacity to transform the institution's ability to create value for society in the twenty-first century. In so doing, the book concludes with a theory of care for the museum.

Notes

1 This is all the more surprising given Eilean Hooper-Greenhill's often cited remark that: 'the balance of power in museums is shifting from those who care for objects to include, and often prioritise, those who care for people. The older ideology of conservation must now share its directing role with the newer ideology of collaboration' (1994: 1).

2 Annemarie Mol uses the logic of care in contrast to the logic of choice in healthcare in order to outline how good care is not only a matter of individual choices but rather it is something that emerges out of collaborative attempts to adapt technologies and ways of working to complex lives and bodies. This idea of a logic of care has deeply inspired the ideas presented in this book, although transposed to a very different setting in the museum. From here, I also develop a contrasting logic to care that of the logic of contribution, which I argue frames the current rhetoric of museum participation.

3 Two authors' book have had a profound impact of shaping my narrative – Annemarie Mol's *The Logic of Care:* Health and the Problem of Patient Choice, and Sara Ahmed, *On Being Included: Racism and Diversity in Institutional Life.* Where ideas have provided inspiration and terminology that these authors have developed is used in my museum context I have clearly signalled this. These books have also provided wider inspiration for how to write about museum work, care work, and institutional work in academic ways.

4 Many toolkits and frameworks were produced by local councils for museums under their responsibility as part of their wider local public engagement strategies. Examples of museum specific toolkits and guides include the 'Community Toolkit' produced as part of the 1807 Commemorated Project (https://www.york.

ac.uk/1807commemorated/commun.html); the Museums Association 'Measuring socially engaged practice: a toolkit for museums' (https://www.museumsassociation. org/download?id=1249262) and 'People Power: a self-assessment framework of participatory practice' (https://www.museumsassociation.org/download?id=1254507). Several toolkits were produced as an outcome of the London 2012 Cultural Olympiad project *Stories of the World*, during which museums across the UK worked with young people to co-produce programmes and exhibitions. These include the Geffrye Museum 'Working and Engaging with Young People' resource (https:// www.geffrye-museum.org.uk/Download.ashx?id=25293) and the British Museum 'Talking Objects Toolkit' (http://www.britishmuseum.org/about_us/community_ collaborations/partnerships/talking_objects/talking_objects_toolkit/the_group. aspx). National Museum Scotland has also produced a toolkit for working with young people https://www.nms.ac.uk/media/353536/sc-toolkit-final.pdf. A more recent resource is the *Our Museum: Communities and Museum as Active Partners* website, which was produced as an outcome of the Paul Hamlyn Foundation funded programme http://ourmuseum.org.uk. I discuss this programme at various points within the book.

5 Outreach team member interview, 2013.
6 The Alliance has now merged with the National Arts for Health and Wellbeing Alliance to create the Culture, Health and Wellbeing Alliance in the UK.
7 Museums on prescription are also being formally developed in Canada.
8 See Ander et al., 2013; Camic et al., 2015, 2017; Eekelaar et al., 2012; Lanceley et al., 2012; Morse et al., 2015; Paddon et al., 2014; Thomson et al., 2012, 2018. There have also been large-scale studies of cultural attendance that suggest a link between life expectancy and cultural participation (see O'Neill, 2010).
9 At the time of the start of the research, the service managed 12 venues. In 2013, one of the five councils, Sunderland City Council, withdrew from its agreement with TWAM, taking three venues into its own management as a cost saving measure in response to local authority cuts.
10 Fleming's influence on the UK sector at the time is marked by his involvement in the Museums Association as President and Board Member and his publications (2001, 2002, 2012). Since then, Fleming has been a strong advocate for the social agency of the museum on an international stage, with positions at ICOM and as President of the Federation of International Human Rights Museums.
11 I conducted 45 semi-structured interviews, including five group interviews, across different museum departments – collections teams, managers (and four from previous management, including two previous directors), learning teams, exhibition project teams, communication and development teams, and curatorial teams. These interviews took place at TWAM between 2011 and 2013 and focused on asking staff what they understood by 'community engagement', how it related to their practice and their perceptions of the barriers to this work.
12 This work was then followed up by additional observations of TWAM that were collected during my time as a postdoctoral research associate for a project entitled 'Not so Grim Up North: investigating the health and wellbeing impacts of taking part in museum activities' (2016–2018).

References

Ahmed S (2012) *On Being Included: Racism and Diversity in Institutional Life.* Durham, NC and London: Duke University Press.
All-Party Parliamentary Group on Arts, Health and Wellbeing (2017) *Creative Health: The Arts for Health and Wellbeing.* Available at: http://www. artshealthandwellbeing.org.uk/appg-inquiry/ (accessed 31 July 2017).

Ander E, Thomson LJ, Blair K, et al. (2013) Using museum objects to improve well-being in mental health service users and neurological rehabilitation clients. *The British Journal of Occupational Therapy* 76(5): 208–216. doi: 10.4276/030802213X 13679275042645.

Barnes M (2006) *Caring and Social Justice.* Basingstoke: Palgrave MacMillan.

Bienkowski, P (2016) *No longer us and them: how to change into a participatory museum and gallery. Learning from the Our Museum programme.* London: Paul Hamlyn Foundation. Available at: http://www.phf.org.uk/wp-content/uploads/2016/07/Our-Museum-Report_April-2016-double-page.pdf (accessed 2 January 2017).

Bourdieu P (1977) *Outline of a Theory of Practice.* Cambridge: Cambridge University Press.

Bowlby S (2012) Recognising the time – space dimensions of care: Caringscapes and carescapes. *Environment and Planning A* 44(9): 2101–2118.

Brandling J and House W (2009) Social prescribing in general practice: Adding meaning to medicine. *British Journal of General Practice* 59(563): 454–456. doi: 10.3399/bjgp09X421085.

Brown K and Mairesse F (2018) The definition of the museum through its social role. *Curator: The Museum Journal* 61(4): 525–539. doi: 10.1111/cura.12276.

Cameron F and Kelly L (2010) *Hot Topics, Public Culture, Museums.* Cambridge: Cambridge Scholars Publishing.

Camic PM and Chatterjee HJ (2013) Museums and art galleries as partners for public health interventions. *Perspectives in Public Health* 133(1): 66–71. doi: 10.1177/1757913912468523.

Camic PM, Baker EL and Tischler V (2015) Theorizing how art gallery interventions impact people with dementia and their caregivers. *The Gerontologist.* Online First. doi: 10.1093/geront/gnv063.

Camic PM, Hulbert S and Kimmel J (2017) Museum object handling: A health-promoting community-based activity for dementia care. *Journal of Health Psychology* 24(6): 787–798. doi: 10.1177/1359105316685899.

Chatterjee HJ (ed.) (2008) *Touch in Museums: Policy and Practice in Object Handling.* Oxford: Berg.

Chatterjee HJ (2015) Museums and art galleries as settings for public health interventions. In: Clift S and Camic P (eds) *Oxford Textbook of Creative Arts, Health, and Wellbeing International Perspectives on Practice, Policy and Research.* Oxford: Oxford University Press, pp. 281–289.

Chatterjee HJ and Noble G (2013) *Museums, Health and Well-Being.* Farnham: Ashgate.

Chatterjee HJ, Vreeland S and Noble G (2009) Museopathy: Exploring the healing potential of handling museum objects. *Museum and Society* 7(3): 164–177.

Cloke P, May J and Johnsen S (2005) Exploring ethos? Discourses of 'charity' in the provision of emergency services for homeless people. *Environment and Planning A* 37: 385–402. doi: 10.1068/a36189.

Conradson D (2003) Spaces of care in the city: The place of a community drop-in centre. *Social & Cultural Geography* 4(4): 507–525. doi: 10.1080/1464936032000137939.

Crang M and Tolia-Kelly DP (2010) Nation, race and affect: Senses and sensibilities at National Heritage sites. *Environment and Planning A.* 42: 2315. doi: http://dx.doi.org/10.1068/a4346.

Crooke EM (2008) *Museums and Community: Ideas, Issues, and Challenges.* New York: Routledge.

Crouch D (2015) Affect, heritage, feeling. In: Waterton E and Watson S (eds) *The Palgrave Handbook of Contemporary Heritage Research*. London: Palgrave Macmillan. pp. 177–190.

Darling J (2011) Giving space: Care, generosity and belonging in a UK asylum drop-in centre. *Geoforum* 42(4): 408–417. doi: 10.1016/j.geoforum.2011.02.004.

Dicks B (2000) *Heritage, Place and Community*. Cardiff: University of Wales Press.

Dodd J (2015) The socially purposeful museum. *Museologica Brunensia* 4(2): 28–31.

Dodd J and Jones C (2014) *Mind, Body, Spirit: How Museums Impact Health and Wellbeing*. Leicester: Research Centre for Museums and Galleries, University of Leicester. Available at: https://www2.le.ac.uk/departments/museumstudies/rcmg/publications/mind-body-spirit-report (accessed 31 October 2016).

Dodd J and Sandell R (2001) *Including Museums: Perspectives on Museums, Galleries and Social Inclusion*. Leicester: Research Centre for Museums and Galleries, University of Leicester.

Dudley SH (ed.) (2010) *Museum Materialities: Objects, Engagements, Interpretations*. London: Routledge.

Dudley SH (2012) Encountering a Chinese horse: Engaging with the thingness of things. In: Dudley SH (ed.) *Museum Materialities: Objects, Engagements, Interpretations*. London: Routledge, pp. 28–42.

Eekelaar C, Camic PM and Springham N (2012) Art galleries, episodic memory and verbal fluency in dementia: An exploratory study. *Psychology of Aesthetics, Creativity, and the Arts* 6(3): 262–272. doi: 10.1037/a0027499.

Falk JH and Dierking LD (1992) *The Museum Experience*. Washington, DC: Whalesback Books.

Fleming D (2001) The politics of social inclusion. In: Dodd J and Sandell R (eds) *Including Museums: Perspectives on Museums, Galleries and Social Inclusion*. Leicester: Research Centre for Museums and Galleries, University of Leicester.

Fleming D (2002) Positioning the museum for social inclusion. In: Sandell R (ed.) *Museums, Society, Inequality*. London and New York: Routledge, pp. 213–224.

Fleming D (2012) Museum missions, values, vision. In: McCarthy C (ed.) *Museum Practice: Critical Debates in the Museum Sector*. Malden, MA and Oxford: Blackwell Publishing, pp. 3–25.

Froggett L and Trustram M (2014) Object relations in the museum: A psychosocial perspective. *Museum Management and Curatorship* 29(5): 482–497. doi: 10.1080/09647775.2014.957481.

Froggett L, Farrier A and Poursanidou K (2011) *Who Cares? Museums, Health and Wellbeing. A study of the Renaissance North West Programme*. Preston: University of Central Lancashire. Available at: http://www.healthandculture.org.uk/publications-case-studies/publications/who-cares-museums-health-and-wellbeing/ (accessed 21 January 2019).

Golding V and Modest W (eds) (2013) *Museums and Communities: Curators, Collections and Collaboration*. London: Bloomsbury.

Graham H (2012) Scaling Governmentality. *Cultural Studies* 26(4): 565–592. doi: 10.1080/09502386.2012.679285.

Gurian EH (2006) *Civilizing the Museum: The Collected Writings of Elaine Heumann Gurian*. London: Routledge.

Hall E (2013) Making and gifting belonging: Creative arts and people with learning disabilities. *Environment and Planning A* 45(2): 244–262. doi: 10.1068/a44629.

Hastrup K (1995) *A Passage to Anthropology: Between Experience and Theory.* London and New York: Routledge.

Hein GE (1998) *Learning in the Museum.* London: Routledge.

Hein H (2006) Museum education. In: Macdonald S (ed.) *A Companion to Museum Studies.* Blackwell companions in cultural studies. Oxford: Blackwell, pp. 340–352.

Held V (2006) *The Ethics of Care: Personal, Political, and Global.* New York: Oxford University Press.

Hooper-Greenhill E (1992) *Museums and the Shaping of Knowledge.* The heritage: care – preservation – management. London: Routledge.

Hooper-Greenhill E (1994) *Museums and Their Visitors.* London: Routledge.

Hooper-Greenhill E (2000) *Museums and the Interpretation of Visual Culture.* Museum meanings 4. London: Routledge.

Janes RR (2009) *Museums in a Troubled World: Renewal, Irrelevance, or Collapse?* Abingdon and New York: Routledge.

Janes RR and Conaty GT (2005) *Looking Reality in the Eye: Museums and Social Responsibility.* Calgary: University of Calgary Press.

Janes RR and Sandell R (eds) (2019) *Museum Activism* (1st edn). Abingdon and New York: Routledge.

Johnsen S, Cloke P and May J (2006) Day centres for homeless people: Spaces of care or fear? *Social & Cultural Geography* 6(6): 787–811. doi: 10.1080/14649360500353004.

Kaplan FS (1994) *Museums and the Making of 'Ourselves': The Role of Objects in National Identity.* London: Leicester University Press.

Karp I, Kreamer CM and Lavine S (eds) (1992) *Museums and Communities: The Politics of Public Culture.* Washington, DC: Smithsonian Institution Press.

Kavanagh Gaynor (2000) *Dream Spaces: Memory and the Museum.* New York and London: Leicester University Press.

Knigge L (2009) Intersections between public and private: Community gardens, community service and geographies of care in the US City of Buffalo, NY. *Geographica Helvetica* 64(1): 45–52. doi: https://doi.org/10.5194/gh-64-45-2009.

Lanceley A, Noble G, Johnson M, et al. (2012) Investigating the therapeutic potential of a heritage-object focused intervention: A qualitative study. *Journal of Health Psychology* 17(6): 809–820. doi: 10.1177/1359105311426625.

Lawrence TB, Suddaby R and Leca B (eds) (2009) *Institutional Work: Actors and Agency in Institutional Studies of Organizations.* Cambridge: Cambridge University Press.

Laws J (2009) Reworking therapeutic landscapes: The spatiality of an 'alternative' self-help group. *Social Science & Medicine* 69(12). Part Special Issue: New approaches to researching patient safety: 1827–1833. doi: 10.1016/j.socscimed.2009.09.034.

Lawson V (2007) Geographies of care and responsibility. *Annals of the Association of American Geographers* 97(1): 1–11. doi: 10.1111/j.1467–8306.2007.00520.x.

Lynch BT (2011a) Collaboration, contestation and creative conflict: On the efficacy of museum/community partnerships. In: Marstine J (ed.) *The Routledge Companion to Museum Ethics: Redefining Ethics for the Twenty-First Century Museum.* London: Routledge, pp. 146–164.

Lynch BT (2011b) *'Whose Cake Is It Anyway?' A Collaborative Investigation into Engagement and Participation in 12 Museums and Galleries in the UK.* London: Paul Hamlyn Foundation.

Lynch BT (2014) 'Generally dissatisfied': hidden pedagogy in the postcolonial museum. *THEMA. La revue des Musées de la civilisation* 1(1): 79–92.

Lynch BT and Alberti SJMM (2010) Legacies of prejudice: Racism, co-production and radical trust in the museum. *Museum Management and Curatorship* 25(1): 13–35. doi: 10.1080/09647770903529061.

Macdonald S (2002) *Behind the Scenes at the Science Museum*. Oxford: Berg.

Marstine J (ed.) (2011) *The Routledge Companion to Museum Ethics: Redefining Ethics for the Twenty-First Century Museum*. London: Routledge.

Marstine J, Bauer AA and Haines C (2011) New directions in museum ethics. *Museum Management and Curatorship* 26(2): 91–95. doi: 10.1080/09647775.2011.566709.

Mason R (2006) Cultural theory and museum studies. In: Macdonald S (ed.) *A Companion to Museum Studies*. Blackwell Companions in Cultural Studies. Oxford: Blackwell, pp. 17–32.

McCarthy C (2015) Grounding museum studies: Introducing practice. In: McCarthy C, Macdonald S, and Leahy HR (eds) *Museum Practice*. Chichester: Wiley Blackwell, pp. xxxv–lii.

McCarthy C (2016) Theorising museum practice through practice theory. In: Burnard P, Mackinlay E, and Powell K (eds) *Routledge Handbook of Intercultural Arts Research*. Abingdon and New York: Routledge, pp. 24–34. doi: 10.4324/9781315693699.ch3.

McSweeney K and Kavanagh J (eds) (2016) *Museum Participation: New Directions for Audience Collaboration*. Edinburgh and Boston, MA: MuseumsEtc.

Message K (2013) *Museums and Social Activism: Engaged Protest*. Museum meanings. New York: Routledge.

Message K (2017) *The Disobedient Museum: Writing at the Edge*. London: Routledge.

Milligan C, Gatrell A and Bingley A (2004) 'Cultivating health': Therapeutic landscapes and older people in northern England. *Social Science & Medicine* 58(9): 1781–1793. doi: 10.1016/S0277–9536(03)00397-6.

Milligan C, Atkinson S, Skinner M, et al. (2007) Geographies of care: A commentary. *New Zealand Geographer* 63(2): 135–140. doi: 10.1111/j.1745–7939.2007.00101.x.

Mol A (2010) *The Logic of Care: Health and the Problem of Patient Choice*. Abingdon: Routledge.

Morse N and Bloore C (2018) How can museums work with hospitals? *Museological Review* 22: 63–67.

Morse N and Munro E (2015) Museums' community engagement schemes, austerity and practices of care in two local museum services. *Social & Cultural Geography*. Online First: 357–378. doi: 10.1080/14649365.2015.1089583.

Morse N, Thomson LJM, Brown Z, et al. (2015) Effects of creative museum outreach sessions on measures of confidence, sociability and well-being for mental health and addiction recovery service-users. *Arts & Health* 7(3): 231–246. doi: 10.1080/17533015.2015.1061570.

Morse N, Rex B and Richardson SH (2018) Special issue editorial: Methodologies for researching the museum as organization. *Museum and Society* 16(2): 112–123. doi: 10.29311/mas.v16i2.2810.

Mygind L, Hällman AK and Bentsen P (2015) Bridging gaps between intentions and realities: A review of participatory exhibition development in museums. *Museum Management and Curatorship* 30(2): 117–137. doi: 10.1080/09647775.2015.1022903.

Newman A and McLean F (2004) Presumption, policy and practice: the use of museums and galleries as agents of social inclusion in Great Britain. *International Journal of Cultural Policy* 10(2): 167–181.

Not So Grim Up North Research Team (2018) *Not So Grim Up North: Investigating the Health and Wellbeing Impacts of Museum and Gallery Activities for People Living with Dementia, Stroke Survivors, and Mental Health Service-Users.* Available at: http://www.healthandculture.org.uk/not-so-grim-up-north/research-publications/ (accessed 1 August 2019).

Onciul B, Stefano ML and Hawke S (eds) (2017) *Engaging Heritage - Engaging Communities.* Martlesham: Boydell & Brewer.

O'Neill M (2010) Cultural attendance and public mental health: From research to practice. *Journal of Public Mental Health* 9(4): 22–29. doi: 10.5042/jpmh.2010.0700.

Paddon HL, Thomson LJ, Menon U, et al. (2014) Mixed methods evaluation of well-being benefits derived from a heritage-in-health intervention with hospital patients. *Arts & Health* 6(1): 24–58. doi: 10.1080/17533015.2013.800987.

Parr H (2008) *Mental Health and Social Space: Towards Inclusionary Geographies?* RGS-IBG Book Series. Oxford: Blackwell.

Peers LL and Brown AK (eds) (2003) *Museums and Source Communities: A Routledge Reader.* London: Routledge.

Phillips L (2008) Reminiscence: Recent work from at the British Museum. In: Chatterjee HJ (ed.) *Touch in Museums: Policy and Practice in Object Handling.* Oxford: Berg, pp. 199–205.

Power A and Hall E (2018) Placing care in times of austerity. *Social & Cultural Geography* 19(3): 303–313. doi: 10.1080/14649365.2017.1327612.

Pye E (2008) *The Power of Touch: Handling Objects in Museum and Heritage Context.* London and New York: Routledge.

Sandell R (2002a) Museums and the combating of social inequality: Roles, responsibilities, resistance. In: Sandell R (ed.) *Museums, Society, Inequality.* London: Routledge, pp. 3–24.

Sandell R (ed.) (2002b) *Museums, Society, Inequality.* London: Routledge.

Sandell R (2003) Social Inclusion, the museum and the dynamics of sectoral change. *Museum and Society* 1(1): 45–62.

Sandell R (2007) *Museums, Prejudice and the Reframing of Difference.* London: Routledge.

Sandell R (2016) *Museums, Moralities and Human Rights.* London: Routledge.

Sandell R and Nightingale E (eds) (2012) *Museums, Equality, and Social Justice.* London: Routledge.

Sandell R, Dodd J and Garland-Thomson R (2010) *Re-Presenting Disability: Activism and Agency in the Museum.* London: Routledge. Available at: https://lra.le.ac.uk/handle/2381/8906 (accessed 21 January 2013).

Schatzki TR (1996) *Social Practices: A Wittgensteinian Approach to Human Activity and the Social.* Cambridge: Cambridge University Press.

Schatzki TR (2001) Introduction: Practice theory. In: Schatzki Theodore R, Knorr-Cetina KD, and von Savigny E (eds) *The Practice Turn in Contemporary Theory.* London: Routledge, pp. 43–55.

Schatzki TR (2002) *The Site of the Social: A Philosophical Account of the Constitution of Social Life and Change* (1st edn). University Park: Penn State University Press.

Shelton A (2013) Critical museology: A manifesto. *Museum Worlds* 1(1): 7–23. doi: 10.3167/armw.2013.010102.

Simon N (2010) *The Participatory Museum.* Museum 2.0.

Smith L (2006) *Uses of heritage.* London and New York: Routledge.

Smith L and Waterton E (2009) *Heritage, Communities and Archaeology.* London: Gerald Duckworth & Co. Available at: http://www.ducknet.co.uk/academic/title.php?titleissue_id=912 (accessed 29 July 2014).

Smith L, Wetherell M and Campbell G (2018) *Emotion, Affective Practices, and the Past in the Present*. London: Routledge.

Solway R, Camic PM, Thomson LJ, et al. (2015) Material objects and psychological theory: A conceptual literature review. *Arts & Health* 0(0): 1–20. doi: 10.1080/17533015.2014.998010.

Strathern M (2000) *Audit Cultures: Anthropological Studies in Accountability, Ethics and the Academy*. London: Routledge.

Thomson LJ, Ander EE, Menon U, et al. (2012) Enhancing cancer patient well-being with a nonpharmacological, heritage-focused intervention. *Journal of Pain and Symptom Management* 44(5): 731–740. doi: 10.1016/j.jpainsymman.2011.10.026.

Thomson LJ, Lockyer B, Camic PM, et al. (2018) Effects of a museum-based social prescription intervention on quantitative measures of psychological wellbeing in older adults. *Perspectives in Public Health* 138(1): 28–38. doi: 10.1177/1757913917737563.

Thomson, LJ, Morse, N, Elsden E, et al. (2020). Art, nature and mental health: Assessing the biopsychosocial effects of a 'creative green prescription' museum programme involving horticulture, artmaking and collections. *Perspectives in Public Health,* 10(11), 1–9. doi: 10.1177/1757913920910443.

Tlili A, Gewirtz S and Cribb A (2007) New Labour's socially responsible museum: Roles, functions and greater expectations. *Policy Studies* 28(3): 269–289. doi: 10.1080/01442870701437634.

Tolia-Kelly DP, Waterton E and Watson S (2016) *Heritage, Affect and Emotion: Politics, Practices and Infrastructures*. Abingdon and New York: Routledge.

Tronto JC (1993) *Moral Boundaries: A Political Argument for an Ethic of Care*. New York and London: Routledge.

Tronto JC (2013) *Caring Democracy: Markets, Equality, and Justice*. New York: NYU Press.

Warner J, Talbot D and Bennison G (2013) The cafe as affective community space: Reconceptualizing care and emotional labour in everyday life. *Critical Social Policy* 33(2): 305–324. doi: 10.1177/0261018312449811.

Waterton E (2014) A more-than-representational understanding of heritage? The 'past' and the politics of affect. *Geography Compass* 8(11): 823–833.

Waterton E and Watson S (eds) (2011) *Heritage and Community Engagement: Collaboration or Contestation?* London: Routledge.

Watson SER (ed.) (2007) *Museums and Their Communities*. Leicester readers in museum studies. London: Routledge.

Wood C (2009) *Museums of the Mind: Mental Health, Emotional Wellbeing, and Museums*. Culture: Unlimited. Available at: http://cultureunlimited.org/pdfs/museums (accessed 20 January 2013).

Part I

The participatory turn in museums

2 The problem of engagement

The museum sector has undergone something of a 'participatory turn' in recent years. An increasing number of museums and galleries worldwide have developed a range of practices that seek to involve visitors, non-visitors and different interest groups in their activities. As this work has developed, these practices have been described through terms such as access, inclusion, consultation, outreach, *community engagement*, co-production and co-curation. At the heart of this participatory turn is the promise of democratising and pluralising of museum spaces and practice, the possibility of disrupting existing power structures and the potential for the radical transformation of the museum. The call for participatory practice is a call for museums to reform themselves as a place for dialogue, for social justice, for democracy and, latterly, for wellbeing. At a time when public institutions are increasingly under pressure to justify their work, it is also seen to secure the contemporary museum's relevance and purpose. The idea of the participatory museum is one that is now becoming well established worldwide. It is seen as a 'good' thing. And yet, at the same time, it is a deeply contested idea that has incited much academic and professional debate. Critical literature has focused on the uneven configurations of power that are manifest in museum-initiated programmes and heritage activities (Clifford, 1997; Fouseki, 2010; Lynch, 2011a; Lynch and Alberti, 2010; Modest, 2013; Sandell, 2007; Smith and Waterton, 2009; Waterton and Watson, 2011). These accounts reveal the inequitable relations between professionals and participants in terms of the control of narratives and resources in the museum, and much of participatory and community engagement practice has been criticised as little more than tokenism or 'empowerment-lite' (Lynch, 2011c). Critiques have ranged from institutional resistance to embedding participatory work, to discussion of the ways in which initiatives end up reinforcing established power structures. Community engagement is therefore a 'problem' in the museum. And yet, as we explore the critical literature, we see that community engagement is presented as the solution to this problem. There is a persistent optimism around participation that runs alongside its critique: more, and better, community engagement is needed to resolve the problem of community engagement and achieve its transformational potential. As Helen Graham suggests, there is 'critique-contest impasse' in museum studies when it comes to participation (2012b: 571). In this chapter, I examine the problem of community engagement, as an ambivalent domain of museum theory and practice.

To understand the recent participatory turn in museums, we can examine a number of different expressions and origins that are not often acknowledged in discussions of community engagement (for an exception, see Onciul et al., 2017).[1] In this chapter, I focus on the different discourses that have influenced ideas of community engagement in the UK museum sector in particular. I use the terms community engagement and participation more or less interchangeably in order to survey a wider field of writing in museum studies. These discourses include the representational critique of curatorial practice and the growth of social history curatorship; governmental demands for the social inclusion of groups that are excluded by the cultural sector and civil society more widely; a growing focus on visitors, within both an economic discourse and as a key area of museological concern; the sharing possibilities of digital participatory cultures; and the renewal of museum ethics and the social justice role of museums. Within these discourses, I also situate the emergence of the recent work of 'museums in health', which is of particular concern to the idea of care that underpins this book. Though distinct in origins, I suggest these discourses co-exist and have evolved closely together. It is important to tease out (as much as is possible) these participatory discourses to reflect upon how they have imagined community engagement practice, its aims and purpose, its participants and the different museum teams involved (either curatorial, education or outreach teams). Indeed, the different uses of community engagement 'betrays a myriad of contrary approaches and understandings' (Onciul, 2017: 1) that animate contemporary museum practice. As Andrea Cornwall (2006: 50) reminds us, 'as an infinitely malleable term, participation can be used to evoke and to signify almost anything that involves people. As such, it can be framed to meet almost any demand made of it'. In this chapter, then, I set the scene of the participatory turn in order to highlight the ambivalence of community engagement, as a term that exists within the complementary and contradictory tendencies that make up the political form of the contemporary museum. This essential ambivalence will later serve to help us understand community engagement in practice at Tyne & Wear Archives & Museums (TWAM) in the following chapters. Next, I consider some of the key theories of community engagement that have informed the critiques of the participatory turn. Then, I address the persistent optimism and the critical impasse in the literature.

This sets up my main argument: I want to suggest that much of the current practice and scholarship frames participation within a *logic of contribution*, where community engagement (and participation more generally) is a form of contribution into the museum (donating an object, a story, an interpretation, etc.).[2] As I will go on to show, within the logic of contribution, participation is framed around ideas of participant choice, control and empowerment, but most of the time, this is organised as a form of contribution to the museum, focused on what communities can bring to the museum, for instance, to complement a gap in the collections or to enhance a public display. It follows that in the logic of contribution, the key aim is to improve the museum. I will also suggest that in returning to more or better participation as the solution to the problem of engagement, the critical literature further entrenches this logic of contribution. As I go forward in the chapter, I consider the limitations of this particular logic, as it is an institutional logic first, aimed at benefiting the museum. This argument points to the need for a closer examination of the museum form (as an institution) and of museum practice (people's institutional work that aims to disrupt institutional arrangements). While I will suggest that the logic of contribution is dominant in contemporary museum practice, I will also highlight some museum trends that exceed this logic in their attempt to reconfigure the institution. This opens up ways forward that break with the critical impasse. Later, I will surface another logic, the logic of care, as an alternative to the practice, discourse and critique of community engagement in the museum.

Museums and community engagement practice: origins and developments

A reading of the literature on community engagement and museums draws out a number of different contexts that have called for the development of community engagement practice in the museum. The first expression emerges from a longer representational critique of the museum in the postmodernism debates of cultural theory from the 1980s onwards, which centred on a critique of the museum's uncontested authority claims to 'truth' and identity (Karp and Lavine, 1991; Karp et al., 1992; Macdonald, 1998; Mason, 2004, 2006). In the museum context, this led to calls to 'deconstruct' museum exhibitions and practices in order to lay bare their knowledge claims as inherently political in pursuit and deployment. This challenge came especially from the many minoritised forces – indigenous, popular, feminist, postcolonial – whose voices had previously been silenced or ignored by museums (Barringer and Flynn, 1998; Coombes, 1994; Hall, 1992; Haraway, 1994; Lidchi, 1997; Lonetree, 2012; Porter, 1996; Samuel, 1994; Sleeper-Smith, 2009). Each movement included calls from outside the sector for more adequate representation and material inclusion in the museum and raised fundamental questions inside the museum about what is collected, how it is catalogued, what is displayed, whose stories are told and who should be involved in making public exhibitions. The challenge to museum representation was therefore a demand for a politics of recognition and often, of restitution. Community engagement emerges here as the institution's response to these varied demands, and as a practice, it has primarily focused on how to democratise the museum's core practices of collection and display (restitution remains a much more fraught area). 'Collaborative museology' has been consciously developed in museums worldwide where there are large indigenous communities such as North America, Canada, Australia and New Zealand, and in museums with ethnographic and archaeological collections through work with more distant 'source' communities (Peers and Brown, 2003). The argument for community engagement is here driven by the necessity that certain objects can only be legitimately interpreted by those communities from which these objects originate (Graham, 2012a: 8; see also Ames, 2003; Kreps, 2003; Krmpotich and Peers, 2013; Phillips, 2003; Peers and Brown, 2003; Tapsell, 2014). This led to the development of collaborative collections management (e.g. Mccarthy et al., 2013) and collaborative exhibition practices (e.g. Phillips, 2003) aimed at decentralising Western viewpoints and bringing new stories into the museum. A number of museums, such as the Te Papa Tongerawa in New Zealand and the Museum of Anthropology at the University of British Columbia, have led the way for this way of working. These forms of community engagement practice are aimed to reform museums into dialogic spaces of exchange with communities and, in their more radical orientation, are part of the wider political project of decolonising museums.

Collaboration with source communities has provided the reference point for discourse in other countries, including in the UK, linked to discourses of multiculturalism and cultural diversity from the 1990s onwards. In the UK, this direction for community engagement work has developed through critical engagement with the legacies of Empire and dominant representations of 'Britishness'. This has included work with communities to re-interpret collections amassed during colonial times, for instance, at the Victoria & Albert Museum (Nightingale, 2006; Nightingale and Swallow, 2003), as well as recent projects such as *Objects Journeys* at the British Museum and *The Past is Now* at Birmingham Museum and Art Gallery, as well as contemporary collecting projects like the Science Museum's collaboration with the African community during the redevelopment of the Information Age Galleries (Bunning et al., 2015). In recent years, there have been specific national events that have provided a platform to develop community engagement practice in the UK, for instance, the bicentenary of Britain's abolition of the slave trade act in 2007 (Lynch and Alberti, 2010; Smith et al., 2014) and the 2012 Cultural Olympiad which involved young people co-curating exhibitions with ethnographic collections (Lynch, 2016; Modest, 2013; for discussion of this work at TWAM, see Morse et al., 2013).[3] The growing interest in migration stories in the UK museums has also provided further impulse for this collaborative work (Golding and Walklate, 2019; Whitehead et al., 2016), for example the *Migration Museum* project and the *Destination Tyneside* gallery at TWAM (Little and Watson, 2016).

Other intersecting trajectories have advanced the democratisation of the museum through new community engagement practices linked to the issue of representation via collecting and display. These are succinctly connected by museum scholar Rhiannon Mason:

> this trajectory begins with a 19th-century interest in non-elite, folk culture which links up with the valorisation of culture and history of the working classes and other marginalised groups promoted by social history from the 1970s and 1980s. Along the way it takes on board an interest in popular culture and everyday collecting habits encouraged by the development of material culture theory.
>
> (2004: 58)

Community engagement practices have emerged in this trajectory through oral history projects, contemporary collecting and polyvocal exhibition practices, linked to efforts to broaden the kinds of culture(s) in the museum, in particular, vernacular and popular cultures (e.g. Boon et al., 2014). More generally, there has been an interest in including 'non-expert' voices across a range of topics: the invitation is for 'ordinary people' to speak for themselves in the museums (Thumim, 2010). The influential discourse of the 'New Museology' has been significant here for the UK sector (McCall and Gray, 2014) in driving demands for wider access and representation of diverse groups (Stam, 1993) as well as demands for a more active role for the public as both visitors and active participants 'in the production of their own pasts' (Walsh, 1992: 161; see also Black, 2005). This re-orientation towards culture in everyday life has particularly influenced social history curatorship in UK museums, where community engagement is used to collect objects and first-person interpretations as a means to pluralise displays and collections. Notable early examples of this work are the Open Museum in Glasgow, the millennium collection project *Making Histories* at TWAM and the community collaboration *Art on Tyneside*, which involved members of the public to create a new multivocal art display (Mason et al., 2013). Work of this kind with geographically close communities or 'communities of interest' has probably accounted for the majority of community engagement work by curatorial teams in the UK, though this practice has not always been written up or recorded beyond museum websites and evaluation reports.[4]

Across these different origins, the first direction for community engagement in museums, then, has been a response to the challenges of representation and attempts to democratise the museum by including more voices – in particular those voices that had previously been systematically side-lined in the museum – in order to better reflect contemporary society and redress previous exclusions. Community engagement practice has emerged through oral history projects, contemporary collecting and collaborative exhibition making, developed primarily within curatorial teams. As such, it has tended to be viewed through objects (curatorial) concerns (Fouseki, 2010) and, as a way to access better knowledge, displays and research for the museum (Graham, 2012a: 6). Underlining this work is a political intent to challenge museum authority, expertise and taken for granted ideas of cultural value, made more or less explicit depending on the project and circumstances.

These shifts in curatorial practice have occurred alongside a more fundamental re-questioning of the social responsibility of the museum. This relates to broader and long-standing discourse about the very definition of museums from 'temples to forums' (Cameron, 1971) to institutions that foreground the responsibilities to the communities that they serve (Knell et al., 2007; Watson, 2007; Weil, 1990). In the UK and in large sections of Europe, where museums have tended to be publicly funded, this discourse has been further inflected in specifically 'public' ways, framed around notions of civic accountability and the public good. The second direction for community engagement I want to highlight here therefore has taken shape within governmental uses of culture, via policy and other governmental directives linked around the idea of community (see also Mason, 2004). Drawing on examples of museums worldwide, Elizabeth Crooke describes how the integration of 'community' within diverse areas of policy, including but not limited to cultural policy, led to the creation of community collections and education officers within large numbers of local government museum services in the 1980s and 1990s, in efforts to create public museums that are more meaningful to a broader range of people and to reverse the elitist view of the museum (Crooke, 2006: 171). This has marked out a reappraisal of the community function of the museum through investment in more public facing activities. In the UK, a further set of governmental contexts since the 1990s has had significant effects on shaping local government museums in particular, which account for a significant proportion (25%) of the sector. Indeed, from the 1990s, in the UK, the increasing demand for accountability grew across nearly all domains of public policy, including housing, health, education and social services, coupled with a focus on public participation in services. Set against this background, there were a number of explicit policy directives that positioned museums as having a key role to play in addressing social policy areas, such as building cohesive communities and contributing to neighbourhood regeneration (see Crooke, 2006; Newman and McLean, 2004; Sandell, 2003; Tlili et al., 2007). Although a longer context to deploying heritage for economic and urban regeneration existed from the 1980s, the instrumental use of museums in wider social policy was most clearly articulated during the New Labour years (1997–2010) (Gray, 2008). Government directives, via the newly formed Department for Culture, Media and Sport (DCMS), placed expectations on museums to work in partnership with third sector and local community organisations to contribute to work around employment, crime reduction, urban regeneration and neighbourhood renewal, rehabilitation, health care and health promotion (Sandell, 2003). This linked to a wider policy agenda of combating social exclusion through cross-sectoral approaches, where culture was seen as part of the policy solutions (Levitas, 2005). At a time when museums were already redefining their purpose in terms of their public, conversely, their activities were explicitly steered by public funders into wider social inclusion agendas where they were charged with instituting programmes to engage groups affected by deprivation and social exclusion. 'Access' was also identified as a key area within DCMS policy efforts giving priority to developing and diversifying museum and arts audiences through a targeted approach focused on disability, lower socio-economic groups, Black Minority Ethnic (BME) groups and young people.[5] Over this time period, community engagement projects in the UK museums emerged as a response to these directives through adult education programmes and outreach-led projects where creative and cultural participation was aimed to empower those involved and provide positive impacts in terms of social capital, self-confidence, citizenship, skills and wellbeing (Dodd and Sandell, 2001; GLLAM, 2000). Discussions of how the museum 'acts on the social' are not in themselves new, since we can trace back commentary advocating a role for the museum in addressing social issues such as urban deprivation, moral improvement and citizenship from the early nineteenth century (Bennett, 1995; Silverman, 2010). However, what distinguished this period from the earlier paternalism in the governmental use of culture was the integration of the representational discourse described above. Indeed, much of the museum education and outreach activities in these years focused not only on widening access but also focused on content and display through collaborative projects based on ideas of self-representation and lived experience (Mason, 2004).

The scale of this work is difficult to quantify, but significant investment at this time meant that many sections of the UK museum sector were quickly drawn into developing a range of new education and outreach programmes (see Durrer and Miles, 2009 on art galleries). I would argue that this period of activity has framed the UK museum discourse of 'community engagement' and its practice to a significant extent and with lasting effects (Morse, 2020). The period marked out a strong sense of the 'socially responsible museum', an idea that has retained currency in the UK sector (Dodd, 2015; Tlili et al., 2007). In later years, changes in government to a Conservative–Liberal Democrat coalition (2010–2015) and a Conservative government (since 2015 to date) changed the policy landscape for museums. This has been marked by policy driven by austerity politics in response to the economic crash of 2008, which included significant cuts to local authority budgets, directly affecting local government museums such as TWAM. Government-led agendas in the coalition years pursued a localism and decentralisation agenda to devolve power over funding and policies to local authorities, with policy statements expressing ambitions to engage local communities in taking over and running local services, such as schools, libraries and indeed museums (see Rex, 2018). Within this political programme, civil society and community organising were encouraged to step in with reduced funding, a phenomenon termed 'austerity localism' (Featherstone et al., 2012; Morse and Munro, 2015). There was also an explicit retreat from New Labour's public investment in culture, with successive cuts to DCMS, signalling the intention to revert culture to a marginal governmental concern (Gordon et al., 2015). Elsewhere, I have suggested that in this climate of reduced government funding and support for culture, community engagement was refocused as a way to stake the relevance of the museum and ensure its sustainability by strengthening its (local) civic function (Morse, 2020). This is exemplified, for instance, in the Museums Association's (the sector support body for museums in the UK) manifesto *Museums Change Lives*, which explicitly links the sector's relevance to the social impact of museums.

Of particular interest to the discussion in this book is the work of 'museums in health' that emerged at this juncture. Recent reforms of the UK health sector through the Health and Social Care Act of 2012 (and later the Care Act of 2014) have extended the variety of provider organisations for health services to include the private sector, charity, voluntary and social enterprise organisations at the same time as the responsibility for public health was transferred from the National Health Service to local authorities. This has opened up opportunities for museums to play an active role in improving the health and wellbeing of their local communities in the contexts of cultural commissioning and social prescribing, integrating arts and cultural activities into a range of services, including mental health and wellbeing, older people services and place-based commissioning (Camic and Chatterjee, 2013). This new policy landscape has led many museums to look towards the health sector for new partnerships, in particular community organisations working with people living with dementia and their carers, individuals accessing mental health services and other support organisations (Desmarais et al., 2018; Lackoi et al., 2016). In one sense, we can view this new area of work as refocusing the socially responsible museum to address public health concerns and working with support organisations for individuals who are marginalised because of physical health or mental health. At the same time, the representational discourse remains important in framing this new work and bringing new stories into the museums, as many projects have included elements of small co-produced displays or collecting oral histories, while others have sought to raise public awareness around health and wellbeing issues. I have suggested that we might consider this form of community engagement practice as evolving directly from the practices developed in museums during the social inclusion years, reformulating social impact in the terms of health and wellbeing (Morse, 2020).

The next direction of community engagement is set in an economic discourse. At the same time as the representational and governmental discourse focused museum work on audiences and excluded groups, a wider economic discourse within the public sector from the 1980s onwards has prompted museums to become more consumer-focused and more accountable to their (tax-paying) publics: 'the results has been the reframing of visitors as consumers and users, the promotion of visitor-oriented focus within the museum sector, and the demand that museums must widen their audiences to reach all potential visitors' (Mason, 2004: 63). As Mason makes clear, here, the emphasis on broadening access was the same as in the representational discourse; however, the ideological thrust was markedly different, framed in the demands of the market and its end-users. At times, community engagement has been oriented in this discourse to positive effects, for instance, linked to marketing, education and outreach strategies to build more diverse, socially inclusive audiences and museum experiences that feel more personally relevant to visitors (for UK examples, see Lang et al., 2006). However, there are clear tensions here in terms of how participation is envisaged within a consumer logic through the work of (well meaning) marketing teams, and it is often pointed out that community engagement should not be conflated with (and reduced to) 'audience development' imperatives (Tlili, 2008). Ideas of commercialism and entertainment reflect a fundamental shift towards audiences and visitors within a longer museological discourse that I noted previously, first marked out in the 'New Museology' (Lumley, 1988; Vergo, 1989) and Stephen E Weil's now famous call for the museum's transformation 'from being about something to being for somebody' (1999). Weil then pointed out that the museum's mission had fundamentally changed 'from one of mastery to one of service' (Weil, 1990: 257). In contemporary museology, museums, once traditionally defined by their function (object-based collecting institutions), have become firmly defined by their purpose (education and engagement) and their relations to the public. This has led to understanding the public as plural and active, rather than homogenous and passive, denoting a shift to 'a new orthodoxy of visitor sovereignty' in which ideas and practices of engagement, collaboration and audience development have taken root (Macdonald, 2006: 8). This has also led to the introduction of a range of new terminology in museum practice (communities, audiences, stakeholders, consumers, visitors, citizens, etc.), each signifying different relationships between the museum and its public. Indeed, across the different origins that I seek to mark out, there are many continuities and cross-overs; however, pointing out the discontinuities is more important to my discussion, as it will allow me to highlight the ambivalence of community engagement.

The next direction of community engagement I want to pinpoint comes out of the growth of social media and the possibilities for digital participatory cultures which have further expanded the focus on audiences. Within this, we find The Participatory Museum movement, which takes its title from Nina Simon's book (2010) and her blog *Museum 2.0*, which have been very influential in the UK context and are often referred to in professional settings and conferences. Simon argues for greater participatory practice within museums, which she describes through case studies of projects and programmes (mainly in the USA) in which visitors actively interpret collections and share memories and experiences in the museum, often using interactive or digital means. For Simon, participation is focused on the visitor experience: it is a *design strategy* to create personalised, creative and social experiences for visitors (2010: iv). In this sense, then, participation becomes an umbrella term for the creative ways that audiences are increasingly involved in shaping and consuming the museum. The very language of this participatory practice, which draws from the design and digital domains, frames the purposes of this work within the wider theories and logics of participatory culture and focuses museum practice on visitor participation and audience connections (Parry, 2007).[6] In this model, every person who walks through the museum's doors is a potential contributor to the work of the museum, and museums should build platforms for visitors to make and share content. Here, community engagement practices are usually developed within digital teams and design teams. Creativity and original content generation are central to this practice, rather than specific knowledge or expertise linked to collections, as in the representational discourse, or redressing wider societal forms of exclusion, as in the governmental discourse; rather, it evolves more closely from the economic discourse of consumer's rights. Simon's vision for the participatory museum is progressive in terms of diversifying audiences but it is also pragmatic – it is about securing the relevance of the contemporary museum, and it is part of a business mandate (new visitors are also new supporters). It should be noted that in Simon's early work, the starting point for participation was with individuals; her more recent writing shifts emphasis to espouse an asset-based model working with close communities of interest and creating museums that are 'of, by and for' the community (Simon, 2016).[7] This focuses the idea of participation back onto a broader sense of public relevance and accountability, with creative approaches to participation set firmly at the heart of how the organisation should function. In the UK, the notion of relevance and putting communities at the centre of museum work came together in the Paul Hamlyn Foundation 'Our Museum' project (2012–2015), which supported a number of organisations, TWAM included, to take an organisation-wide approach to engaging communities. The project evaluation reports describe a range of activities and programmes that the museum set up to involve communities more directly in the functioning of the museum, from alternative management teams to collaborative training events (Bienkowski, 2016).[8]

The final direction of community engagement is best understood within the renewal of a contemporary museum ethics, 'founded on the concept that museums can have moral agency' (Marstine, 2011: 5). This is linked to calls for museums to reform themselves to become places of social justice and human rights. In the UK, we might postulate that this final direction has evolved closely from the practice developed during the social inclusion years and within the representational discourse, but the difference arises from the clear positioning of the museum as having an explicit 'moral leadership role' in combating prejudice and supporting social justice (Sandell, 2007: 189). Here, community engagement occurs in response to demands led by activist movements both inside and outside the museum to develop more socially inclusive forms of museum practice around issues of gender, diversity, LGBTQ and disability (Janes and Sandell, 2019; Sandell, 2002, 2007, 2016; Sandell and Nightingale, 2012). This practice has developed across a range of different teams, and it calls for all staff to be involved in the transformation of the museum institution in more profound ways – from its public facing displays, the content of its collections, to its workforce diversity and to scrutinising sponsorship deals. Collectively, this scholarship articulates the generative potential of the museum in actively reconfiguring moral standpoints and their capacity to positively impact the lived experience of those who have experienced prejudice and discrimination. Central here is the sense that museums do not only reflect society but have the potential (and responsibility) to actively shape societal discourses. This work has been linked to new forms of democratic pluralism and moral activism in the museum, alongside urgent calls for the redistribution of power and authority in response to current societal concerns and emergencies (Janes and Sandell, 2019; Marstine, 2011). In this discourse, participation features centrally through collaboration with different civil society groups and campaigning organisations, and community engagement practice takes on a more explicit activist inflection, working with small groups to affect wider societal change. In the UK, there are a growing number of museum-based project that describe themselves as 'activist' or 'campaigning' projects, enabled, in part, by the wider support of campaigns and initiatives of the Museums Association (Morse and McCann, 2019).

As I first indicated, the concept of community engagement in the UK has a number of origins set across different discourses. The notion of participation as an organisational priority for museums was clearly announced in more recent Museums Association publications such as *Power to the People* (2018), their first framework for participatory practice in the museum. It states that 'engaging communities in the life of your museum will make it a more responsive, dynamic and sustainable institution. Meaningful community engagement and participation will raise the profile of your museum and will have a positive impact on how you are perceived by stakeholders, funders and the public' (2018: 5). In this way, community engagement has moved beyond the concerns of representation or social inclusion only, combining the economic discourse with discourses from public policy and using public resources for public good, all of which are brought together to position community engagement as a means of securing the museum's relevance in the twenty-first century. The museum's political form today is firmly set within claims to representation, access and social impact.

Overall, what is clear from my discussion above is that community engagement (and participation more generally) in the UK is made up of a number of distinct origins that have shaped a strong sense of a model of practice founded on concepts of inclusion, diversity and tolerance. However, as we begin to tease these apart, it becomes clearer how in each context, community engagement is framed and deployed in relation to different goals – whether these are about gaining better knowledge of collections;

celebrating local history; as part of developing a socially responsible role or opening up the museum as a platform for visitor experiences; as a means of supporting inclusion and wellbeing; or as a route to activist practice and moral leadership. In each case, the conception of community differs from local communities to targeted groups to consumers to everyone. What unites all these discourses is a desire to pluralise and democratise museums by inviting more people to take part in and contribute to the museum. At one time or another, they can all be in operation; they may dovetail into the same opportunities or they may present conflicting demands. These tensions often appear only in the messiness and specificity of the practice itself. For now, then, we might usefully consider community engagement as an expansive yet ambivalent term that exists within the complementary and contradictory tendencies that make up the political form of the contemporary museum. In the next two chapters, I work through this ambivalence in the language and management of community engagement at TWAM during the period of my ethnographic research.

Theories of engagement in the museum

Critical academic discussions of participation in the museum can be said to have focused on two areas: first, the centre/periphery dynamic in the museum and, second, the priority of participant choice and control. A significant theory of engagement for museums can be found in James Clifford's (1997) notion of the museum as 'contact zone'. Borrowing the phrase from Mary Louise Pratt (1992), Clifford used the contact perspective to examine the nature of post-colonial encounters in the museum, based on his observations of a Tlingit visit to the Portland Art Museum in Canada. For Clifford, the relationships between museums and their communities have historically been characterised by radically asymmetric relations of power, 'usually involving conditions of coercion, radical inequality, and intractable conflict' that are embedded in the museum's catalogues and displays (Clifford, 1997: 192). Clifford makes clear that contemporary relationships are still characterised by uneven power relations and that these must be recognised as the starting point to any cross-cultural engagement. Emerging from the representational discourse, the contact zone is articulated through the principle of (uneven) reciprocity and the potential for shared authority, agency and collaboration in asymmetrical power relations. For Clifford, reciprocity is fundamentally 'a power-charged set of exchanges of push and pull', in which 'what exceed the apparatus of coercion and stereotypes in contact relations may perhaps be reclaimed' towards more equitable forms of exchange and mutual benefit (Clifford, 1997: 192, 200). The possibilities of the contact zone as a 'dialogic space' have provided much optimism for collaborative work in the museum across the world (Witcomb, 2003). As Robin Boast suggests, it is a central idea of postmodern museology, either explicitly or often implicitly, especially in cross-cultural and multicultural work (Boast, 2011: 59; Hutchison and Collins, 2009; Peers and Brown, 2003; Phillips, 2005). The concept of the contact zone has also been very influential in shaping UK museums' approaches to working with diaspora communities (Lynch, 2011a; Lynch and Alberti, 2010; McLean, 2008; Purkis, 2013). Following such influence, the concept has been extensively debated,[9] but it has also been instructively used to examine the forms, processes and products of collaboration (Boast, 2011; Lynch and Alberti, 2010). For some scholars, it holds the possibility for the renegotiation and contestation of complex relationships with communities in museum settings (Krmpotich and Peers, 2013; McCarthy, 2007; Schorch, 2013; Witcomb, 2003). It has also been extended in interesting ways to recognise the forms of cultural engagement and negotiation that take place beyond the museum and which also influence its processes (for example, see Krmpotich and Peers, 2013 on the 'third space'; and Onciul, 2015 on the 'engagement zone'). In another context, Dodd et al. (2017) have used the concept of the 'trading zone' (borrowed from science and technology studies) as a space through which different forms of expertise (for instance, the expertise that derives from lived experience of impairment and disability) can come together on equal terms with collection knowledge in museum interpretation. Here, we might also draw parallels with the long running notion of the contact zone. The key point I want to raise is that the concept of the contact/trading zone as a theory of engagement draws attention to the centre/periphery dynamic in the museum – the museum as the centre and the community at its periphery. This centre/periphery dynamic has also animated wider discussions of community engagement in museums that have demanded that participation must move from the margins of the institution to the core. I address these critiques further below.

Another focus of theories of engagement has been around categorizing 'types' of engagement along a spectrum based on the level of power that is shared. A common typology of participation for community engagement in the public sector is Sherry Arnstein's (1969) Ladder of Citizen Participation, which, although dated, remains a key model to theorise participation, and one that has been widely adopted and adapted in museum research (Gibson and Kindon, 2013; Govier, 2009; Onciul, 2013). Arnstein describes a hierarchical model across three main categories with different steps. The lowest part of the ladder represents 'non-participation' (steps 1–2: manipulation and therapy), moving up to 'tokenism' (steps 3–5: informing, consultation, placation) and finally, up to 'citizen power' (steps 6–8: partnership, delegated power, citizen control). In Arnstein's model, participation is equated with the concept of power sharing within determined projects in public institutions. Applied to the museum, it is used to assess participation in different aspects of a museum project, for instance, an exhibition. The ladder centres on the question of 'how much' participation: how much power is shared? Implied in this model is the redistribution of power as the ultimate aim of participation, and so the measure of participation is the power for participants to make unrestricted decisions, and this is the desirable end point. Indeed, concerns over the redistribution of power have focused much of the museum literature on community engagement, particularly in account of co-producing exhibitions (Lynch and Alberti, 2010; Peers and Brown, 2003) and community-led heritage projects (Smith and Waterton, 2009). These discussions are based on the values of 'choice' and 'control': the capacity of individuals or groups to make decisions on narratives, choice of objects, etc., and the role of participants in controlling the processes of production of a heritage project or an exhibition, for example. Following the ladder/spectrum model, a range of new terminologies have been introduced to describe the higher levels of engagement as they apply in the museum, from co-curation, co-production and co-creation, each term having different emphases in terms of how much authority and control is shared between the museum and communities. The model of the ladder has been critiqued for its limitation as a linear model, and more complex theories of participation have been presented to acknowledge the messy nature of participatory processes and their power dynamics within non-homogenous groups (Bovaird, 2007; Burns et al., 1994; Tritter and McCallum, 2006; Wilcox, 1994). Burns et al.'s (1994) ladder is particularly interesting in focusing attention to the quality of engagement process, which is also my focus later in this book (a focus on the 'how' rather than the 'how much' engagement). Nonetheless, the ladder model of participation remains influential in museum thinking, positioning participant choice and control as the pinnacle of involvement and as key measures of success in community engagement practice.

A third and significant model of engagement in the museum field is Nina Simon's typology of participation, developed in her influential book *The Participatory Museum* (2010). Simon presents four forms of institutionally defined participation in museums: Contributory, where communities have a specific and often limited input in an institutionally controlled process; Collaborative, where visitors become active participants in shaping a museum project that is ultimately controlled by the museum; Co-creative, where communities work with museum staff from the beginning to define the project's goals; and Hosting, where the museum opens its facilities and resources for communities to develop projects themselves. In her view, these different participatory categories are not progressively more valuable or better than each other. Simon's main argument is that museums must consider the implications of community work and develop models that best fit their institutional goals. In this way, Simon's model is mostly pragmatic rather than influenced by the democratic imperatives of Arnstein's ladder. The influence of Simon's work can be understood through her focus on the institution: she provides inspiration for organisational change as well as direction for strategic approaches. This call has been taken up by UK initiatives such as the Paul Hamlyn Foundation 'Our Museum' project and the Museums Association's publication *Power to the People* (2018), which present a framework through which museums can move towards a 'holistic approach' to community engagement, as part of core work and strategic programming, with community involvement in decision-making on projects and wider strategy. This whole organisation 'theory of change' approach marks out the final key theory of engagement in current museological discussion (Lynch, 2015). This goes back to the dynamic of centre/periphery by demanding that participation is brought into the centre of the organisation to affect change, focusing on the key tenets of sharing control and decision-making with communities and bringing together the two areas that have animated different theories of engagement.

Dissatisfied yet optimistic

As I contended earlier, the participatory turn in museums has inspired a range of community engagement practices promoted as a means for advancing the plurally democratic museum. At the same time, scholars have questioned the extent to which participation realises these goals in practice. Two practical critiques are levelled at the practice: the first is about the levels of involvement (i.e. the ladder theory), and the second is about the limited scale of impact, where participatory work remains at the surface without addressing institutional practice due to a lack of strategic leadership (see also Graham, 2019). In the UK, an influential report, *Whose Cake Is It Anyway?*, found that:

> Despite presenting numerous examples of ground-breaking, innovative practice, the funding invested in public engagement and participation in the UK's museums and galleries has not significantly succeeded in shifting the work from the margins to the core of many of these organisations.
>
> (Lynch, 2011c: 5)

Despite its promises, community engagement disappoints. Participatory processes are co-opted, consensus is manipulated, the museum only works with the usual suspects, the results are often little more than tokenism, and everyone – participants and museum practitioners – is left 'generally dissatisfied' (Lynch, 2014: 79). In fact, the museum's invitation to participate is met with disappointment precisely because it promises so much, invoking the ideas of community choice, control and self-representation and, ultimately, the museum's reform. Community engagement is therefore a problem in the museum.

In their edited book on participatory development, *Participation: The New Tyranny?* (2001), Bill Cooke and Uma Kothari contend that since the first attempts at genuine participation, the concept has been appropriated, as suggested by the Arnstein's ladder. Participatory initiatives tend to be in name only, since they are often 'top-down' and extractive. Cooke and Kothari make clear that participation itself is a form of power, and as such, it most often ends up reproducing the inequalities it seeks to challenge. In their words, participation masks 'continued centralization in the name of decentralization' (Cooke and Kothari, 2001: 7). Cooke and Kothari's call for participatory practice to begin with a more serious consideration of power relations is one that has been taken up in the museum studies literature, drawing on a longer scholarship that has examined the role of discourse in the reproduction of exclusion (Boast, 2011; Clifford, 1997; Karp and Lavine, 1991; Peers and Brown, 2003; Sandell, 2002; Smith and Waterton, 2009). For many commentators, the failure of participatory practice more generally, and beyond the critiques of scale and level of involvement, is its failure to analyse and dismantle institutional power – or put another way, its failure to address the power at the core of the institution. Bernadette Lynch is an important commentator here who has focused the debates in the UK museum sector and beyond, drawing on her own experience working at the Manchester Museum and her extensive research with the Paul Hamlyn Foundation (Lynch, 2011b, 2015). In the widely referenced *Cake* report (2011c), Lynch argues that museums' participatory efforts have so far only practised 'empowerment-lite' (citing Cornwall and Coelho, 2007) because museums continue to retain institutional control, resulting in work that is paternalistic and/or tokenistic (reflecting the ladder idea). The power imbalance is revealed in the processes of collaboration, with projects often heavily museum-led, where the final right to edit any content produced collaboratively is retained by the museum (Fouseki, 2010; Lynch, 2011b; Lynch and Alberti, 2010). Lynch brings to attention two strong analyses of power in the museum. First, she highlights how participation takes shape within the 'invited spaces' of the museum (c.f. Cornwall, 2008; Fraser, 1990; Gaventa, 2004), where the rules of engagement are always already pre-defined by those who create these spaces and those who issue the invitation:

> When we invite others into our space, from the outset the relationship is permeated with the power effects of difference – them and us – us and them. Thus, while an illusion of creative participation is what is on offer, decisions tend to be coerced or rushed through on the basis of the institution's agenda or strategic plan, manipulating a group consensus of what is inevitable, usual or expected.
>
> (Lynch, 2011b: 451)

Second, her central argument is that participation, as it is currently imagined, is flawed because it operates within a 'welfare model':

> A culture of 'giving', doing 'for', 'on behalf of' (...) runs throughout the cultural sector, infecting both curatorial and educational practices alike. (...) the rhetoric of 'service' continues to place the subject in the role of 'supplicant', 'beneficiary' or 'learner' and the provider (the museum and its staff) in the role of teacher/carer', perpetrating a 'deficit' model which assumes that people, 'learners' have 'gaps' which need

filling or fixing through museum intervention, rather than a theory of change that places people at the centre, as active in their own right.

(Lynch, 2016: 256)

Lynch diagnoses this welfare model across museum and policy practice and in the language that museum professionals use when describing their work, which in turn forms the institutional habits that limit current approaches to participation (Lynch, 2011c, 2016). This welfare model is based on a deficit perspective as part of a wider socio-political ideology that approaches exclusion based upon perceptions of individuals' personal shortcomings or 'incompleteness' (Levitas, 2005). In this perspective, the institutional response is to produce a needs-based programme of museum activities as a form of cultural compensation. The positioning of participants as beneficiaries underpins Lynch's characterisation of participation work as 'empowerment-lite'. I will return very directly to this welfare critique in the final chapter of the book, where I seek to reclaim the welfare notion in my own discussion of care – but this comes later.

For Lynch, the main challenge in participatory practices resides in addressing the 'invisible power' at play in museums (after Lukes, 1974). The more overt use of institutional power includes agenda-setting and top-down decisions. For instance, in some cases, public participation is manipulated as a means to 'rubber-stamp' pre-existing plans (see also Fouseki, 2010). Invisible power operates as a more subtle form of consensual power that convinces or co-opts both museum professionals and participants into what is 'common sense' or inevitable. This power is implicit in understandings of 'how things work' in the museum (Lynch, 2011a: 153), underpinning the taken for granted nature of the 'welfare model' of participation. This subtle form of power also aligns communities with the values and agenda of the institution. In this way, while museums invite participation, they also control it. Writing about her own experience at the Manchester Museum during a collaborative exhibition *Myths about Race*, Lynch reflects a perhaps typical scene that has played out in numerous museums:

This particular meeting at the Manchester Museum took place at a late stage in the exhibition planning process, when pressure was high to resolve and implement decisions. Community members voiced dissatisfaction with the process, and what they perceived as the museum exercising a veto based on its power to make decisions off-agenda, outside the meetings. It is entirely likely that staff members had little or no awareness of the ways in which such a 'veto' operated.

(Lynch, 2011a: 148)

This lack of awareness is echoed in the *Cake* report, which suggests that museum professionals have little understanding of how power shapes the development and delivery of community engagement work, and the ways in which it is influenced by institutional 'habits of mind' and the values that are considered normal or desirable. Against the invisible power of the institution, the good intentions of museum professionals appear to have little force since 'a subtle and coercive power at work in the museum obscures the view, creating and recreating the hegemony of the museum/gallery as institution so that those involved feel powerless to really analyse or challenge it' (Lynch, 2011b: 444; see also Boast, 2011: 67). We should note, however, that other times in her writing, it appears that the failure of participation is the museum's fear of loss of control, with staff more or less implicated. This critique resonates in other writings too. For instance, a follow-on study from the *Cake* report highlighted cross-departmental staff resistance to participatory work as 'both conscious and unconscious – it can be poor understanding of community engagement, lack of interest [or] fear of participation as a perceived threat to professional expertise and status' (Bienkowski, 2016: 8).

The next set of challenges identified by Lynch concerns the organisation and management of participation in the museum. The *Cake* report suggests that the UK funding model kept participation at the margins of the institution through short-term project-based funding with unsustainable impact. The report also suggests that engagement practice is risk-averse and characterised by high levels of control (a more predictable top-down form of power here). This is further exacerbated by funding regimes that are seen to discourage critical reflection: 'Museums are rewarded for "success," not for their risk-taking or the challenges and failures they face. Nor are they encouraged (in project funding reports) to honestly and openly reflect on the difficulties in their work' (Lynch, 2011b: 445). Other practical issues that affect participation are restricted budgets and timeframes, which are often not clearly described to participants, leading to tensions later on in the project (Lynch and Alberti, 2010). Mark O'Neill has further reflected on the organisation of participation in UK museums. He also invokes the core/periphery metaphor to suggest that current forms of participatory work via temporary exhibitions and outreach activities have so far remained at the margin as small-scale targeted projects and, as such, have become the way the core is protected from change (O'Neill, 2010). As previously mentioned, the idea of the 'core' is significant, and I return to it in a moment.

Despite the trenchant critiques levelled at participation in the museum, Lynch and other scholars present a number of ways forward. Building on her work from the *Cake* report and to counter the argument of empowerment-lite, the Paul Hamlyn Our Museum project advocated a more strategic approach where communities are seen as active partners and community engagement is made central to all of museum work (in terms of staff roles, budgeting, programming, etc.) (Bienkowski, 2016). From an academic perspective, in order to move forward, the argument is that museums need to 'unlearn their privilege' through reflective practice that questions habits of mind and established ways of working in collaboration with community partners (Lynch, 2011a, 2011b). This requires the practice of 'radical trust' and 'reciprocity', where the museum accepts it cannot control the outcome (Lynch and Alberti, 2010: 16). Following political theorist Chantal Mouffe, Lynch argues that 'conflict must be allowed to be central to democratic participation if museums are to view participants as *actors* rather than *beneficiaries*' (2011a: 160 emphasis in original). In this way, museums can become spaces 'not only for collaboration but also for contestation' (Lynch and Alberti, 2010: 16), breaking out of the welfare model. For Lynch, conflict is the very site of interaction that enables reciprocity and trust. To this end, she reconfigures Clifford's contact zone as a 'political space between adversaries, where the power relations which structure these encounters are brought to the fore, creating a liberating effect for museums and their community partners' (2011a: 155). By creating these political spaces, museums can in turn harness their wider potential to act as training grounds for agency and participatory democracy more generally (Lynch, 2011b; see also Simon, 2016). In more recent work, Lynch has also presented critical pedagogy as a route to disrupting the welfare model of participation, particularly in the context of the decolonising practice led by curatorial and educational teams (Lynch, 2016). And so, despite being 'generally dissatisfied' with participation, the museum studies literature has returned to participation as the solution to the problem of participation, or, as Ben Dibley puts it, as the route to the museum's 'redemption' (2005). Helen Graham clearly summarises this optimistic return:

> It is a specific site where (the story goes) *if* museums' 'neocolonial legacy' is fully recognized (Boast, 2011, p. 67), *if* a museum recognizes its role in combating 'social inequality' and 'prejudice' (Sandell, 2002, p. 3), *if* community co-production is conducted with 'honesty, dialogue, recognition of power, a holistic and integrated approach, and a critical regard for the social and political context of community engagement' (Smith and Waterton, 2009, p. 139) and in the spirit of 'reciprocity' and 'radical trust' and with an acceptance of conflict (Lynch and Alberti 2010, p. 16) – the promise of heritage and/or the museum as really democratic will be realized.
>
> (Graham, 2012b: 566)

What is interesting and significant to note here is how the critique of participation returns to its original promise. There is a sense that more, better or modified participation can secure the participatory museum as originally intended. Graham reveals how the current critique of museum participation is caught in a persistent cycle of critique-contest, followed by optimism for the 'always-yet-to-be-realized' practice that will guarantee the democratic museum in a normative sense (i.e. an adjusted practice of participation that will secure the participatory museum). Graham relates this persistent critique-contest dynamic to Tony Bennett's description of the 'political rationality of the museum'. Bennett's key contribution to museum studies is his discussion of the museum through Foucault's analysis of governmental-ity as applied to the logic of culture. For Bennett, the museum is 'constantly subject to demands for reform' (1995: 90). Since the nineteenth century, the museum has been animated by a number of contradictory demands; namely, the 'demand that museums should be equally open and accessible to all' and 'the demand that museums should adequately represent the cultures and values of different sections of the public'. Bennett concludes that the museum is essentially an 'unamenable' institution, being configured as both a 'vehicle for popular education' *and* simultaneously an 'instrument for the reform of public manners' (1995: 90). A persistent contradiction ensues between its rhetorical form (democratic or participatory or otherwise) and its pedagogical form; 'between exchange and narration or reciprocity and imposition' (Miller and Yudice, 2002: 158). The museum presents an insatiable mismatch between rights and reform.[10] Added to this is the particular custodian function of museums, where decisions are to be made not only in relation to people in the present, but also on behalf of everyone, now and future generations (Graham, 2017).

Graham transposes Bennett's position on the early public museums onto contemporary participatory discourses in museums:

> When seen through this lens rather than being counter to the logics of the museum, calls for greater participation and empowerment are fully consonant with the rationality of the museum. In short those who animate the demands Bennett describes are not so much vanguardists as confirming and restoring the very institutional purposes of the museum. The counter-hegemony is, in this sense, already factored in.
>
> (2012b: 567)

For Bennett, then, much of participatory work is simply reconfiguring the relations between museums and forms of governmentality. It is a 'programme of the same type' (Bennett, 1998: 212).[11] For Graham, a key effect of the critique-contest cycle is that it has produced a critical impasse in museum studies (hegemony/counter-hegemony; critique/reform/critique/and so on). It is this impasse that I am most interested in for now. The consequence of this is the reinforcement of certain dominant conceptual pathways, notably a persistent return to the idea of the 'core', 'with participation being understood as being constantly, centripetally, in a contest-mode with a fixed centre' (Graham, 2019: 86), and where the proposed solution is more and better participation at the centre. In a moment, I will go further to suggest another persistent idea in the literature where the current ideal of participation and its critique are formulated within a 'logic of contribution', whereby the museum remains at the centre, therefore restoring the institution. The issue in both cases is a narrowing of the object of study. At one level, it isolates the museum from broader networks of democracy and therefore simultaneously overplays and mutes its potential by misappropriating the ideas of scale, as

Graham notes: 'Once the institutional critique phase has been completed then the hoped for co-production practice is imagined as reworking the dynamics between museum and public so effectively at a micro level that it is as if it might simply be scaled up to then transform the museum and power in general' (2012b: 568). But far from suggesting that there is no politics to be done in the museum, Graham calls for a 'contingent micropolitics for museum practice' in order to focus discussion of participation at the level of 'in-practice dynamics themselves – how [culture] is calibrated and, specifically, the scale on which that calibration is predicated' (2012b: 569). Viewed up close, other readings of participatory work are possible that eschew a disciplinary reading and may provide a way out of the critique-contest impasse. A close-up view also opens up conceptual space to focus on the frontline worker in museum practice – in my case, community engagement practitioners. At this level, we can consider the specifics of museum work and their own particular logics in practice. Following Graham's lead, as I move onto a discussion of community engagement in practice in the remainder of this book, I am looking at the possibilities of participatory forms of practice 'at the level of practicalities (how projects are conceived and organized) and practice (how projects are made up through interactions)' (Graham, 2012b: 569), and the work of calibration that takes place within existing institutional contexts.

In bringing us close-up to practicalities, we move from discursive forms of museum practice (and theory) to engagement with nondiscursive, emotional and embodied experiences of the museum and museum work. This, in itself, opens up a different conceptual path forward for participatory practice outside of the current critical impasse. I will also be moving in and out of the museum – therefore locating community engagement across different spaces, and into broader networks, where its potential can be explored along yet other conceptual paths, in a way that reworks the core/periphery discussion (Chapter 6). Additionally, the current critique-then-desired-contest cycle is reflective of a problem of totalising 'all or nothing' dichotomies – curated/co-produced, curator/community and museum control/community control. However, it does not serve us well to work with such binaries and neither does it serve to view the museum as a homogenous rational machine. Museums are made up of multiple and contradictory people and practices. It is therefore possible for multiple forms of the museum to be made at any one time (c.f. Mol, 2002). By focusing on people, practicalities and practice, a much more nuanced and contingent discussion of participatory work comes to the fore.

The logic of contribution

The review of the literature around community engagement has traced a long tradition of demanding more, and better, participatory practice in museums. To this point in the chapter, I have considered a number of different directions and discourses that have underpinned these demands. Reflecting on these together, I want to suggest that many of these discourses are animated by a common and persistent logic – the logic of contribution – and that this logic extends through the critical impasse, further entrenching it. In the end, however, I will turn to approaches that begin to exceed this persistent logic and set out a possible alternative – the logic of care.

The logic of contribution defines the evolution of the public museum as a participatory place that individuals and groups input into through donations, bequests, through telling their stories, through to visitor-generated content and co-produced collaboration.[12] The forms of the contribution have evolved over time as the museum has opened up to more and more diverse forms of contributions, responding to different demands (representational or governmental or ethical or otherwise), to include much wider range and types of contributions: new types of objects, stories and re-interpretations of collections. However, and this is the key point, the relationship between the museum and its communities has in the main remained focused on a relationship of contribution from one into the other. While the rhetoric and ethics have extended through reciprocity, mutuality and dialogue, underpinning much of the practice, we can still discern a contributory logic, aimed towards the reform of the institution – creating more responsive, more inclusive, more relevant museums. It is the particular *institutional form* of the museum (and its political rationality) that I aim to consider closely in this final discussion, and which I suggest we need to understand as primarily shaped and upheld in a logic of contribution.

The logic of contribution can be found across many of the discourses that I described earlier. The representational discourse has pluralised and diversified the number of contributors to the museum who in turn contribute to making more knowledgeable, more relevant and 'better' institutions. This work has been, and continues to be, critical in expanding representation and the stories that are told in museums. However, we might consider whether these community engagement efforts are perhaps on the whole mostly demotic rather than democratic, as more and more ordinary and diverse people are represented in museums (see Turner, 2010). In this expansion, the form of the museum has not much changed: it remains an institution that collects, preserves and displays. The economic and digital discourses also operate within the logic of contribution, albeit here contribution is opened up on different terms, either via customers' rights or through the idea of the digital commons or through direct appeals to visitors to create content in the museum. Across these discourses, the museum has been required to shift its ways of working, but in the main, this work has been about reforming the institution rather than transforming its purpose.

In the logic of contribution, community engagement is therefore instigated by and focused on the institution: contributions are sought on the museum's invitation, and community engagement is imagined through certain codes, languages and knowledges that are expected as valid and valuable forms of contribution. For example, the form of an interpretation for an object, whether museological or non-expert or even inviting critique and challenge (I explore this more in Chapter 4). The logic of contribution reflects the core/periphery dynamic that animates the museum: bringing contributions from the outside into the centre. In this logic, the contribution is unidirectional, from the outside-in. While contribution might semantically be considered as framing two directions, in the logic I am describing here, it is firmly linked to the dynamic of core/periphery and focused on the contribution of the community into the museum. Fundamentally, the logic of contribution asks: 'what can the community do for the museum?' so as to lead to its betterment and reform. As such, it is always oriented to the centre; contributions go to the core, and in doing so, they build, improve and restore the museum. In this logic, participation begins and ends with the museum. Viewed through this lens, the core/periphery that participatory practices seek to dislodge in fact defines participation in the logic of contribution.

The logic of contribution is also perpetuated within discussions and critiques of museum participation. As I discussed above, referring Graham's and Dibley's arguments, the critique of participation is hopeful, and, in its optimism, it redeems the museum's institutional form. If Graham is right that calls for greater participation (in a modified sense) confirm the institutional purposes of the museum, and I think she is, then the logic of contribution is replicated in the critique of participation *and* its proposed solutions, further entrenching the impasse. I want to suggest that the critique-contest discourse as it stands does not fully recognise the logic of contribution that underpins current debates of participation, and because it does not recognise it, it does not seek alternatives, and the proposed solutions to participation and community engagement remain framed within the same logic.

Current debates around community engagement, I have suggested previously, focus on two areas: a desired move from the periphery to the centre and a focus on participant choice and control. These are reflected in the dominant models of participation: the contact zone and the ladder of participation. Across museological writing, the stated aim is to move participation from the margins of the organisation to the core, into policies, strategies and museum operations. The way to do this is to ensure that participants are in control – to move towards the top of the ladder. In the logic of contribution, participants choose what they contribute and control how they contribute. To be clear, this can radically alter what museums collect, and the stories that they tell, so that they become different kinds of knowledge institutions. The logic of contribution is not necessarily regressive, or entirely compromised: it can reform many different areas of museum practice. However, it leaves the institution mostly intact. Ultimately, contribution will ameliorate the museum (and for some, this might be enough), but it will not change its institutional form. Viewed in this way, calls for embedding or mainstreaming participation are fully consonant with the logic of contribution. Projects like the Paul Hamlyn Foundation 'Our Museum' programme extends the logic further: by placing communities 'at the heart of the museum', communities are asked to contribute to museum management functions through their contribution to boards, strategy development and other forms of decision-making mechanisms.

The second dimension of the critical mode is the focus on participant choice and participant control. Here, the desired form of contribution is one that is shaped through free choice and in a manner where participants have control. Indeed, and well beyond the museum, individual choice is widely celebrated as an ideal. This is an explicitly normative celebration: choice is a good that offers autonomy and control affords emancipation. But they have also been questioned (e.g. Clarke et al., 2007; Mol, 2010). In the museum, however, this is rarely the case. For now, we might consider some immediate concerns. Choices presented to participants are rarely about themselves, more often they are about the museum, or what is possible to do within the museum. As such, we often lack the material resources required to choose. Choice also assumes that we are knowledgeable and self-directing subjects, capable of easily identifying and articulating wants or desires as rational choices that can be translated into the language of the institution. In the same way, presenting participants with a supposed 'blank canvas' is often disingenuous and equally disempowering. Choice and control in the museum tend to be equated with decision-making (such as an interpretive label, a choice of object, etc.) but often, deciding something is rarely enough to actually achieve anything. Furthermore, satisfying participants with 'choice' may not be the same thing as providing opportunities and tools for fulfilling engagement – these might lay elsewhere. The notion of participant choice also presupposes museum professionals as neutral facilitators, which is rarely the case, and here, I also believe that something important is lost that is fundamental to the quality of community engagement work. Finally, we might also wonder about the continued reliance of the community to improve the museum through more expansive forms of participation where the museum is not in control, rather than the museum perhaps taking control (and responsibility) to seriously fix itself through collaboration and other means. These are immediate concerns. As I go through the book, I come back to these ideas of choice and control to consider how they circulate and play out in the museum, and in the practice of community engagement at TWAM.

The two main foci of the critical mode require further questioning; I follow these ideas in practice throughout the book. But to fully consider the contributory logic of the museum, and to understand the persistence of this logic in both the discourse and critique, we also need to reflect further on the political rationality of the museum, and in particular, how the museum has sought to establish its legitimacy. Indeed, many strands of the discussions around participation have emerged within a more fundamental questioning of the institution's legitimacy and its responsibilities towards communities. I come back to Helen Graham (2012a) here. She suggests that there are three main arguments that museums put forward for participation: 'good for us', where participation sustains better knowledge institutions and more relevant institutions; 'good for them', which sustains more socially responsible institutions; and 'good for us all', which sustains new forms of legitimacy based on museum ethics and activism. The different discourses I presented earlier can be considered through these museum claims. In Graham's sense, the most significant remark is that in each case, these claims set out to secure the museum's political legitimacy, or, following a critique of current participatory practice, to redeem its political legitimacy. Linking to this idea of legitimacy, I want to suggest that much community engagement work in museums still remains within a 'good for the museum' argument, reflecting the logic of contribution, where contribution is intimately bound up with securing the legitimacy of the museum. In this sense, the logic of contribution reflects the contemporary political rationality of the museum – it aims to pluralise the numbers of people involved at the same time as holding on to its legitimacy as a public institution that collects, preserves and displays. As Dewdney et al. (2012: 156) state, the museum remains a 'place to which tribute must be paid'.[13]

It would be possible to read the logic of contribution quite simply through the critical lens described previously and view the museum as an institution that manipulates, co-opts and retains power. I am not exactly in dispute with these arguments. It is critical to name power in the museum and trace both overt and invisible power dynamics that shape museums and their work. My argument however points to a closer examination of the museum form to consider what other interpretations might be possible. It is useful at this juncture for me to turn to social geography's engagement with participation in the context of Participatory Action Research (PAR) to draw out this argument further (Kindon et al., 2008). Here, participation is understood along different lines, drawing on other genealogies of political thought. In the context of academic research, PAR draws on emancipatory pedagogy (such as Paulo Friere), where participation is grounded in people's struggle and local knowledges, and research is turned into a means of social transformation. While PAR is increasingly viewed as one answer to the recent questioning of relevance and legitimacy in academic work (so similar to the museum), at the heart of the PAR project is the focus on connecting research and knowledge production with social change. The object of the participation is agreed collaboratively, as researchers and participants identify an issue or situation in need of change, since PAR 'aims to change practices, social structures, and media which maintain irrationality, injustice, and unsatisfying forms of existences' (Kindon et al., 2008: 90). While it is context-bound, it often identifies institutions that are part of the practices, structures and media that are in need of change, as well as working consciously within multiple scales. This marks out a different beginning and end point from the logic of contribution: the 'key point here is that while people's participation in research is important (and an ethical necessity), unless it translates into action that somehow improves their lives on their own terms, it serves to perpetuate (perhaps even exacerbate) existing inequalities' (Kindon et al., 2009: 94). Museum participation in the logic of contribution does not fully hold this capacity. That is not to say that engaging in museum projects does not have significant benefits for participants, particularly in terms of self-representation, and as we will see thought this book, in terms of sense of self and wellbeing; rather, it indicates that participation operates within the limitations of the museum form. In the museum's modes of participation, the action is always ultimately oriented at ameliorating the institution, rather than necessarily having the capacity to move beyond it. Central to PAR is the need to hold together its three elements; in museum participation, the 'action' imperative is often held apart, as it is already predetermined and set on fixing the institution.

Towards another logic of practice

While I contend that the logic of contribution is the dominant logic that frames the majority of community engagement work in museums, there are also approaches that begin to exceed this logic. First is the museum's claim that participation is 'good for them', which posits the contribution in the other way whereby the museum is contributing to the community (so this is a different sense of contribution to the logic I am describing). The social inclusion discourse, as a governmental discourse, is founded in this claim, as is much of the recent work around museums in health.[14] Within the argument that participation is 'good for them', the most damning critique suggests that despite good intention, this form of community engagement work represents a 'welfare model' that places participants in a passive role as 'beneficiaries', reinforcing existing power relations and resulting only in 'empowerment-lite' for participants (Lynch, 2011c, 2016). In this book, I want to revisit and challenge this critique to explore a much more sympathetic view to recover the idea of welfare and, more broadly, the potential of the museum in relations of social care. To do so, I am again inspired by PAR approaches to participation, which see the relationship with participants as the most significant. While recent discussions in museums have determined the need to look at the *processes* of engagement/participation over the forms and products only (Govier, 2009; Knudsen, 2016), I would still suggest that the dominant focus on contribution and improving the museum has been at the expense of serious engagement with relations. Or rather, the attention to relations has focused more or less exclusively on 'choice' and 'control' (or their opposite, 'empowerment-lite'), at the expense of a wider relational approach that is attentive to grounded and embodied engagements. Within PAR in social geography, we can pick out the importance of relations and relational praxis, and more particularly, the conception of PAR as an 'ethics of care', going beyond the research ethics principle of 'doing no harm' only, 'in which primacy is placed upon relationships and the responsibilities involved in working with communities' (Cahill, 2007: 361). This brings us to a word, an idea, a practice, that is the key concern of this book: care.

The second claim that starts to exceed the dominant logic of contribution is the 'good for us all' mode, represented in the final direction for community engagement and linked to the renewal of a contemporary museum ethics and the growth of activist and campaigning practice in museums. Drawing together ideas of museums as training grounds for wider democratic engagement and the concept of the museum with a moral leadership role, this claim begins to disrupt the logic of contribution because its activities are oriented beyond the institution as they consider the ways in which museums both reflect and shape society and influence societal conversations. The community engagement practice is here focused on direct relations with people that often go beyond issues of representation only, to focus on empowerment and forms of action outside the museum. This represents a small, but increasingly vocal and growing area of museum practice in the UK and internationally. This work has also demanded institutional change in explicit terms as well as calling for the transformation of the museum sector and society more broadly. Here, the work of community engagement can be found in different types of logic that may include contribution but which also far exceed it (see Janes and Sandell, 2019; Simon, 2016).[15]

In the following chapters, taking TWAM as the case study, I examine how the logic of contribution plays out in the language and management of community engagement, drawing together three decades of practices across the museum service (Part II). The scale, structures and history of TWAM, with multiple venues managed through local authority arrangements in a service with a strong sense of its civic role, make this a particularly interesting example through which to reflect on the museum form and the ambivalence of community engagement as discourse and practice. Taking my second concern and returning to Graham's call for a 'contingent micropolitics for museum practice' (2012b: 569), in Part III, I focus on the practice of community engagement workers at TWAM which again I trace over several decades, and its evolution into the broad area of museums in health. It is from this particular practice that I want to outline another logic for community engagement work that can operate as an alternative to the logic of contribution – the logic of care.

To develop this idea, I look at the everyday practice of community engagement workers, and the ways in which this practice develops as an ethics of care, focused on close relations with marginalised and other community groups where care is central, but in a way that breaks firmly away from the disempowering notions of 'passive beneficiaries' and which views the welfare model in more sympathetic ways. My aim in developing an alternative is to present a different conceptual path to the current critical discussions of participation. The alternative path I develop works within the current institutional rationality and form of the museum. It also works within an acceptance that participation is a form of governance with potentially negative effects. But rather than abandon the 'problem' of community engagement, I suggest that we look for different logics in order to reorganise the forms of the relations between the museum and its community in order to re-theorise the empowerment sought through participatory approaches. This is where care comes into the museum. The logic of care might be considered across the 'good for them'/welfare claim (that I wish to reclaim) and, in its more activist form, as part of the 'good for us all' claim, for instance, in initiatives linked to combating health inequalities. I will suggest that an alternative such as the logic of care can be developed within *existing* institutional politics to open up forms of museum community engagement practice that can be at the same time governmental and ethical. The logic of care is focused less on sweeping reform, and more on the creative work of tinkering, working around and within existing museum structures on the ways to transforming the institution. At the very end of this book, I will take this further to explore how an alternative way of thinking – care thinking – can offer a way out of the critical impasse of the problem of engagement, with possibilities towards transforming the museum more completely, into space of social care: a form of the museum that puts relations and practices of care as central, and where the museum plays an active role in broader landscapes of formal and informal care provision.

Notes

1 There are longer-standing debates in museum studies about 'community' (Crooke, 2008; Karp et al., 1992; Watson, 2007). For the purpose of this book, the essential defining characteristic of a community is a sense of belonging that links those who are a part of it (after Kavanagh, 1990). Communities are created around the needs, interests and wishes of people. Communities may exist outside of the museum, or they may emerge through specific museum projects (after Witcomb, 2003). It is not the target audiences, which is often a reductive set of demographics; it is not the public, which is too general. There is something about community that implies immediacy and connection: for me, it is a term that links diverse individuals with a common purpose/need/interest, and I am interested in how the museum can become more responsive to communities.

2 In the previous chapter, I draw on Mol's idea of logic as it relates to practice, and this approach is followed through the book to consider the logic of care in practice. Here, however, the argument set up around the logic contribution is best understood as a logic of argumentation as much as a logic of practice per se.

3 Of note in these papers was a particular 'three-way' configuration of participation between young people, originating communities and the museum.

4 The recent edited volume *Museum Participation: New Directions for Audience Collaborations* (McSweeney and Kavanagh, 2016) provides a good overview of numerous UK case studies written from practitioner perspectives.

5 Tlili (2008) has written about how the understanding of social inclusion was often mediated through the notion of 'access' and the more limited concept of 'audience development', leading to more limited practice in this area.

6 It is important to note here that web logics themselves operate outside of institutional spaces, in that they are 'post-commodity' productions. And yet, this very significant difference is rarely recognised as ideas from digital circulate back

into other areas of museum practice with little discussion of wider institutional power and contexts.

7 Simon describes this as OF/BY/FOR ALL, a 'global movement and a set of tools' to transform museums into vibrant community centres. https://www.ofbyforall.org/.

8 At TWAM, this led to the establishment of an 'Alternative Management Team' made up of TWAM staff, volunteers and community partners that works alongside the formal management structure to provide an alternative voice for key operational decisions.

9 Some have suggested that the contact zone idea has become 'fetishized' (Message, 2017: 77), while critics have argued that it extends a neo-colonial (Boast, 2011) and reformist agenda of the museum (Bennett, 1998; Dibley, 2005)

10 This particularity of the museum and its multiple and at times contradictory functions have been picked up (though not always explicitly) as areas of dilemma presented in a number of studies of museum participation. It is revealed in specific moments when the participatory process becomes 'public', and the museum must negotiate its wider responsibilities to its publics (both present and in the future) – for instance, when participants are resistant to access requirements in exhibition texts (Strachan and Mackay, 2013), or when participants are asked to interpret museum objects for which they do not have any legitimate knowledge (Morse et al., 2013) or when a public interest argument unsettles collaborative practices in the art gallery (Graham et al., 2013).

11 In Bennett's views, campaigns related to diversity or climate change, for instance, or Clifford's ideal of the contact zone, are informed by the same logic of public education and improvement as the public health or public housing exhibitions that were early features of the public museum, relocated as 'variant formulations of contemporary reordering of the relations between museums and liberal forms of governmentality' (Bennett, 2015: 11). As such, Bennett's disciplinary reading of the museum does not necessarily close down all possibilities; rather, they are already accounted for. Dibley argues that Bennett's discourse is also, ultimately, redemptive of the museum. As he states, 'For Bennett this is no bad thing and he commits himself to this process' (2015: 16). Disciplinary readings of the museum are difficult to escape, and it may be possible to read my argument for the logic of care as another variant of governmentality. However, by drawing close attention to the contingencies of practice, I hope to show that care does in fact provide another way of ordering the museum.

12 The logic of contribution could even be traced back to the nineteenth century European museum and its expansionist form, where the museum was a central 'point of gathering' (Bennett, 1998: 203; Clifford, 1997: 193) (in part, to create a self-fashioning citizenry linked to the reform of public manners).

13 Dewdney et al. (2012: 156–160) present a study of Tate Britain in which they call for post-structuralist thinking to reconceptualise the museum as distributed, where the institution itself is a space of circulation. They set this model against 'the established model of the contributive museum' founded in the early public museums and their colonial histories, where 'at the centre of such a model lies the deposit of artworks held on reserve'. The distributed museum 'acts more like a port, setting out a vast array of flights paths, rail-tracks, shipping lines and airwaves that in themselves link the different aspects of the fragmented subjects distributed across the world'. The authors start to consider how the 'transmigrating subject' comes up against the contributive museum, which 'becomes redundant to the needs of a subject-position constructed around continual differentiation'. There are interesting possibilities in terms of reading Dewdney et al.'s work alongside the argument I am making in this book; however, our subject matters and concerns are different and therefore take us to different places.

14 Significant critique has been applied to highlight the instrumentalisation of culture within this framing (Belfiore, 2002; Gray, 2008). My argument, however, points to a closer examination of the museum form, so I do not directly engage with this debate, preferring instead to explore alternative views on the social work of the museum.

15 The question of scale raised by Graham (2012b) here remains important, linked to the project-based nature of this work (Lynch, 2011c) and suggestions by some commentators that often little is learned from working intensely with small targeted groups (O'Neill, 2010).

References

Ames MM (2003) How to decorate a house: The renegotiation of cultural representation at the University of British Colombia Museum of Anthropology. In: Peers LL and Brown AK (eds) *Museums and Source Communities: A Routledge Reader*. London: Routledge, pp. 171–180.

Arnstein SR (1969) A ladder of citizen participation. *Journal of the American Institute of Planners* 35(4): 216–224. doi: 10.1080/01944366908977225.

Barringer TJ and Flynn T (eds) (1998) *Colonialism and the Object: Empire, Material Culture and the Museum*. Museum Meanings. London: Routledge.

Belfiore E (2002) Art as a means of alleviating social exclusion: Does it really work? A critique of instrumental cultural policies and social impact studies in the UK. *International Journal of Cultural Policy* 8(1): 91–106. doi: 10.1080/102866302900324658.

Bennett T (1995) *The Birth of the Museum: History, Theory, Politics*. London: Routledge.

Bennett T (1998) *Culture: A Reformer's Science*. London and Thousand Oaks, CA: Sage Publications.

Bennett T (2015) Thinking (with) museums: From exhibitionary complex to governmental assemblage. In: Witcomb A and Message K (eds) *The International Handbooks of Museum Studies*. Wiley-Blackwell, pp. 3–20. doi: 10.1002/9781118829059.wbihms101.

Bienkowski P (2016) *No Longer Us and Them: How to Change into a Participatory Museum and Gallery. Learning from the Our Museum Programme*. Paul Hamlyn Foundation. Available at: http://www.phf.org.uk/wp-content/uploads/2016/07/Our-Museum-Report_April-2016-double-page.pdf (accessed 2 January 2017).

Black G (2005) *The Engaging Museum: Developing Museums for Visitor Involvement*. The heritage: care, preservation, management. Abingdon: Routledge.

Boast R (2011) Neocolonial collaboration: Museum as contact zone revisited. *Museum Anthropology* 34(1): 56–70. doi: 10.1111/j.1548-1379.2010.01107.x.

Boon T, Vaart M van der and Price K (2014) Oramics to electronica: Investigating lay understandings of the history of technology through a participatory project. *Science Museum Group Journal* 2(02). doi: 10.15180/140206.

Bovaird T (2007) Beyond engagement and participation: User and community co-production of public services. *Public Administration Review* 67(5): 846–860. doi: 10.1111/j.1540-6210.2007.00773.x.

Bunning K, Kavanagh J, McSweeney K, et al. (2015) Embedding plurality: Exploring participatory. *Science Museum Group Journal* 3(03). doi: 10.15180/150305.

Burns D, Hambleton R and Hoggett P (1994) *The Politics of Decentralisation: Revitalising Local Democracy*. Public Policy and Politics. Basingstoke: Macmillan.

Cahill C (2007) Repositioning ethical commitments: Participatory action research as a relational praxis of social change. *ACME: An International Journal for Critical Geographies* 6(3): 360–373.

Cameron DF (1971) The museum, a temple or the forum. *Curator: The Museum Journal* 14(1): 11–24. doi: 10.1111/j.2151–6952.1971.tb00416.x.

Camic PM and Chatterjee HJ (2013) Museums and art galleries as partners for public health interventions. *Perspectives in Public Health* 133(1): 66–71. doi: 10.1177/1757913912468523.

Clarke J, Newman J, Smith N, et al. (2007) *Creating Citizen-Consumers: Changing Publics and Changing Public Services.* London: Sage Publications.

Clifford J (1997) *Routes: Travel and Translation in the Late Twentieth Century.* Cambridge, MA and London: Harvard University Press.

Cooke B and Kothari U (eds) (2001) *Participation, the New Tyranny?* London: Zed.

Coombes AE (1994) *Reinventing Africa: Museums, Material Culture, and Popular Imagination in Late Victorian and Edwardian England.* New Haven, CT and London: Yale University Press.

Cornwall A (2006) Historical perspectives on participation in development. *Commonwealth &Comparative Politics* 44(1): 62–83. doi: 10.1080/14662040600624460.

Cornwall A (2008) Unpacking 'Participation': Models, meanings and practices. *Community Development Journal* 43(3): 269–283. doi: 10.1093/cdj/bsn010.

Cornwall A and Coelho VS (2007) *Spaces for Change?: The Politics of Citizen Participation in New Democratic Arenas.* London: Zed Books.

Crooke E (2006) Museums and community. In Macdonald S: *A Companion to Museum Studies.* Oxford: Blackwell Publishing, pp. 171–185.

Crooke EM (2008) *Museums and Community: Ideas, Issues, and Challenges.* New York: Routledge.

Desmarais S, Bedford L and Chatterjee HJ (2018) *Museums as Spaces for Wellbeing: A Second Report from the National Alliance for Museums, Health and Wellbeing.* London. Available at: www.museumsandwellbeingalliance.wordpress.com (accessed 30 June 2018).

Dewdney A, Dibosa D and Walsh V (2012) *Post Critical Museology: Theory and Practice in the Art Museum.* London and New York: Routledge.

Dibley B (2005) The museum's redemption Contact zones, government and the limits of reform. *International Journal of Cultural Studies* 8(1): 5–27. doi: 10.1177/1367877905050160.

Dodd J (2015) The socially purposeful museum. *Museologica Brunensia* 4(2): 28–31.

Dodd J, Jones C and Sandell R (2017) Trading Zones: Collaborative ventures in disability history. In Gardner JB and Hamliton P (eds) *The Oxford Handbook of Public History*, pp. 87–104.

Dodd J and Sandell R (2001) *Including Museums: Perspectives on Museums, Galleries and Social Inclusion.* Leicester: Research Centre for Museums and Galleries, University of Leicester.

Durrer V and Miles S (2009) New perspectives on the role of cultural intermediaries in social inclusion in the UK. *Consumption Markets & Culture* 12(3): 225–241. doi: 10.1080/10253860903063238.

Featherstone D, Ince A, Mackinnon D, et al. (2012) Progressive localism and the construction of political alternatives. *Transactions of the Institute of British Geographers* 37(2): 177–182. doi: 10.1111/j.1475–5661.2011.00493.x.

Fouseki K (2010) 'Community voices, curatorial choices': Community consultation for the 1807 exhibitions. *Museum and Society* 8(3): 180–192.

Fraser N (1990) Rethinking the public sphere: A contribution to the critique of actually existing democracy. *Social Text* (25/26): 56–80. doi: 10.2307/466240.

Gaventa J (2004) Towards participatory governance: Assessing the transformative possibilities. In: Hickey S and Mohan G (eds) *Participation: From Tyranny to Transformation? Exploring New Approaches to Participation in Development.* London: Zed books, pp. 25–41.

Gibson S and Kindon S (2013) The mixing room project at Te Papa: Co-creating the museum with refugee background youth in Aotearoa/New Zealand. *Tuhinga* 21: 65–83.

GLLAM (2000) *Museums and Social Exclusion: The GLLAM Report.* Leicester: Department of Museum Studies, Leicester University.

Golding V and Walklate J (2019) *Museums and Communities: Diversity, Dialogue and Collaboration in an Age of Migrations.* Cambridge Scholars Publishing.

Gordon C, Powell D and Stark P (2015) The coalition government 2010–2015: Lessons for future cultural policy. *Cultural Trends* 24(1): 51–55. doi: 10.1080/09548963.2014.1000585.

Govier L (2009) Leaders in co-creation? Why and how museums could develop their co-creative practice with the public, building on ideas from the performing arts and other non-museum organisation. Available at: http://www.cloreleadership.org/cms/user_files/fellow_fellowship_research_projects_download_report/74/Louise%20Govier%20-%20Clore%20Research%20-%20Leaders%20in%20Co-Creation.pdf (accessed 11 October 2010).

Graham H (2012a) *'Participation', Intellectual Property and Informed Consent: A literature review.* Available at: http://partnershipandparticipation.wordpress.com/ (accessed 8 January 2013).

Graham H (2012b) Scaling governmentality. *Cultural Studies* 26(4): 565–592. doi: 10.1080/09502386.2012.679285.

Graham H (2017) Horizontality: Tactical politics for participation and museums. In: Onciul B, Stefano ML and Hawke S (eds) *Engaging Heritage - Engaging Communities.* Martlesham: Boydell & Brewer, pp. 73–90.

Graham H (2019) Breaking out of the museum core: Conservation as participatory ontology and systematic action enquiry. In: Glenn H and O'Neill M (eds) *Connecting Museums.* London: Routledge, pp. 80–94.

Graham H, Mason R and Nayling N (2013) The personal is still political: Museums, participation and copyright. *Museum and Society* 11(1): 105–121.

Gray C (2008) Instrumental policies: Causes, consequences, museums and galleries. *Cultural Trends* 17(4): 209–222.

Hall C (1992) *White, Male and Middle-Class: Explorations in Feminism and History.* Cambridge, MA: Polity.

Haraway D (1994) Teddy bear patriarchy: Taxidermy in the Garden of Eden, New York City, 1908–36. In: Dirks NB, Eley G and Ortner SB (eds) *Culture/Power/History: A Reader in Contemporary Social Theory.* Princeton, NJ and London: Princeton University Press, pp. 49–95.

Hutchison M and Collins L (2009) Translations: Experiments in dialogic representation of cultural diversity in three museum sound installations. *Museum and Society* 7(2): 92–109.

Janes RR and Sandell R (eds) (2019) *Museum Activism* (1st edn). Abingdon and New York: Routledge.

Karp I and Lavine SD (eds) (1991) *Exhibiting Cultures: The Poetics and Politics of Museum Display.* Washington, DC: Smithsonian Institution Press.

Karp I, Kreamer CM and Lavine S (eds) (1992) *Museums and Communities: The Politics of Public Culture.* Washington, DC: Smithsonian Institution Press.

Kavanagh G (1990) *History Curatorship.* Washington, DC: Smithsonian Institution Press.

Kindon S, Pain R and Kesby M (2008) Participatory action research. In Kitchin R and Thrift N (eds): *International Encyclopaedia of Human Geography.* Amsterdam and London: Elsevier, pp. 90–95.

Knell S, Macleod S and Watson S (eds) (2007) *Museum Revolutions: How Museums Change and Are Changed.* London and New York: Routledge.

Knudsen LV (2016) Participation at work in the museum. *Museum Management and Curatorship* 31(2): 193–211. doi: 10.1080/09647775.2016.1146916.

Kreps C (2003) *Liberating Culture: Cross-Cultural Perspectives on Museums, Curation and Heritage Preservation.* London: Routledge.

Krmpotich C and Peers LL (2013) *This Is Our Life: Haida Material Heritage and Changing Museum Practice.* Vancouver, BC: UBC Press.

Lackoi K, Patsou M and Chatterjee HJ (2016) *Museums for Health and Wellbeing. A Preliminary Report.* Available at: https://museumsandwellbeingalliance.wordpress.com/ (accessed 31 October 2016).

Lang C, Reeve J and Woollard V (eds) (2006) *The Responsive Museum: Working with Audiences in the Twenty-First Century.* Aldershot and Burlington, VT: Ashgate.

Levitas R (2005) *The Inclusive Society?: Social Exclusion and New Labour* (2nd edn). Basingstoke: Macmillan.

Lidchi H (1997) The poetics and the politics of exhibiting other cultures. In: Hall S (ed.) *Representation: Cultural Representations and Signifying Practices.* Culture, Media and Identities. London: Sage in association with the Open University, pp. 155–222.

Little K and Watson I (2016) Destination Tyneside - Stories of Belonging: The philosophy and experience of developing a new permanent migration gallery at Discovery Museum in Newcastle Upon Tyne. In: Whitehead C, Eckersley S, Lloyd K, Mason R (eds) *Museums, Migration and Identity in Europe: Peoples, Places and Identities.* London and New York: Routledge, pp. 183–206.

Lonetree A (2012) *Decolonizing Museums Representing Native America in National and Tribal Museums.* Chapel Hill: The University of North Carolina Press.

Lukes S (1974) *Power: A Radical View.* London: Macmillan.

Lumley R (1988) *The Museum Time Machine: Putting Cultures on Display.* London and New York: Routledge.

Lynch BT (2011a) Collaboration, contestation and creative conflict: On the efficacy of museum/community partnerships. In: Marstine J (ed.) *The Routledge Companion to Museum Ethics: Redefining Ethics for the Twenty-First Century Museum.* London: Routledge, pp. 146–164.

Lynch BT (2011b) Custom-made reflective practice: Can museums realise their capabilities in helping others realise theirs? *Museum Management and Curatorship* 26(5): 441–458. doi: 10.1080/09647775.2011.621731.

Lynch BT (2011c) *Whose Cake Is It Anyway? A Collaborative Investigation into Engagement and Participation in 12 Museums and Galleries in the UK.* London: Paul Hamlyn Foundation.

Lynch BT (2014) 'Generally dissatisfied': Hidden pedagogy in the postcolonial museum. *THEMA. La revue des Musées de la civilisation* 1(1): 79–92.

Lynch BT (2015) *Our Museum: A Five-Year Perspective from a Critical Friend.* London: Paul Hamlyn Foundation. Available at: http://ourmuseum.org.uk/about/a-five-year-perspective-from-a-critical-friend/ (accessed 27 July 2019).

Lynch BT (2016) 'Good for you, but I don't care!' radical museum pedagogy in educational and curatorial practice. In: Morsch C, Angeli Sachs, and Sieber T (eds) *Contemporary Curating & Museum Education.* Bielefeld, Germany: Transcript Verlag, pp. 255–267.

Lynch BT and Alberti SJMM (2010) Legacies of prejudice: Racism, co-production and radical trust in the museum. *Museum Management and Curatorship* 25(1): 13–35. doi: 10.1080/09647770903529061.

Macdonald S (ed.) (1998) *The Politics of Display: Museums, Science, Culture.* London: Routledge.

Macdonald S (2006) Expanding museum studies: An introduction. In: Macdonald S (ed.) *A Companion to Museum Studies.* Oxford: Blackwell, pp. 1–13.

Marstine J (ed.) (2011) *The Routledge Companion to Museum Ethics: Redefining Ethics for the Twenty-First Century Museum.* London: Routledge.

Mason R (2004) Conflict and complement: An exploration of the discourses informing the concept of the socially inclusive museum in contemporary Britain. *International Journal of Heritage Studies* 10(1): 49–73. doi: 10.1080/1352725032000194240.

Mason R (2006) Cultural theory and museum studies. In: Macdonald S (ed.) *A Companion to Museum Studies.* Blackwell companions in cultural studies. Oxford: Blackwell, pp. 17–32.

Mason R, Whitehead C and Graham H (2013) One voice to many voices? Displaying polyvocality in an art gallery. In: Golding V and Modest W (eds) *Museums and Communities: Curators Collections and Collaboration.* London: Bloomsbury, pp. 163–177.

McCall V and Gray C (2014) Museums and the 'new museology': Theory, practice and organisational change. *Museum Management and Curatorship* 29(1): 19–35. doi: 10.1080/09647775.2013.869852.

McCarthy C (2007) *Exhibiting Maori: A History of Colonial Cultures of Display.* Oxford and New York: Berg.

McCarthy C, Dorfman E, Hakiwai A, et al. (2013) Mana Taonga: Connecting communities with New Zealand Museums through Ancestral Māori Culture. *Museum International* 65(1–4): 5–15. doi: 10.1111/muse.12028.

McLean F (2008) Museums and the representation of identity. In: Graham BJ and Howard P (eds) *The Ashgate Research Companion to Heritage and Identity.* Ashgate Research Companions. Aldershot and Burlington, VT: Ashgate, pp. 283–296.

McSweeney K and Kavanagh J (eds) (2016) *Museum Participation: New Directions for Audience Collaboration.* Edinburgh and Boston, MA: MuseumsEtc.

Message K (2017) *The Disobedient Museum: Writing at the Edge.* London: Routledge.

Miller T and Yudice G (2002) *Cultural Policy.* London and Thousand Oaks, CA: Sage.

Modest W (2013) Co-curating with Teenagers at the Horniman Museum. In: Golding V and Modest W (eds) *Museums and Communities: Curators, Collections and Collaboration.* London: Bloomsbury, pp. 98–109.

Mol A (2002) *The Body Multiple: Ontology in Medical Practice.* Durham, NC: Duke University Press.

Mol A (2010) *The Logic of Care: Health and the Problem of Patient Choice.* Abingdon: Routledge.

Morse N (2020) The social role of the museum: From social inclusion to health and wellbeing. In: Glenn H and O'Neill M (eds) *Connecting Museums*. London: Routledge, pp.48–65.

Morse N and McCann M (2019) *Becoming a Change-Maker in Museums: Experiences, Opportunities and Challenges – Reflections on the Museums Association's Transformers Workforce Development Initiative*. Leicester: University of Leicester. Available at: https://leicester.figshare.com/articles/Becoming_a_Change-Maker_in_Museums_ Experiences_Opportunities_and_Challenges_-_Reflections_on_the_Museums_ Association_s_Transformers_Workforce_Development_Initiative_/10304777 (accessed 23 January 2020).

Morse N and Munro E (2015) Museums' community engagement schemes, austerity and practices of care in two local museum services. *Social & Cultural Geography*. Online First: 357–378. doi: 10.1080/14649365.2015.1089583.

Morse N, Macpherson M and Robinson S (2013) Developing dialogue in co-produced exhibitions: Between rhetoric, intentions and realities. *Museum Management and Curatorship* 28(1): 91–106. doi: 10.1080/09647775.2012.754632.

Museums Association (2018) *Power to the People*. Available at: https://www.museumsassociation.org/download?id=1254507 (accessed 14 August 2019).

Newman A and McLean F (2004) Presumption, policy and practice: The use of museums and galleries as agents of social inclusion in Great Britain. *International Journal of Cultural Policy* 10(2): 167–181.

Nightingale E (2006) Dancing around the collections: Developing individuals and audiences. In: Lang C, Reeve J, and Woollard V (eds) *The Responsive Museum: Working with Audiences in the Twenty-First Century*. Aldershot and Burlington, VT: Ashgate, pp. 79–91.

Nightingale E and Swallow D (2003) The Arts of the Sikh Kingdoms: Collaborating with a community. In: Peers LL and Brown AK (eds) *Museums and Source Communities: A Routledge Reader*. London: Routledge, pp. 55–71.

Onciul B (2013) Community engagement, curatorial practice, and museum ethos in Alberta, Canada. In: Golding V and Modest W (eds) *Museums and Communities: Curators Collections and Collaboration*. London: Bloomsbury, pp. 79–98.

Onciul B (2015) *Museums, Heritage and Indigenous Voice: Decolonizing Engagement*. New York: Routledge. doi: 10.4324/9781315770246.

Onciul B (2017) Introduction. In: Onciul B, Stefano ML, and Hawke S (eds) *Engaging Heritage – Engaging Communities*. Martlesham: Boydell & Brewer, pp. 1–10.

Onciul B, Stefano ML and Hawke S (eds) (2017) *Engaging Heritage - Engaging Communities*. Martlesham: Boydell & Brewer.

O'Neill M (2010) Cultural attendance and public mental health: From research to practice. *Journal of Public Mental Health* 9(4): 22–29. doi: 10.5042/jpmh.2010.0700.

Parry R (2007) *Recoding the Museum: Digital Heritage and the Technologies of Change*. Routledge. doi: 10.4324/9780203347485.

Peers LL and Brown AK (eds) (2003) *Museums and Source Communities: A Routledge Reader*. London: Routledge.

Phillips R (2003) Community collaborations in exhibitions: Towards a dialogic paradigm. In: Peers LL and Brown AK (eds) *Museums and Source Communities: A Routledge Reader*. London: Routledge, pp. 156–170.

Phillips RB (2005) Re-placing objects: Historical practices for the second museum age. *The Canadian Historical Review* 86(1): 83–110.

Porter G (1996) Seeing through solidity: A feminist perspective on museums. In: Macdonald S and Fyfe G (eds) *Theorizing Museums: Representing Identity and Diversity in a Changing World*. Sociological review monograph 43. Oxford: Blackwell/ The Sociological Review, pp. 105–26.

Pratt ML (1992) *Imperial Eyes: Travel Writing and Transculturation*. London: Routledge.

Purkis H (2013) Making contact in an exhibition zone: Displaying contemporary cultural diversity in Donegal, Ireland, through an installation of visual and material portraits. *Museum and Society* 11(1): 50–67. doi: 10.29311/mas.v11i1.222.

Rex B (2018) Exploring relations to documents and documentary infrastructures: The case of museum management after austerity. *Museum and Society* 16(2): 187–200.

Samuel R (1994) *Theatres of Memory*. London and New York: Verso.

Sandell R (ed.) (2002) *Museums, Society, Inequality*. London: Routledge.

Sandell R (2003) Social inclusion, the museum and the dynamics of sectoral change. *Museum and Society* 1(1): 45–62.

Sandell R (2007) *Museums, Prejudice and the Reframing of Difference*. London: Routledge.

Sandell R (2016) *Museums, Moralities and Human Rights*. London: Routledge.

Sandell R and Nightingale E (eds) (2012) *Museums, Equality, and Social Justice*. London: Routledge.

Schorch P (2013) Contact zones, third spaces, and the act of interpretation. *Museum & Society* 11(1): 68–81.

Silverman LH (2010) *The Social Work of Museums*. New York: Routledge.

Simon N (2010) *The Participatory Museum*. Museum 2.0.

Simon N (2016) *The Art of Relevance*. Museum 2.0.

Sleeper-Smith S (2009) *Contesting Knowledge Museums and Indigenous Perspectives*. Lincoln: University of Nebraska Press.

Smith L and Waterton E (2009) *Heritage, Communities and Archaeology*. London: Gerald Duckworth & Co.

Smith L, Cubitt G, Fouseki K, et al. (eds) (2014) *Representing Enslavement and Abolition in Museums* (1st edn). New York: Routledge.

Stam DC (1993) The informed muse: The implications of 'the new museology' for museum practice. *Museum Management and Curatorship* 12(3): 267–283. doi: 10.1080/09647779309515365.

Strachan A and Mackay L (2013) Veiled practice: Reflecting on collaborative exhibition development through the journey of one potentially contentious object. *Museum Management and Curatorship* 28(1): 73–90. doi: 10.1080/09647775.2012.754981.

Tapsell P (2014) Ko Tawa: Where are the glass cabinets? In: Silverman R (ed.) *Museum as Process: Translating Local and Global Knowledges*. London and New York: Routledge, pp. 262–278.

Thumim N (2010) Self-representation in museums: Therapy or democracy? *Critical Discourse Studies* 7(4): 291–304. doi: 10.1080/17405904.2010.511837.

Tlili A (2008) Behind the policy mantra of the inclusive museum: Receptions of social exclusion and inclusion in museums and science centres. *Cultural Sociology* 2(1): 123–147.

Tlili A, Gewirtz S and Cribb A (2007) New Labour's socially responsible museum: Roles, functions and greater expectations. *Policy Studies* 28(3): 269–289. doi: 10.1080/01442870701437634.

Tritter JQ and McCallum A (2006) The snakes and ladders of user involvement: Moving beyond Arnstein. *Health Policy* 76(2): 156–168. doi: 10.1016/j.healthpol.2005.05.008.

Turner G (2010) *Ordinary People and the Media: The Demotic Turn*. London: Sage Publications. doi: 10.4135/9781446269565.

Vergo P (ed.) (1989) *The New Museology*. London: Reaktion.

Walsh K (1992) *The Representation of the Past: Museums and Heritage in the Postmodern World*. London: Routledge.

Waterton E and Watson S (eds) (2011) *Heritage and Community Engagement: Collaboration or Contestation?* London: Routledge.

Watson SER (ed.) (2007) *Museums and Their Communities*. Leicester Readers in Museum Studies. London: Routledge.

Weil SE (1990) *Rethinking the Museum and Other Meditations*. Washington, DC and London: Smithsonian Institution Press.

Weil SE (1999) From being about something to being for somebody: The ongoing transformation of the American museum. *Daedalus* 128(3): 229–258.

Whitehead C, Eckersley S, Lloyd K, et al. (2016) *Museums, Migration and Identity in Europe: Peoples, Places and Identities*. London and New York: Routledge.

Wilcox D (1994) *The Guide to Effective Participation*. London: Joseph Rowntree Foundation. Available at: http://www.partnerships.org.uk/guide/ (accessed 31 July 2014).

Witcomb A (2003) *Re-Imagining the Museum: Beyond the Mausoleum*. London: Routledge.

Part II
The institutional life of community engagement workers

3   The language of community engagement

In this chapter, I take a look at the the institutional life of community engagement in the museum, by looking at the language of community engagement, and how it circulates in the institution. The chapter sketches out the multiple meanings of community engagement in Tyne & Wear Archives & Museums (TWAM) through different museum professionals' experiences and perceptions of this work. My discussion in particular focuses on three main groups: senior management, curatorial staff[1] and outreach, as those groups most often involved in this practice, either directly or those who manage it at an operational level at a distance. I am interested here in how different groups of museum professionals define 'community engagement' in order to gain a sense of how practice is imagined in its institutional context. The chapter reveals the way in which different teams purposively claim different meanings in relation to their working practices as managers, curators or outreach workers. It also reveals the term's capacity to hold together the general, public function of the museum *and* its more specific work of engagement with marginalised and excluded communities. My aim in this chapter is not to provide a final definition or model for community engagement; instead, I suggest that it is more productive to look at how the language of community engagement operates in the museum and its effects. To highlight different meanings might seem obvious, but it also requires that we delve further into the consequences of these differences in meaning in relation to how they frame the purpose of practice, ideas of 'community' and the associations and dissociations with other words and practices (such as inclusion or diversity). This then enables me to begin to address the paradox presented by community engagement workers: staff experience continued resistance to their work *despite* the prevalence of community engagement in the official language of the museum. Indeed, the typical goal for participatory practice is to embed or 'institutionalise' this practice: to integrate it into the daily routines of an institution (to bring it to the 'core' of the museum). This work is done through institutional language, through official statements and policies that mark out an institutional commitment to this work. In this chapter, I ask whether such commitments are 'performative': whether they do what they say. The question of what community engagement is, as language, then, is also a question about what it does in the museum. I correspondingly ask whose role it is to enact this commitment. Finally, I consider how institutional cultures frame the value of community engagement work. How are the skills of community engagement understood within an organisational setting? How is this practice valued across the institution?

Multiple meanings

As I briefly discussed in the introduction, TWAM has an established practice of community engagement that developed from the early 1990s, with a national and international reputation for this work. Community engagement practice evolved within different teams – curatorial, learning, audience development teams and (from 1992 onwards) the Outreach team – sometimes working together, but often working apart, each team developing their own sense of community engagement 'in practice' (I discuss this history of practice in more detail in the following chapter). Community engagement is writ large across institutional documents, annual reports, corporate plans and in funding bids, more or less consistently across the years. A typical response across the institution was to first describe community engagement by referring to the mission statement:

> *Our mission is to help people determine their place in the world and define their identities, so enhancing their self-respect and their respect for others.*

> I suppose it all has to do with TWAM's mission statement... All of our collections, they don't belong to us they belong to the people of Tyne and Wear so we should be promoting access in whatever way is possible.[2]

At a basic level, then, the purpose of community engagement is to make the museum accessible and relevant: 'we do community engagement to make our collections and displays relevant to the public which we serve'.[3] It links to the representational discourse (Chapter 2) and the notion of custodianship: the duty of care for collections as well as the duty to make these accessible and relevant. In this way, community engagement was often first used across the organisation to refer more generally to the public function of the museum as a locally relevant institution. Across interviews, I was first struck by the association with the mission statement and reference to the longer tradition of this type of work in the museum, as a way to make another statement: that the museum is committed to community engagement. Yet on a strategic level, the museum did not have a community engagement policy or action plan that might lay out a definition of community engagement.[4] When asked to define community engagement, staff offered a whole range of different events, activities and programmes as examples of community engagement:

- A year-long co-produced exhibition project working with young people as young curators
- The museum putting on a free annual firework display for the local community

- A curator receiving an object donation from a member of the public
- The museum's public Flickr account
- A talk for the Friend's groups
- A gallery redevelopment consultation
- A curator's blog entry about an object in the museum collection
- The schools' programme
- Supporting volunteers on work placements
- A ten-week reminiscence project with a dementia patient group, culminating in a series of digital stories that are accessioned in the collections
- A member of the corporate hire team liaising over a wedding booking
- *The People's Gallery*, a space programmed and co-curated with local communities

The examples above represent a broad range in terms of scale, time-length, number of people and their levels of participation as well as the level of involvement of staff, revealing stark differences in terms of what can be considered 'community engagement'. At the same time, it presents an over-arching sense of commitment across all areas of work. In the museum, the term encompasses a whole range of activities from one-off events, short-term projects to more in-depth partnerships and transformative encounters. There is no single or coherent definition. On first reading, we might suggest that such a broad range of activities could mean that the museum is working towards the same goal (the museum mission) and that different parts complement the whole. However, this is not necessarily the case. I want to suggest that these multiple meanings of community engagement are not trivial; they have consequences for how the work of engagement is oriented in terms of its participants, how it is distributed and managed across the museum organisation, which 'versions' are valued and resourced and which are side-lined and obstructed. I will develop this argument as I go through this chapter and the next.

When asked to further describe their understanding of community engagement in the museum, many staff highlighted the ambiguity of the terms. Identifying 'community' was frequently the first stumbling bloc, and staff often deflected with the question 'what do you mean by community?' Defining community was an inherently 'tricky thing'[5] and it was variously defined: 'It's always going to be difficult because the whole concept of community is very different to different people... We can really stretch the definitions here in terms of communities of interest; there are communities defined by geography, there are communities defined by disadvantage'.[6] These three defining categories – interest, geography and disadvantage (also described as 'hard to reach') – were the ones most often highlighted. All three imply commonality between their members through either spatial or social ties. Communities of interest were seen as self-defined, while communities of geography and disadvantage were seen as externally defined, with the boundaries of geography associated with local wards, while disadvantage was framed through policy, funding and local authority priorities. It should be noted that the Outreach team favoured the term 'under-served' communities, referring more explicitly to the responsibility of the museum towards these communities rather than an externally framed deficit label. The views of professionals in the museum also reflected many of the challenges highlighted by social science theory: that communities are fluid, contingent and unstable; that people can belong to more than one community; and that communities can also have negative connotations as exclusive (see Watson, 2007).

Recognising different types of communities therefore implied a need to establish different types of activities to engage different needs. As one senior staff member put it:

> Now arguably your community of interest you can engage simply by putting on a conference. Your community in the area, if you do it right you can engage simply by opening your doors. Your community of need you probably have to do something else as well.

While this could in theory involve all teams in the work of community engagement (as the earlier list suggested), for significant numbers of staff across the museum, community engagement was first associated with the work of the Outreach team, which was itself associated with targeting specific groups or 'communities of need':

> People have different understandings of community. So if you say 'have you worked with a community group?', people will immediately think it's a specific group, it's like NEETs [Not in Employment, Education of Training] or it's just the West African community.[7]

But as our conversations progressed, community engagement was linked to a much wider range of participants:

> What we just mean by working with the community we just mean **everyone** who is in our region.[8]

> In its broadest sense it means interacting with **any visitor** that walks through the door and anybody who comes online and wants to have some interaction with the museum.[9]

> We talk about communities but it's about **the individuals** that we are doing work with.[10]

Community is here alternatively used to signify 'the public' (everyone – albeit usually a specifically local version), 'the audience' (visitors – in person or virtual) and 'participants' (individuals). Other terms were also discussed in the same breath as community, including 'customers' and sometimes even 'councillors' as community representatives. These 'discursive displacements'

(Tlili, 2008) between public/audience/visitors/customers/community are not trivial since the use of each term allows for (and impedes) different forms of work. They map onto the recipients of the particular forms of engagement. The tensions begin to appear around how these different positions orient benefits towards different aims and different actions: community engagement is either directed at everybody in an undifferentiated manner (the 'public' as unknown others) and can therefore justify anything the museum does; or it is directed at 'visitors' and might be resolved by simply opening the doors; or it is aimed at specific groups and individuals and may require more sustained, specific work. Drawing attention to the question of 'who' community engagement is imagined for can reveal much about what community engagement 'is'. Specifically, the use of different language can reveal the different legitimacy claims that are made around community engagement, which are shaped within different discourses that inform the stakes of participation (see Chapter 2). Significantly, the case of TWAM reveals how community engagement holds together the general public function of the museum (in terms of access and representation) *and* its specific work of inclusion with communities that are excluded from the institution. At times, this duality operated unproblematically in the museum. At other times, however, tensions appeared in the particular calibration of these claims (Graham, 2012). For instance, the 'public' was sometimes used in opposition to community when community came to stand in for excluded or under-served groups. The question often overheard would become 'but how are we serving the general public?' with the implication that community engagement – by its small-scale nature – was taking attention and resources away from engaging regular museum visitors. As one senior staff member suggested: 'It's not all about working with the hardest to reach groups because if you work just with the hardest to reach groups you miss out all the other groups in society absolutely need to be engaging'. Discussions across the museum reveal the ambivalence in the language of community engagement: it is a capacious term, but this also underlines its ambiguity.

At some level of course, the diversity in meaning was recognised by staff, who would refer to each other's professional perceptions as either 'narrow' or 'expanded' views of community engagement. In terms of defining the *work* of community engagement, staff replicated a distinction that might be expected between community engagement inside the museum (focused on developing wider and more diverse audiences) and community engagement outside the museum, also referred to as *outreach*. More broadly across the organisation, the practice of community engagement was imagined through the metaphor of the ladder, or spectrum, of participation, as one curatorial staff member described it: 'you are going through a spectrum of community engagement there, from entitlement to basically you still have to take the initiative right through to something where people are actively engaged in a partnership with it'. Staff recognised that while different activities might be described as community engagement, there was an implied hierarchy of practice, whereby:

We engage with communities in lots of different ways at the most basic level by inviting them in to see what we have got ... But strictly speaking community engagement is about allowing people to have more of a voice and an influence over what services they are being provided with. So I don't think we have cracked that at all really.[11]

Across the museum, it was recognised that community engagement takes on different forms linked to the level of involvement and influence of participants in projects and the impact of projects on the museum. As the senior staff member commented above, managing this practice across the institution was not yet resolved. In the next chapter, I will examine a number of tensions that arise in the museum as it aims to work within the ladder model of participation.

What was most notable in conversations and interviews with organisational actors across the museum was how ideas of community engagement were inflected in different teams and their demarcated work:

I guess the way that [History] differs from other teams is that other teams might have more set audiences that they are trying to reach. So for Outreach it's harder to reach audiences, under-represented audiences, with Learning they have their targets with school groups so I think [curators] are well placed to be able to offer to a wider more core audience of the museum.[12]

In terms of the story of community engagement I think there have been different stories in the museum. In Outreach there has been a story - in other departments there has been another story I think about the way they engage with communities. (...) Some people think it's about working with the public; others it's about working with a targeted group; and there is also this whole global online virtual communities. I think over the years these things have tried to come together, and other times they have collided.[13]

This collision is where difference in meaning becomes relevant. By relating community engagement to different areas of work, practice becomes reconfigured within other elements of museum work and other kinds of constituencies.

Three organisational actors' perspectives

To consider these reconfigurations, let us explore three perspectives: managers, curators and outreach staff. For senior managers, community engagement was mostly discussed in two related manners: in terms of representative forms of relationships with communities via elected officials and in terms of public funding and 'value for money'. In TWAM, governance is assured by a Joint Committee made up of elected representatives from the member councils, a structure that is common across UK local authority museums. The museum's governance structures derive legitimacy from having elected councillors sitting on committees who have a mandate from the people by virtue of having been democratically elected. This was often described by managers as the mechanism through which the museum was accountable to the (local) communities it served.[14] For managers, community engagement was imagined, at one level, as part of their work of securing the relevance of the museum via political support, especially at a local level. In turn, this political support secures the core funding (c. 40–50%) of the museum from cross-council contributions by aligning with key local council priorities:

> The whole advocacy side of community engagement is important because it helps you to justify your existence. There are different levels to it and the most obvious one is outreach but I see it as much wider than that. And probably my role is (…) in general advocacy and increasing awareness of the service and what we actually do.

> There's no point having a mission statement and a corporate plan if you are not going to have measures to check whether you are following them. Ultimately, community engagement, part of it has to be to demonstrate to the people who have given you the money in the first place that you have spent the money in the way that you said you were going to and that you added value to them in however they wanted to engage with you.

It is interesting that management, although necessarily detached from the direct delivery of engagement work, associated with community engagement through an advocacy role. In this way, the idea of community engagement was quite directly linked to securing the relevance and accountability of the museum as a publicly funded institution. Within this managerial frame, the claim is that value for money should deliver a utility return to the public. On paper, in strategies, and in annual reports, community engagement becomes an instrumental activity through which museum work is aligned to council priorities such as 'stronger and safer communities' or 'strengthening public life'. Because of the distance from direct practice, managers' descriptions of community engagement tended to focus on visitor number and types of demographic engaged ('400,000 community people come in [to the museum every year] — so that's engaging with people isn't it?'). But for other professionals in the museum, this advocacy view of community engagement was felt as a narrow interpretation of community engagement focused on 'getting them in'. Indeed, equating participatory practice with marketing or audience development is a commonly reported misunderstanding of this work (Lynch, 2011; Tlili, 2008). But it does not serve us well to interpret it only in this way in TWAM. Managers' understanding of community engagement is perhaps better understood as part of their managerial practices and the structures of public accountability that shape their day-to-day work (or put simply, what the museum requires them to do). This frames community engagement work at a distance and in a more abstracted manner. It is reconfigured within the structures of public administration, removed from the relational and immediate understandings in teams that work with communities on the ground.

In fact, there was a widely held sense of public accountability across all the teams in the museum, linked to the responsibility of working in a publicly funded local authority service:

> For me [community engagement] is fundamentally around the fact that the public pay for these services out of their taxes full stop.[15]

> I think there is a commitment to making a difference in the local community and wanting people to feel ownership and to make a more resilient organisation because we are responding to people's needs because at the end the day if there isn't a demand for your product then why would you continue to deliver it? So again, that ties into value for money but I do think there is a social ethos behind the organisation.[16]

As noted in the second quote, the perspective of public accountability in the museum was not simply a managerial view, it was also woven into a long-standing 'social ethos' of the institution and the ways in which different parts of the museum understand its public (local) relevance.[17]

For those professionals working more directly with collections (the second organisational perspective I want to explore), including curators and collections management staff, community engagement was described more precisely as part of the museum's ethos of social history practice, as suggested by these two curators:

> I would see community engagement being mainly in the sense of content in a museum's terms so that history is what people's everyday lives were (...) I think that it offers value for money in a local authority museum that you are engaging people to make sure you are offering a service that they want and a story that they want to hear.

> Community engagement in that sense is about working with people to tell everyday stories about everyday Newcastle and that's the main premise of social history and that's its strength - so I would see community engagement being mainly in the sense of content in a museum so that history is what people's everyday lives were.

The first purpose of community engagement within the social history ethos is described as 'building content': community engagement is a tool used by curators to add to the value of the museum and to add to knowledge in the museum. For many staff, this was also a self-conscious attempt to disrupt claims of professional expertise and authority, especially in relation to the curator's role. The purpose of community engagement according to member of the History (curatorial) team was 'to give voice to communities which have previously been under-represented; so in the past that has been women and working-class people and more recently it has been minority ethnic groups and disabled groups, gay, lesbian groups'. There is an ethical necessity here, since, as one curatorial staff member simply put it, 'if it's about someone's life you should consult them'. Examples of community engagement practice included a range of activities that could be considered along the ladder of participation from donations and oral histories to first-person interpretation and more proactive collaborative exhibitions processes. Involving local people in telling their own stories was seen by curatorial and collection staff as fundamental to the museum's relevance. Within this, staff recognised co-curation as an important practice to further develop in the museum and as a 'higher level' of community engagement, referring back to the ladder of engagement model. Overall, community engagement was understood first through objects and stories, linked to content and representation, as a method to gather 'better knowledge' for the museum:

> I exist as a curator to collect objects but I think the way I do that sometimes is through community engagement... so it's a method, it's something that legitimises what I collect – so sometimes I can't justify buying something without asking someone. If we are talking about a community or a person or a group, I feel like I am not doing it factually correctly unless I have asked that community.

> With social history we are asking for people's story but we are not always involving people in the design of things and I think it's hard for us to involve people from that idea stage right through because perhaps the way that we work... I think we drop people off once we have the ideas.

As I suggested in Chapter 2, this particular orientation of participation as a way of accessing 'better knowledge' is focused on securing the museum's authority in relation to more inclusive and more accurate forms of collecting and interpretation. In this way, the language of community engagement in the curatorial/collection management team reflected the logic contribution as a method to secure the relevance of the collection and to improve the museum. As I described in Chapter 2, a relation of contribution is not always or necessarily regressive, and within the museum, 'better knowledge' was very clearly framed as a democratic argument around inclusion and plural representation. At the same time, the logic of contribution shapes relationships in a singular way, with the focus on communities improving the museum and a focus on objects (and their stories) first, above relations with people – as the second curator noted, people get 'dropped off'. In the curatorial view, then, community engagement is imagined both at a distance through notions of public accountability and in a more proximate way, through objects and stories, but not necessarily individuals or groups. Here again, the practice is reconfigured within the role that these teams are required to do in the museum (i.e. to care for collections and tell local stories through the work of display).

For the Outreach team (those I later describe interchangeably as community engagement workers), the definition of community engagement was formulated differently. It goes beyond the logic of contribution and is formed more directly in relation with people:

> We set the conditions for creative ways of working with people who maybe had never thought about museums and galleries as places where they belonged in, or could contribute to, [or] could offer them anything that could benefit them in their lives.

For Outreach, the focus of community engagement was working with underserved groups and communities that have largely been excluded from the museum. The most visible work of community engagement by the team was defined through bespoke projects developed with participants and through facilitating community-led or co-produced exhibitions. Community engagement projects used varied museum collections as inspiration for creative projects such as arts and crafts, creative writing or photography. The team defined community engagement as 'crossing the disciplines, since culture is all these different things for people'. Collections of any kind were the tools that helped them to do their work. This work was oriented towards enabling the creative conditions for people to explore ideas of identity, place and belonging. The team further described their work explicitly against a deficit model of engagement, as enabling opportunities for participants to identify their own interests and nurture their capabilities. In this sense, this is the work of setting the conditions for people to empower themselves (a key semantic they would explain at length – 'we don't empower people, people empower themselves'). In this way, the team viewed their work as part of an active dynamic focused on supporting individuals, groups and wider communities. Community engagement was strongly defined by its impact. Simply put: 'we want to make a difference to people's lives and believe we can do this through art and culture'. This practice was focused on facilitating people to decide for themselves how to engage with the museum, as one staff member put it, 'I think it is important not to be seen as going out and almost like Lady Bountiful giving people something that they "need". It has to be collaborative'. This collaboration included participants and the different community organisations and community services that support them and took shape from community development approaches. Community engagement was seen as mutually beneficial rather than strictly contributory. It was explicitly positioned as a 'different model' to curatorial forms of community engagement: '[we] don't go to them and say "we [the museum] think this is important what do you think?", [we] go to them as say 'what do you want to talk about?'. This reversal in language actively reverses the logic of contribution in the museum by presenting a different starting point in the community.

Outreach staff spoke clearly about community engagement as more than a set of museum activities or a means to develop collection knowledge; it is a powerful allegiance to communities. The ethos was underpinned by a clearly articulated commitment to inclusion, equality and diversity, reflected in the groups the team worked with, from diaspora communities to young offenders or adults in addiction recovery, and a collaborative approach to identify what those marginalised or otherwise excluded groups might want from a relationship with museum. More fundamentally, community engagement was understood as a duty of care towards communities. As one staff member put it: 'there is a sense of responsibility to the people you work with on the ground – if you lose that you lose the point of what's being done'. In this direct sense of responsibility and allegiance to communities 'on the ground', we begin to hear another logic of practice being articulated. In the Outreach team, this responsibility was felt both in relation to the institution (indeed they also connected it to the mission statement) but also through a personal and emotional register: 'why do community engagement? There are reasons at the organisational level, the team level … sometimes it is the personal level that is the most interesting and important, but there is no room for that'. Adding further depth and detail to this practice and making room for its alternative logic is my next concern in this book. Examining the second sentiment that there is 'no room' for personal and emotional registers in the museum is also another concern as I move into the next chapter.

By taking a closer look across three teams, it becomes clearer how the meanings of community engagement are defined through alignment to different team's remits, priorities and the value-rationalities that animate the work that they do in the museum. Community engagement practice becomes refracted through the work that the institution requires them to do. They each view community engagement through different lenses – whether in terms of number of people engaged and its equivalent value for money, in terms of objects and 'better knowledge' of collections or a more people-centred approach found in a duty of care for communities. There are different scales at play within understandings of community engagement. Managers tend to imagine this at the organisational scale of public administration, while curators (and other collections-focused staff) relate to objects first and the wider role of the museum as an institution of knowledge, while Outreach staff reflect on the in-practice and micro-scale of the people, relations and objects enrolled in museum engagement projects. These different sites and scales of practice reveal the constitutive dynamic of community engagement as distance *and* proximity. At a distance, community engagement is described through ideas of public accountability and becomes a practice of advocacy, rendered through annual report and other institutional statements. In curatorial work, the focus on objects sets a distance from a sustained engagement with communities; instead, this relation is more often maintained (again at a distance) through the custodial role, keeping objects safe *on behalf* of communities and keeping collections and exhibitions updated to reflect contemporary communities. For the Outreach team, community engagement is a more direct, immediate and deeply involved practice with communities who are currently not visiting or are otherwise excluded from the museum. Here, it is a practice that is formed through proximity. The distance/proximity of community engagement is another element of the term's ambivalent nature.

Taking a closer look at three areas of the museum further reveals this ambivalence of community engagement in relation to its attachment across different types of museum work and different museum functions. We might also consider how the different discourses I described in Chapter 2 frame meanings in the museum. Across each team, we can discern the economic and governmental discourses in managers' perspectives, the discourse of representation (in particular a social history impetus) in curatorial teams and ideas of social inclusion and empowerment in Outreach. At times, these discourses are held together in the museum in temporary arrangements so that the museum can describe a whole range of different activities as community engagement. On the surface, it might appear that all parts of the institution are working together towards the same goal. But does this mean that community engagement is institutionalised?

Institutionalising community engagement?

While there lacked a shared understanding of the term across the institution, at the same time, community engagement was clearly identified as a key element of the museum's work and its institutional goal.[18] At a most basic level, community engagement was defined through the very purpose of the museum, linking notions of 'publicness' to the notion of custodianship: the duty of care for collections and the duty to make these accessible and relevant to local audiences. As I commented earlier, museum professionals' first response to describing community engagement was to do so by focusing on the museum's mission statement. Through attachment to the mission statement, it comes to stand in as an institutional commitment – as it was put to me by a middle manager: 'everything we do is community engagement'. While staff recognised that community engagement was often activated through commitment to external drivers – such as local and central policy and funder priorities – it was also positioned as central to what the institution is. As one senior staff member suggested, 'our intentions have been very good in terms of community engagement – and it's not just about meeting funders agendas it is a genuine commitment to want to explore these kinds of relationships'. In broader discussion of museums, the typical goal for participatory practice is to 'embed' or 'institutionalise' participation. The aim is to make practice routine across the work of an organisation. At one level, this is done through routinised statements of the importance of this work. The routinised utterance or evoking of the term presents the museum as committed to this work, with policies and practice responsive to an implied coherent way of working with communities. But the routinisation of the language can remain just this; as the concept becomes applied as routine, it becomes a catch-all signifier and leads to an indiscriminate tagging of all kinds of activities as 'community engagement'. This may account for the wider variety of work presented earlier as community engagement in terms of form, timescale and intensity and the term's ready attachments to different domains of museum work. The routinisation of the concept of community engagement is moade clear in the statement that it is 'everything we do' which, paradoxically, makes it so self-evident, and at the same time muddles it.

In her book, *On Being Included* (2012), Sara Ahmed explores the issue of commitment in institutions through the lens of diversity in universities.[19] She examines the language of diversity by attending to the official claims made by institutions, drawing on John Austin's work on speech acts (1975). Austin outlines two forms of speech: constative utterances, which are descriptive statements that can be true or false, and performative utterances, which exist as acts in themselves that bring something into existence by virtue of the utterance. Austin's examples of performatives include the acts of naming, marrying, bequeathing and betting as those utterances that bring a state of affairs into existence, rather than simply describing a state of affairs (1975: 5). Such speech acts are uttered not simply to say something but rather to perform an action. Ahmed builds on Austin's work to outline 'institutional speech acts' that make claims about and on behalf of the institution: 'institutional speech acts, in making claims about the institution (for instance, by describing the institution as having certain qualities, such as being diverse) might also point toward future action (by committing an institution to a course of action)' (2012: 54–55). We can think of community engagement as an institutional speech act in museums: a statement of purpose and a pledge to do this work and a commitment to this course of action. In TWAM, it appears in the statement 'everything we do is community engagement' and via its widespread attachment to the mission statement. The link between the mission statement and community engagement is explicit: community engagement is the tool to achieve this institutional goal. By attaching a whole host of activities in the museum to the mission, community engagement becomes a routine description of the institution. For Ahmed, such routine descriptions enable institutional speech acts to become a convention of speech. Their utterance by senior staff in particular enables them to further acquire importance, generating institutional cultures around the word (Ahmed, 2012: 52). Reflecting on commitment to diversity in Higher Education institutions, Ahmed makes clear that committing to diversity (in the sense of 'pledging') is not the same as being committed to diversity (in the sense of 'being bound'): 'a commitment does not necessarily commit the institution to doing anything' (2012: 116). Ahmed puts forward the argument that statements of commitment are often 'non-performatives': 'they do not bring about the effects they name' (Ahmed, 2012: 114–121). Returning to Austin, she explains:

> For Austin, failed performatives are unhappy: they do not act because the conditions required for action to succeed are not in place (for example, if a person who apologizes is insincere, then the apology would be unhappy). In my model of the non-performative, the failure of the speech act to do what it says is not a failure of intent or even circumstance, *but actually what the speech act is doing.* Such speech acts are taken up as if they are performatives (*as if* they have brought about the effects they name), such that the name comes to stand in for the effects. As a result, naming can be a way of not bringing something into effect.
>
> (2012: 117 emphasis in original)

In this way, committing to community engagement in the museum, through saying that community engagement is a key value and referring to the mission statement, does not necessarily evoke commitment to action. The description of commitment as genuine in the previous senior manager's quote ('our intentions have been very good in terms of community engagement – and it's not just about meeting funder's agendas it is a genuine commitment to want to explore these kinds of relationships') describes its quality, at the same time as implying that this work is difficult and incomplete. In this way, the museum aims to set the conditions through which action can succeed – the condition through which it can become performative. However, by naming everything it *already does* as community engagement, it comes to stand in for the effects it names, unintentionally not bringing it into effect: it becomes non-performative. In particular, naming, through reference, the tradition of community engagement in the museum, which occurred at a different time and under different conditions (see also Chapter 3), *as if* practice is mainstreamed becomes a way of further muting a commitment to present action. Bernadette Lynch (2011) and other scholars have discussed the issue of embedding community engagement in museums, focusing on structural issues relating to project-based funding and the 'invisible' power of the institution that co-opts commitment into other agendas. Seeing commitment as a non-performative offers another lens to examine the institutional power in museums by paying close attention to the more diffuse yet potent impact of language and the effects of institutional speech acts. It presents another view into how institutions are maintained, not through failure of intent directly, but through the prevalence of institutional speech acts themselves. Indeed, naming, through speech acts, means that the institution does not have to do or change anything, but it does so in such a way that organisational actors may feel that this commitment is institutionalised, since as the speech act has become routine. The speech act is configured internally for external presentation. This joins a contention I made earlier (Chapter 2): that most of the participatory impulses in the museum are bound inside the institution's own boundaries (they are contributory), with no real intent to change the institution.

Reflecting on the influence of this practice on TWAM, one staff commented:

> I see [community engagement] as just making people feel good and getting them into the museum. And other than the relationship and what people think about museums, that doesn't affect what we are doing inside the museum.[20]

'Making people feel good' and 'getting people in' are two rather narrow senses of community engagement shared by only small sections of the museum. While reductive they perhaps are not reflective of the wider institution, and it does not serve to over interpret these comments. What is more instructive is the far more commonly shared sense in the quote above that community engagement is externally facing, and so, it does not affect what happens inside the museum. Community engagement is that which happens in the public spaces of the museum, in its relations with communities outside the museum's walls, rather than in the organisational backrooms or offices. We might follow a sociological lens here to paraphrase the terms of Erwin Goffman's (1971) 'front stage'. The implication of the imperative to institutionalise or mainstream engagement and participatory practice is premised on the demand that community engagement (and participation) must move in from the periphery or from what happens only on the surface of the institution to become embedded within organisational processes and institutional procedures within the museum and its 'back stage'. The argument here is that such a move is required to sustain practice and to ensure that the whole organisation is acting towards this same goal. In becoming an institutional speech act ('everything we do is community engagement'), it moves to the centre where it is taken up as if it is performative (*as if* it has brought about the effects it names), such that the name comes to stand in for the effects. Again, following Goffman, we might consider how the non-performative nature of community engagement can work towards keeping this practice as a form of 'impression management'. What is perhaps most significant to note then is the way in which community engagement comes to describe the nature and quality of the contemporary museum (more precisely in the UK, in a local authority context) as an institution and as an idea. This generates an institutional culture around the word; but we must then ask again, why do community engagement workers experience their institutions as resistant?

Across my conversations with staff, while there was a shared sense of commitment, there was also recognition that the museum could do better in relation to this commitment. As one middle manager put it, 'the things we like to say can be quite radical but end up being conservative'. Why and how does commitment end up in a more compromised place (beyond, that is, structural issues)? Why does it not affect what people are doing inside the museum? We can relate this back to the different value-rationalities previously uncovered across different teams' working definitions of community engagement – whether it is focused on an abstracted version of the public, on visitor numbers, on objects and collections knowledge, or whether it is more directly involved with specific groups – so that the aims and objectives are so different that to assess change in any one area would be meaningless in another. Within the model of the non-performative, we can also think of these effects as a function of the institutional speech acts – they do not bring about the effects that they name. I want to suggest that the non-performative nature of institutional commitment in the museum is itself further complicated by the multiple understandings of community engagement and *the effects they ought to have*. These multiple meanings relate to the more essential distance/proximity ambivalence of community engagement (and by extension, participation) within the museum, holding together the museum's public function *and* its specific work of inclusion. This brings me to another set of considerations about words and associations. Some staff suggested that community engagement had gained currency just as 'social inclusion' and 'diversity' had lost their rhetorical appeal as they faded from government policy and wider sector speak.[21] When staff outside of the Outreach team did speak of social inclusion and indeed 'outreach' (rather than the more general 'community engagement'), this was most directly associated in staff's minds with hard-to-reach groups, which in turn inferred groups that are difficult to work with. For some, this was seen as moving the museum away from work on objects and collections and into areas of work where the museum (on the whole) was not resourced, skilled or equipped. The appeal of community engagement can therefore be understood in relation to other words. Its first appeal is that it is seen as an easier, less confronting and more positive term than social inclusion. There is a sense of vagueness that displaces it into a euphemized form; the previous 'hard-to-reach targets' are replaced by a (perhaps romanticised) sense of 'community' and the exclusion/inclusion dynamic shifted into 'engagement'. As a less problematic term, it also gains institutional appeal. This goes some way to explaining its attachment to a wide range of activities within the museum. But as an amenable term used so flexibly across such varied contexts, it can lose its edge. In the museum, talking about community engagement could also become a way to circumvent or to avoid talking directly about equality, inclusion and diversity. There is a real danger here that in becoming so amenable, the language of community engagement risks erasing inclusion and diversity work in the museum.

Following a shared statement of commitment – 'community engagement is everything we do' – but having established its non-performative nature, the most significant question then becomes where the locus of commitment is situated: how is commitment distributed as a task to action and whose role it is to enact the institutional commitment? As it emerged through the interviews, there were two principal, but distinctive, approaches to conceptualising the role of community engagement in the museum. They seemingly co-exist and were often referred to by staff in the same sentence, as in this short quote from a senior staff member:

> Everything we do is community engagement as far as I am concerned, *and* Outreach is a specialist branch of community engagement that spearheads our routes to the hardest to reach groups and sets a good example to the rest of the organisation.

The first conceptualisation of community engagement sees it as an overarching ethos or *ideal*, one that places community at the centre of the museum's functions, via the mission statement: 'community engagement is everything we do'. In this conception, all staff and the institution itself are enlisted (in the sense of 'pledging' to the commitment). The second view of community engagement is as *a set of activities, techniques or tools* designed to involve more people in museums: here, community engagement is designated as a specialised practice and the primary responsibility of the Outreach team. The quote reflects a paradoxical statement that was made across my time in the museum: the announcement that community engagement is 'everything we do' – it is institutionalised – and at the same time, it is the specific role of the Outreach team – it is a separate, specialist concern. In this way, the institution was committed to community engagement, but the responsibility for community engagement remained with a single team. Indeed, staff beyond Outreach rarely had 'community engagement' within their job descriptions. While, in rhetoric, it was presented as core, it was at the same time placed at the periphery. Outreach team members described a common perception from other museum workers that Outreach 'acts of the consciousness of the organisation', as the team responsible for embodying and enacting the wider institutional commitment of the museum towards communities (in the sense of being 'bound' to the commitment). One member of the team further described how Outreach was often positioned to fulfil the 'corporate social responsibility' of the organisation through its work with disadvantaged or minoritised groups. 'Everyone's' commitment quickly becomes diffused and reallocated to Outreach. Rather than consciousness being at the centre, it is pushed outwards.

The question of whose role it is to 'do' community engagement drew interesting responses. It was once mentioned, in a room that responded with emphatic body language to signal a shared concern, that there was a 'danger' in extending this role and 'reducing' everyone to an engagement officer. There is much bundled up in this statement that is revealing of the place of community engagement and community engagement workers in the museum. While of course there will be differences in how staff can become involved in community engagement work within their current job remits and workloads, there remains something in this statement that reverberates uncomfortably about how this work is valued within the museum that it risked 'reducing' staff to engagement workers. Rhetoric of commitment further broke down when I asked staff whether they felt that community engagement work was recognised across the organisation, which, overwhelmingly, they felt it was not – this applied to responses from both those working in Outreach and those outside of this team. Here again, we are confronted with the ambivalence of community engagement within an institution that is both committed to this work, yet where the experience within the institution is of work that is undervalued.

The value of work

> Outreach is the poor cousin of the museum service. The value is not always seen in what we do.
>
> (Outreach team member interview)

Outreach workers spoke of the different ways in which they felt their skill sets were undervalued in the museum based on a number of misunderstandings about their work. A first set of misunderstandings was linked to a sense of this work not being visible in the museum because of its nature as outreach work, outside of the museum's wall and within communities:

> I think there are stereotypes of Outreach and what we do [...] it's maybe something that is airy-fairy and that's not part of the core. Maybe as well because we are not venue based and we flit about, we are not in the museum every day, we are not getting the objects out on display so it is maybe something that is not so visible so it is maybe not seen as valuable by certain individuals.

These misunderstandings were recognised by senior managers also:

> There are tensions in our staff as well in, how should I put it, in terms of the core work of the organisation, where some of them may see Outreach and certainly just going out and talking to people and doing advocacy as not being as important as opening the doors and letting people in and cataloguing the records so that they are accessible.

Community engagement is invisible both because it happens outside of the museum walls, but also because it does not fit easily within professional categories of museum work, such as work relating to venues and access, collections/objects and display/cataloguing work. There is a discernible subtext in both quotes of a procedural notion of professional skills versus more relational, open and uncertain forms of work. Here, the stereotyping of outreach practice as 'airy-fairy' is framed against more technical forms of museum work such as collections management and care, venue management and the work of display. Because the work of 'doing' community engagement is foremost about engaging with people, it does not fit easily within current definitions of work that is museum-like or 'museographic'[22] – defined here as the range of creative and technical work that is unique to museum practice, materials and resources and that takes place within its unique protocols (of conservation, display, ethics and so forth) (after Tlili, 2015). At the same time, it also does not fit easily within the parameters of administrative work that are framed by public administration structures that have also come to define much of contemporary museum practice, for instance, writing corporate plans, filing funder reports or measuring impact through targets and metrics (Morse et al., 2018). Within TWAM, there was a perceived privileging of codified forms of skills and knowledge that are clearly recognisable as 'museographic' and even 'administrative', as those areas most readily understood across the operational structures of the museum. This in turn led to devaluing the knowledge-base and practice of the more relational work with communities that did not fit so easily in either category. This devaluing also happens precisely because community engagement work exceeds the institution and its structuring practices, since it partly takes place outside of institutional spaces. What is notable here is that although outreach workers do in fact work with collections and with communities to create (or co-curate/co-produce) displays and other forms of exhibition work, there were certain persistent perceptions about the 'quality' of this work: outreach work was the 'papier mâché' gallery. The question of quality is one that pervades many discussions of how community engagement is managed in the museum, which I return to in the following chapter. What is clear for now is how such qualifying of community engagement work devalues its skills, expertise and accomplishments. Even where work might be museum-like, it appears to be not of the same value as more traditional museographic work.

To further consider the value of community engagement work in the museum, I turn to two moments from practice. 'Proggy mats' – a type of rag rug common in North East England – was used as a shorthand by outreach workers to highlight one of the ways community engagement practice was devalued in the museum, linked to the implied (low) quality and expectation for community engagement:

> The curatorial staff here don't understand what my job is and they expect me to be going out and doing stuff with the communities that they want to work with. There was an exhibition meeting and they asked us: 'Would one of your groups fancy doing a proggy mat?' and I was thinking I can't just magic up a group that wants to do a proggy mat, and then sit and do a proggy mat – that takes ages! But the curatorial team just sit there and say 'we'll just get Outreach to do that' – there's communities just waiting to sit and do a proggy mat… It's not really helping the community, it's helping the museum.

Within this exchange, the labour of engagement is presented as straightforward and focused on the output, as if the only 'work' is the task of facilitating a simple craft activity as part of a public programme linked to the exhibition. Or perhaps, more significant is the last statement that 'it's not helping the community, it's helping the museum' – to imply the ways in which outreach workers felt that their work was most readily recognised where it brought value to the museum rather than to the community itself. 'It's like with the Yemeni community' became another humorous shorthand (and humour was often used to cope with institutional life) to describe a lack of understanding of community engagement work through accounts that would go something like this:

> One of the museums is situated in an area with a large Yemeni British community settled since the 1890s, however it remains under-represented in the museum audience and collection. One day there is a meeting about a touring exhibition from one of the National Museum, and some of the budget is allocated to outreach work. In the meeting a manager exclaims 'How can we get the Yemeni community involved with this?' and turns expectantly to the Assistant Outreach Officer and says:
> 'Just run off some digital stories with the Yemeni community'
> And I remember saying to my line manager, I don't understand what they want us to do? There isn't a Yemeni community sitting in a room waiting for me to say 'let's do some digital stories!'

This (mis)perception of communities 'waiting in a room to be engaged' or be 'magic-ed up' was felt by the team as a significant barrier to recognising community engagement work as it negates the practices required to build up relationships and bespoke projects with communities, not least the requirements of time. It also simplifies the view of community into a very static and fixed sense and in turn reduces the work of engagement as being only about engaging a community through a singular identity trait. For the Outreach team, a key element of their practice was the slow and careful work of building up and sustaining relationships with different groups, meeting them in their own spaces and building on a community development approach through partnership with other local community organisations. However, this way of working fits uneasily within the time-limited schedules of museum projects that govern many teams' experience of professional work. I discuss some of these issues further in the next chapter.

Misunderstanding was also exacerbated by the differentiation of teams through their separation as areas of specialised skills, knowledge and expertise. Indeed, one feature of TWAM which is not uncommon in museums, is the deep organisational silos that frame its institutional life. These silos are maintained by staff's perceptions of their roles and the roles of other teams: 'curators do this, and I do that', or 'Outreach should only do things outside venues, and Learning should only do things inside venues'. This compartmentalisation of teams according to work specialisations and their priorities has strongly influenced the construction of team-based staff identities in the museum (captured for instance in the sentiment, 'we are a small team, we have got to stick together'). Within the museum, boundaries are tightly drawn up around different kinds of museum work and who gets to do it. One Outreach staff member recalled a day where an exhibition they had led (co-curated with the community) was written about in the *Museums Journal* (a professional magazine): 'someone from the History office came down and they were all like "you're not a curator, this is an outrage!"', again, laying bare the value judgements around where curatorial work can take place, and who can lay claim to this professional work, even in co-curated projects. Across my interviews, staff would often make statements (directly or implied) such as '"what I/we do is more important than we they do"', or 'what I/we do has more value/importance than what they do'. This was re-lated, at least in part, to the uneven pressures of performance management; for example, the high targets for school numbers or visitor figures, which are pressures felt by the Learning team, curators and managers, but are not a shared concern with Outreach, linked to different funding and reporting. But there is also something more pernicious in the earlier quote stating that staff 'flit about' outside the museums. It represents a view of community en-gagement work as unmanaged and perhaps unmanageable: staff flit about, we are led to presume, outside of the museum's internal rules of conduct and outside of management's line of vision. Because work takes places outside of the museum, it disrupts clear hierarchical lines of organising and man-aging work and workers, leading to tensions around professional autonomy, at both the team level and the individual level. The Outreach team felt particularly strongly that this key aspect of their work – outside, within communities – was not understood, and therefore not valued, at a senior management level. More specifically, the team felt a lack of trust, which they described as not having faith in the Outreach Officers themselves. This was felt deeply by staff and in turn could take a very personal toll as staff negotiate the devaluing of their work on a daily basis.

Skills or disposition?

During my time in the museum, I observed two tendencies (held more or less equally across the institution) that further marginalised and devalued the work of community engagement. One tendency was to assert that only certain people within the organisation can work with communities. In this view, community engagement practice is an abstract set of specific skills based around relationship-working that only a select few possess: 'let's face it: some people are people-people, and some people aren't'; 'it's about having that expertise in talking to people, which you build up and some people will never ever be very good at it'. Staff outside the Outreach team would express anxieties in relation to 'doing' this work, describing a feeling that they did not have the skills required, or the confidence to work with communities, typically viewed as 'hard to reach' and therefore 'hard to work with'. Within these comments, heard around the museum (and indeed beyond, in sector conferences I attended at the time), community engagement is framed as natural *disposition*. It shifts emphasis away from the learnt and the technical to the more personal aspects of work. It is conceived as an aptitude that some possess, and others do not, and so it comes to be expected of some people but not of others. A second tendency counters this by arguing that community engagement is a *straightforward task* that anyone in the organisation can do. In this version, community engagement is simply about sitting down with someone for a cup of tea and listening to their stories or collecting their objects. However, this belies the subtlety of high-quality engagement practice and underplays the knowledge required to do so in a meaningful way. Both tendencies have for effect the devaluing of community engagement through its attribution as unskilled work, in one way or another. In my conversations with community engagement workers, we explored these two tendencies. In response, Outreach staff felt that their practice was in fact situated somewhere in between: it is a set of skills and an area of specialised knowledge as well as an attitude. The team also recognised that there was a pressing need to articulate their practice, which up to this point had not clearly been communicated within the museum, leading to the misrecognition and undervaluing of this practice, despite the language being widely adopted across the institution. Describing this practice from their perspective is my next concern (Chapter 5 and 6). But first, I want to examine how the language of community engagement is translated into the management of this practice. What are the consequences of the multiple meanings of community engagement in relation to how this work is organised in the museum? How do community engagement workers experience their institution in the process of 'doing' community engagement work? By focusing further on the institutional life of the museum, we come to see more clearly how the museum is made, as an organisation, as an institution and, more fundamentally, as an idea, in the tussle between different teams working towards the same supposed institutional goals.

Notes

1 I focus primarily on social history curators as the largest team in the Museum and as the team most often involved in engagement work.
2 Learning team member interview. All interviews presented in this chapter took place between 2011 and 2013.
3 History team member interview.
4 In fact, at the time of this research, very few UK museums had a Community Engagement Strategy with the exception of the Manchester Museum. To this day still, very few museums seem to have publicly accessible community engagement strategies.
5 The concept of 'community' is one that has animated much scholarly work in museums studies. Community is a term that is completely fundamental to and yet entirely elusive in museums. Sheila Watson (2007: 3), alongside other authors,

has argued that identities are strongly tied to communities as they define a sense of belonging. A core element of a community is the sharing of certain criteria such as historical and cultural experience, ethnicity, socio-economic status, gender, age and geographical location; it is also defined by exclusions from other communities (Mason, 2005: 206–207). Communities are fluid and relational, and individuals belong to more than one at any time: 'some communities are ours by choice, some are ours because of the way others see us' (Hooper-Greenhill, 2007: 4). Communities are also imagined (Anderson, 2006): for example communities based on a geographical location, like the nation, will include people who may never interact or know each other, yet they share in common a nationality. In different ways, such commentators have presented a view of community as emergent; however, certain conceptual tensions remain: 'the links between museums, heritage and community are so complex that it is hard to distinguish which one leads the other – does heritage construct the community or does a community construct heritage?' (Crooke, 2008: 1). For authors such as Tony Bennett, the museum is as much about producing and inventing a notion of community as it is about representing it: community and museums are necessarily constitutive of each other (Bennett, 1998: 205). Such a view is useful to my particular project of uncovering the work of community engagement practitioners and recognising their part in this dynamic (see Chapter 6 in particular).

6 Collections team member interview.
7 Venue Manager interview.
8 Senior Management team member interview.
9 Venue Manager interview.
10 Curatorial (History) team member interview.
11 Senior Management team member interview.
12 History team member interview.
13 Outreach team member interview.
14 It should be noted that since 2016, as a result of their involvement in the Paul Hamlyn Foundation 'Our Museum' Programme, the museum operates an Alternative Management Team that sits alongside the formal management team to further increase the museum's accountability to its communities and enable them to provide alternative opinions on certain issues. This is undoubtedly a significant development and one that is quite unique for a local authority museum.
15 Collections team member interview.
16 History team member interview.
17 I have explored the different registers of accountability in TWAM in another paper (Morse, 2018).
18 As part of the research, an online survey and report were produced on the perceptions of community engagement at TWAM in February 2013 (67 respondents). Within this survey, 85% of respondents stated that community engagement was a strategic goal of the organisation, and a further 80% stated that it was important to their job.
19 Universities are perhaps not so different from the museum in some sense, as educational institutions of knowledge increasingly bound by bureaucratic structures, with some degree of focus on public engagement and where we might view 'research' as standing in for collections as the object of concern. As such, I have found Ahmed's work readily applicable to my context of the museum.
20 History team member interview.
21 I trace these changes in the policy shifts from this time in another paper (Morse, 2020). Diversity has recently been repositioned as a key language of concern in museums, but only in the last few years, since c.2018, in the context of sector debates around decolonising museums and diversifying the workforce.

22 Professionalism in museum practice is a little-studied domain. 'Museum practice' was first understood in what Anthony Shelton (2013) referred to as 'operational museology', where the attention was on museum practice as technique, derived from a disciplinary body of knowledge, rules of application, ethical protocols and so forth, that constituted exhibitions and collections management. This was followed by a 'critical museology', which Shelton describes in sharp contrast to the operational dimensions of the field, and which redefined the museological project as an reflexive practice based on the ongoing intellectual deconstruction of the museum institution. However, as Anwar Tlili states, 'what has received limited attention is the question of what it is that constitutes the unique mode of professionalism of museum work ... with regard to the nature of the expertise base that can and should support museum work and its claim to professionalism, and the nature of the creative work unique to museum professional practice' (2015: 444). 'Community engagement', in particular, is one area that has been consistently overlooked.

References

Ahmed S (2012) *On Being Included: Racism and Diversity in Institutional Life*. Durham, NC and London: Duke University Press.

Anderson B (2006) *Imagined Communities: Reflections on the Origin and Spread of Nationalism*. Rev. ed. London: Verso.

Austin JL (1975) *How to Do Things with Words*. Cambridge, MA: Harvard University Press.

Bennett T (1998) *Culture: A Reformer's Science*. London and Thousand Oaks, CA: Sage Publications.

Crooke EM (2008) *Museums and Community: Ideas, Issues, and Challenges*. New York: Routledge.

Graham H (2012) Scaling governmentality. *Cultural Studies* 26(4): 565–592. doi: 10.1080/09502386.2012.679285.

Goffman E (1971) *Relations in Public: Microstudies of the Public Order*. London: Allen Lane/Penguin.

Hooper-Greenhill E (2007) Intrepretive communities, strategies and repertoires. In: Watson SER (ed.) *Museums and Their Communities*. Leicester Readers in Museum Studies. London: Routledge, pp. 76–94.

Lynch BT (2011) *'Whose Cake Is It Anyway?': A Collaborative Investigation into Engagement and Participation in 12 Museums and Galleries in the UK*. London: Paul Hamlyn Foundation.

Mason R (2005) Museums, galleries and heritage: Sites of meaning-making and communication. In: Corsane G (ed.) *Heritage, Museums and Galleries: An Introductory Reader*. Abingdon: Routledge, pp. 200–2014.

Morse N (2018) Patterns of accountability: An organizational approach to community engagement in museums. *Museum and Society* 16(2): 171–186.

Morse N (2020) The social role of the museum: From social inclusion to health and wellbeing. In: Glenn H and O'Neill M (eds) *Connecting Museums*. London: Routledge, pp. 48–65.

Morse N, Rex B and Richardson SH (2018) Special issue editorial: Methodologies for researching the museum as organization. *Museum and Society* 16(2): 112–123. doi: 10.29311/mas.v16i2.2810.

Shelton A (2013) Critical museology: A manifesto. *Museum Worlds* 1(1): 7–23. doi: 10.3167/armw.2013.010102.

Tlili A (2008) Behind the policy mantra of the inclusive museum: Receptions of social exclusion and inclusion in museums and science centres. *Cultural Sociology* 2(1): 123–147. doi: 10.1177/1749975507086277.

Tlili A (2015) Encountering the creative museum: Museographic creativeness and the bricolage of time materials. *Educational Philosophy and Theory* 48(5): 443–458. doi: 10.1080/00131857.2015.1031068.

Watson SER (ed.) (2007) *Museums and Their Communities*. Leicester Readers in Museum Studies. London: Routledge.

4 Managing community engagement

The everyday organisational practices of museums are rarely written about,[1] and yet, they distinctively shape institutional life, enabling certain ways of working as routine and creating barriers for other kinds of practice. In this chapter, I consider how community engagement is managed in the museum. I do this by looking back at the different policy structures that shaped work at TWAM (from the 1990s to the time of writing) and in particular, the effects on practice of the introduction of performance management in museums, which focused demands for publicly funded organisations to provide evidence of their public value and the impact of their work. The argument I want to make here is that these performance regimes have created far-reaching 'audit cultures' (Strathern, 2000) that continue to shape museum practices today. As one member of the staff simply stated: 'performance culture is institutional culture in the museum'. In turn, I also consider the other features of the museum-as-organisation, including bureaucratic features such as organisational silos and hierarchical authority. I focus on the impacts of these on the practice of community engagement.

During a conversation, one member of the Outreach team commented on their experience of doing community engagement work in the museum: 'sometimes things flow, and other times there are big black lines'. Such black lines express the institutional resistance to community engagement work, and how this resistance is made solid as barriers to doing this work. I identify four areas of tension in the museum that result in these black lines: ideas of knowledge and expertise; the notion of quality in the museum; the need to manage the expectations of participants in community engagement projects; and the ideas of choice and control. Each area reveals deeper questions about how the museum is made in practice. The final part of the chapter considers how community engagement workers negotiate institutional life.[2] As Sara Ahmed (2012: 15) reminds us, working in institutions is also about working *on* institutions. The 'institutional work' (Lawrence et al., 2009a) of community engagement workers are attempts to move around black lines, to keep things flowing, through tinkering with practice as they negotiate their organisations (see Mol et al., 2010). I also consider how community engagement workers negotiate external policy and fiscal environments on their way to reworking the museum, in particular, the new opportunities that have led the team to develop their work through strategic partnerships with health and social care partners in a period of wider austerity politics.

A (short) history of community engagement

In order to understand community engagement at TWAM, it is important to understand something of the institutional history of community engagement. Such a history highlights the complexity of the contexts within which contemporary museums operate, including the role of government policy, the influence of local council agendas and the requirements of funders on practice (see also Gray, 2012). One notable feature of TWAM is the ways in which particular UK policy shifts have shaped its work of community engagement. As one previous member of the team commented: 'the trajectory of policies...they are very poorly written about, but they are the number one skewer of projects, as in skewing because people will frame their projects in whatever way they can to get the money'.[3] As I briefly go through an account of the more recent influences on the museum's work, I do not wish to imply a simple top-down narrative of policy implementation. Rather, it is clear that policies are also a site of contest for museum staff, and that museum professionals (both directors and front-line staff) actively manage policy requirements to their own ends (Belfiore, 2012; Gray, 2014; Nisbett, 2013).

The work of community engagements at TWAM begins most explicitly during the directorship of David Fleming (1991–2001). Over this period, Fleming developed what he termed 'an institutional approach to inclusivity':

> We took collections off the pedestal where museums have them and we said we want audiences on the pedestal. (...) At this time I was talking about widening access. And being an agent of social change.

The notion of inclusivity (as opposed to exclusivity) focused on breaking down public perceptions of museums as elitist and irrelevant (c.f. Bourdieu and Darbel, 1990) and moving towards the redevelopment of a cultural institution in the service of the public, freely accessible to all. From the beginning of the 1990s, the issue of 'access' in public institutions became a mainstream political issue under the Conservative government's New Public Management policies, based on a view that any public service should respond to customer needs to deliver high standards. Policy at this time concentrated on increasing access (especially schools) and audience development, with a particular focus on data collection about visitors to government subsidised cultural provision (Belfiore, 2004; Lang et al., 2006). Under Fleming, TWAM was one of the first museums to start systematically analysing their visiting audiences in a move to develop a visitor profile that was more representative of local communities, focused particularly on families and lower socio-economic groups (Fleming, 1999, 2002). This work was aimed towards a long-term ambition of creating a 'popular' museum – in the sense of 'for and of the local people'. Between 1989 and 2002, audiences went up about half a million a year to 1.4 million a year, and the proportion of C2, D and E visitors doubled from around 20% to 40% of the core audience across the museum service.[4] One approach to widening audiences was to reinvigorate the core programming of the museum service to better reflect local communities. Over this period there were a number of major contemporary collecting initiatives and smaller projects that invited individuals to interpret objects from multiple perspectives in temporary displays.[5] A second agenda that influenced work at the time was local regeneration initiatives, which funded the first dedicated outreach post in 1992 within the Education team. This role was attached to the creation of a new temporary community exhibition space, *The People's Gallery,* described at the time as 'a pioneering community facility' to engage the West End neighbourhood of Newcastle and 'encourage participation regardless of age, gender, race or ability' (TWM Annual Report, 1993: 24). Many of the first outreach-led activities were focused on the *People's Gallery,* including exhibitions of photographs carried out by community groups and displays addressing contemporary social issues, primarily curated by staff but with input from Occupational Therapists, mental health service user networks, the prison service and recovery service users in the local area. These different activities framed Fleming's second ambition of developing the museum as 'an agent of social change'.

When the New Labour government came to power in 1997, the emphasis on access shifted from customer services towards education and a focus on diversifying audiences (Lang et al., 2006). The New Labour years (1997–2010) were characterised by a number of social policies aimed at tackling social exclusion. Government defined social exclusion as the multidimensional and interlinked problems of unemployment, poor skills, low incomes, poor housing, high crime environments, bad health, poverty and family breakdown, and the wider processes that create a lack of confidence or belonging in society (SEU, 1998, 2001). The solution promoted by government was a multi-agency approach to bring about social change. The most important influence for museums and galleries came through the newly formed Department for Media, Culture and Sport (DCMS), which officially extended this approach through explicit demands that cultural organisations further government objectives through funding agreements. An early DCMS publication, *Centres for Social Change: Museums, Galleries and Archives for All* (2000), articulated the vision for museums to deliver social outcomes and set out the sector's new social roles and social responsibilities:

> Our objective is wider than simply encouraging under-represented groups to come into museum, gallery and archive buildings. If museums, galleries and archives are to make a difference, their goal should be to act as vehicles of positive change.
>
> (DCMS, 2000: 9)

Within this document, TWAM is set out as one of the exemplars of what the social agency of the museum could – and should – look like, building on the work developed under Fleming.[6] Within policy, the social agency of museum was formulated across three inter-related levels (Sandell, 2003): at an individual level, 'soft' outcomes (confidence, self-esteem and wellbeing) derived from engagement with museums can lead to individuals engaging more fully in other aspects of society. At a community level, it is argued that museums can foster inter-community dialogue and social cohesion as well as act a catalyst for regeneration (DCMS, 2002, 2004). At a societal level, museums can promote tolerance and challenge prejudice through inclusive collections and displays. Museums in England were now required to work in partnership with local community organisations to contribute to areas such as employment, urban regeneration and neighbourhood renewal, rehabilitation and health promotion. (As a note of relevance to my later discussions, within early DCMS statements, the role of museums in contributing to health care and health promotion is mentioned briefly, but there are no direct recommendations for taking forward this work.) DCMS set out categories of 'priority groups' for museum projects such as disability, Black Minority Ethnic (BME), Not in Education, Employment or Training youth (NEET) and lower socio-economic groups. This targeted approach to community engagement would deeply shape the organisation of community engagement work in at TWAM. Over this period, significant funding was made available through initiative such as *Renaissance in the Regions* administered by the Museums, Libraries and Archives Council (MLA), which was launched with an investment of almost £150 million aimed to support major regional museums in England in implementing the social inclusion agenda (Resource, 2001). TWAM took the lead in the North East Regional Museums Hub. This period was sometimes referred to as the 'golden age' for the museum: revenue funding from both central and local government rose from c.£5 million in 1997/1998 to c.£12 million in 2009/2010. Over the same period, the number of employees rose from c.200 to c.330 staff.

The museum activities over these years reveal how TWAM approached the task of social inclusion. First, through audience development and access based on equalities areas such as race, gender, LGBT, religion and disability, supported by dedicated posts (a Disability Access Officer and a Cultural Diversity Officer) and advisory groups. Second, through the Learning team and an expanded schools programme (see Hooper-Greenhill et al., 2004). Third, in terms of exhibitions: over this period, the curatorial teams developed further opportunities to include communities in a range of collecting initiatives, public consultation, advisory panels, digital projects and co-curated exhibitions.[7] This work built upon the ethos of social history already established in the museum: 'we embraced it – we opened up things in that way. It was about letting go: about trusting people' (Alec Coles, Museum Director 2001–2009). 'Letting go' was a phrase often used by staff recounting this period. It refers to expanding the idea of authority over collections and museum narratives, working with people to tell their own stories using first-person interpretations and personal objects, and exploring new modes of sharing decision-making in exhibition processes.[8] This form of community engagement placed objects at the centre.[9] Perhaps most significantly, the fourth manner in which the social inclusion policy discourse influenced TWAM was linked to the formal establishment of the Outreach team in 2004. The team's remit was to develop partnerships with local statutory bodies such as the probation service, social services, local authority youth teams, with voluntary social and health organisations and with community organisations. One full-time Assistant Outreach Officer (core funded) was assigned to each of the five districts of Tyne and Wear in order to facilitate contact between the local communities and the museum service, and a dedicated part-time post for *The People's Gallery* was also re-newed (again funded through a council regeneration initiative). Additional project funding over the years enabled the creation of temporary outreach posts for project-specific work, which resulted with the team reaching 17 staff members at one point in 2008. Projects over the years included work with residential homes for young and older people, women's groups, lads' and dads' groups, the probation service and youth referral units, disability support groups, homeless people's projects and culturally diverse groups. Team members were recruited from a variety of backgrounds to do this work: nursing, youth work, community development and artists working alongside individuals with a background in museum practice. The *People's Gallery* became a key space through which the Outreach team developed its practice of community engagement in terms of exhibitions. Over the years, it included a collaboration with local punk fans, young skaters, refugees, prisoners and prison officers and individuals with mental health issues.[10] Each exhibition addressed issues regarding how these different groups were represented in the media or wider society and sought to challenge these views through personal stories. Over this period, the team developed what was routinely referred to around the organisation as 'an Outreach way of working' with communities, positioned as it were in relation to a curatorial way of working: a way of working focused on people, rather than objects. Through the work of the Outreach team, TWAM gained further recognition across the sector for its commitment to socially engaged forms of museum practice and community engagement work.

Performing community engagement

'We were always driven by targets...'

One of the most significant effect of the New Labour cultural policies for museums was the further introduction of performance management re-gimes to the existing calculative practices of New Public Management as a means of evidencing the social impact of the museum alongside its 'value for money' (Selwood, 2002; Tlili, 2008). Measuring performance against standardised quantitative indicators across the sector was part of the government's focus on accountability that became central to DCMS activity over these years. Drawing on the principle of evidence-based policy, government (at arm's length via DCMS Public Service Agreements[11]) insisted on measurable outcomes to demonstrate value for money and to assess efficiency in relation to government objectives, namely monitoring access initiatives for priority target groups. At TWAM, this new regime led to the growth of a quantitative audit culture of audience attendance, the implementation of key outcomes-based targets in nearly all areas of museum work and the adoption of an economic language of Key Performance Indicators and Best Value as a way of talking about the public value of the museum. Performance was recorded against visitor numbers, in particular priority groups, alongside revenue generated per visitor, made publicly available through annual reports and benchmarking surveys. Beyond this public facing data, each team had their own targets outlined within team plans, usually set over the year and reported quarterly. While the rationale of these reforms appears incontestable (making museums more accountable to the public), they have had unanticipated consequences. The anthropologists Marilyn Strathern and Cris Shore have written about how new systems of measuring performance in the workplace profoundly reshape the ways organisations and individuals operate through the establishment of pervasive audit cultures of 'institutionalized expectations and instruments' (Strathern, 2000: 3) that derive legitimacy from claims to accountability and transparency based on the principles of financial audit.[12] In audit culture, 'good practice' correlates with meeting quantifiable targets, documenting the attainment of these goals and sharing reports with management and funders. As the techniques and values of audit become central organising principles, 'new kinds of relationships, habits and practices' are created (Shore, 2008: 279). The impact of instrumental policies on museum practice has been widely discussed in terms of their coherence, feasibility and suitability for the sector (Belfiore, 2002; Gibson, 2008; Holden, 2004; Tlili et al., 2007; West and Smith, 2005). What I am interested in here is how audit culture shapes the particular working environments of community engagement workers and its effects on workplace subjectivities in the museum.

For the Outreach team, community engagement work priorities were organised primarily in relation to the DCMS priority groups such as people with a long-standing limiting illness or disability, people from lower socio-economic groups, people from Black and Minority Ethnic groups (BME) and NEET. Members of the team recalled the influence of these targets on developing their practice when they started in the late-2000s:

My experience of the last 6 years within Outreach: you have people who are funded by *Renaissance*, and they will have specific targets where you need to be working with 'engaging with x amount of people over a period of time'. And there will be definitions of what that means, 'engagement':

for a long time, this was when we were under the Labour Government it was specific targets like Black Minority Ethnic communities and those kind of terms; working with older people. It seems to me that over the past there has been a heavy emphasis on targets and numbers – which serves a purpose... But as I observed the Outreach team have been in the past under pressure, for example, 'you have to work with some Sikhs now, you have to work with some old people with dementia'... and I have problems with that way of working.

I was part of *Renaissance*, the remit was four categories under the social inclusion agenda and they were BME communities, to engage with young people and disaffected youth, older people, and people with disabilities. I remember very much soon after social inclusion you had that push towards cultural diversity (...) I know that my yearly remit was twenty-two small projects, seven medium projects (that's more long term), and three large projects which was more about public engagement in terms of festivals that sort of thing. So we had definite targets to meet.

The quotes capture a sense of the frenetic pace of development of community engagement practice over the last ten years. Funder requirements specified priority groups, while the form of community engagement was mainly dictated by project structures, mostly short-term projects (usually over ten weeks, with very small groups, six per project). In one year, the team was expected to engage 4,000 people, with targets equally divided across team members and across different project size (large, medium or small), with results presented in quarterly reports.

Reflecting back on this time, three vivid metaphors were used to describe how conditions shaped community engagement practice in the museum. First, the team described a 'scatter-gun' approach as a response to the constant pressure to find groups to fit with national policy priority areas. Linked to this, practice developed through a 'conveyor-belt' of projects (a second metaphor), as one staff put viscerally: 'we used to churn people through a mince machine'. Staff would have to rapidly move from one project to the next, with few opportunities for follow-up work or opportunities to develop sustainable relations with groups and organisations. This also worked against longer-term planning as the pressure was to go straight into delivery work:

With the money there was always a need to rush into spending – so bam this project has to happen, there is this money, and you have to engage with this many people and you have to come to the gallery and they have to do something and it would be a bit wham bam book them in.

Because of their quick turn-around, the structures of projects also made it difficult to develop community-led activities: 'in the old days, we had some key aims and we always matched up with what the [external] organisations wanted to get out of the project. But there wasn't much from the bottom-up in terms of what the group wanted to do'. Projects generally tended to focus on the museum's agenda rather than being more fully co-produced: 'I suppose [it was] bespoke with a very small 'b' because it didn't actually come from that group or sector'. Outreach staff also expressed their frustration at 'dropping' people at the end of a ten-week project:

> You feel like you are dipping in and out, like you are parachuting in then zipping off and doing something else whereas there were some organisations that really wanted us to continue working with them.

This problematic dynamic also applied to exhibitions where Outreach and curatorial teams often worked together on externally funded projects. In the management structures of exhibition projects, especially Heritage Lottery funded ones, a proportion of budget would usually be allocated to community engagement work. This tended to produce what Outreach described as a 'bolt-on' form of community engagement (the third vivid metaphor):

> You get touring exhibitions like the Bollywood posters exhibition, and part of that grant would be X amount of outreach work within in. So you would get boards who are organising that kind of project, and they would get Outreach along to it and we will be involved in some of the meetings. I don't want to keep sounding negative but you keep coming in and out: they bring you in as an Outreach Officer, you do the community bit of that exhibition, and then it's gone. It's like: 'we need to find some Asian kids to work with this'. You'll get an application put in by a curator or a senior manager – 'we need Outreach to do something'.

Within the project management timeline and its Gantt charts, community engagement was nearly always placed at the end of the exhibition process, as a means to deliver specific outputs to be used in the exhibition, for example, an oral history (or a proggy mat, see Chapter 3). Project briefs were often written and signed off by management before going out to communities and therefore without consultation (as the outreach workers further noted: 'They were asking the Assistant Officer at the time if they could deliver: you did this before for a another project could you do it again? Almost copying parts of another bid into a new bid'). As one outreach worker put it: 'it's an incidental way of working rather than thinking who will be interested'. It was also rarely possible to change the project objectives or activities once funding had been agreed. Outreach described this model of engagement work as 'singing the tune of the museum service', where the parameters of the project would be entirely set by the museum agenda, its timetable and its ways of working. These were not always compatible with more open ways of working with communities and often resulted in tokenistic approaches to engagement. Tokenism is a central issue in the critique of participatory practice (Chapter 2). The case of TWAM reveals how the mundane bureaucracies of project management, set within a wider audit culture, further entrench these problems. As staff explained, the early DCMS focus on 'access' meant that it was not possible to work with groups long term or on consecutive projects, as a senior staff member made clear: 'they were very suspicious of museums working with the same groups all the time and just counting them over and over again'. The audit culture inferred that only 'unique engagements' could be counted, with the paradoxical effect of discouraging practices to sustain engagement with museums, leading the Outreach team to ask:

> It felt to me as it became just too much about numbers – where people want to get the numbers in, and tick the boxes – and are the projects we're doing really having any kind of legacy with people? Are they affecting people's lives?

Community engagement practice became about *performing* community engagement through data. Quarterly reports and evaluation case studies were the key administrative tasks within the team, and as I observed, a significant portion of work time was dedicated to compiling these documents. Documents such as these reports are crucial to audit culture, as they aim to maximise accountability to managers and funders. But these documents only ever partially represent the work that they are meant to capture. The evaluation report, for example, contains the number of people engaged, some participant quotes and some photographs. It functions performatively as a record of the event but tells us little about the *practice* of community engagement. Within TWAM, there was an additional sense (common across the museum) that evaluation reports needed to be 'happy' documents so as to function as advocacy. As one manager commented, the organisation was encouraged to 'blow its own trumpet', especially when the outcomes were ambitious. Any admission of project challenges, mishaps and even failures were not easily accommodated, especially in a climate of competitive funding, as one member of the Learning team recalled: 'there is always a whole falseness: that evaluations are written to fit. There is always that with any funding'. What is left out of evaluation documents is just as essential to producing impact; however, the things that are left out exist mostly in undocumented spaces, while the workplace identities of community engagement workers are shaped by the dynamic between what must be documented (their administrative work) and what is talked about and practised (reflected in the quote above by the question 'are we affecting people's lives?'). What serves as evidence in audit culture determines a limited view of the practices that comes to define 'good practice', which then circulates within organisations.

Writing about the implementation of the social inclusion agenda in museum, Tlili (2008) has described how museum professionals across the sector began to relate meeting numerical targets with social inclusion itself. He suggests that audience development and marketing strategies at the time became rationalised as having social inclusion functions by simple virtue of increasing visitor numbers, as targets came to stand in for the complex practice of social inclusion itself. In the previous chapter, I spoke of how managers in particular understand community engagement at a distance through an advocacy lens, where data comes to stand in as the primary understanding of practice. As Shore makes clear, while the rationale for audit culture is to promote organisational transparency and efficiency, the extent to which it transforms the workplace practices and relationships means that it often has the reverse effect. He goes on to suggest that 'once introduced into a new setting or context, [audit culture] actively constructs (or colonizes) that environment in order to render it auditable. The effects are irreversible. One of those effects is the loss of room for creativity and initiative' (2008: 291). At the time of these social inclusion policies, the then-director Alec Coles stated that a consequence of the increasing need to justify the receipt of public funding in the museum led to a state where 'sensible evaluation evolved into a performance management regime that was considered, by many, as both unnecessary and draconian' (Coles, 2008: 330). The various operational requirements of the performance agenda had the effect of exhausting the Outreach team:

> We were doing too many projects and we were running around between one thing and another (...) Just a feeling that we were being overworked and doing a lot of projects and none of it was necessarily being recognised or being communicated in the museum.

The audit cultures that aimed to professionalise the museum and evidence social inclusion thus had a corrosive effect on autonomy and creativity in the work of the Outreach team and led to a deep sense of professional dissatisfaction where, ironically, the value and impact of this work was not recognised by the institution.

Museum bureaucracies

Mundane management structures, systems and processes all affect the daily work of museum workers. They shape institutional life. Procedures must be followed to ensure compliance and safety to efficiently manage projects, and reports must be produced to evidence impact, effectiveness and accountability. I have already discussed some of these effects. To understand something more about the experience of community engagement workers, we need to pay further attention to the bureaucratic nature of the museum, which is so often overlooked in scholarly accounts of museum practice (Gray and McCall, 2018). One particular feature of TWAM as a local authority museum is that it shares its systems (from IT to HR) with the council, and at the same time, it must juggle the different requirements of multiple funders – local and central government and other organisations (charities or public bodies such as the Arts Council or Heritage Lottery Fund), each with their own reporting processes, sometimes requiring the same data but often reported in different ways. One senior management staff described the push and pulls of different processes and procedures having produced 'system Kafka' – a bureaucracy marked by disorienting and at times sense-less complexity. It is within this operational complexity that community engagement practitioners must negotiate their practice. At times, it was felt that processes were too rigid ('It's hard to balance the corporate pro-cedures with the flexibility you need to work with a community') or bur-densome ('work with communities is ridden over with the red tape, delays and procedures that we find ourselves plagued with'). In fact, these feelings were shared across many sections of the museum, who felt that certain el-ements were negatively impacting on professional autonomy and creativity ('[the museum] is so tied up in its own paperwork and procedures it feels like we can't breathe sometimes'). Procedures, as a feature of public accounta-bility, were not in themselves seen a problematic; rather, it was their layered bureaucratic effects that were felt as stifling. As I observed it, the museum functioned as a culture that emphasised chains of top-down leadership, effi-ciency and control, where processes and procedures were managed through hierarchical layers of sign-off. A 'culture of hierarchy' was often identified as a barrier to innovative ways of working and professional creativity across the museum more generally. Staff used various images to describe how they experienced the 'sluggishness' of their institution: 'cumbersome', 'turning around the Titanic' or 'pushing a boulder up a mountain' – 'slow to operate, slow to rally people, slow to change'. In another sense, the phrase 'system Kafka' is equally revealing of the cultures of organising in the museum. Over time, procedures become engrained as common sense and a sense in common; simply 'the way things are done'. As one staff member reflected:

> It's not so much the processes and procedures themselves – although they are really frustrating and difficult to manage – but it's more the long-standing beliefs that come along with them. There are some really posi-tive, progressive staff in the museum who are really excited about change and about having wider conversations [with communities], but then there are others who don't want to change their ways of working because of the effort it requires. Perhaps it's one big circle – the processes and procedures create so much of a barrier that only some can climb it successfully.

There is a sense then, that to make the museum (and to answer the fun-damental question about 'what is a museum'), practitioners must also ne-gotiate its bureaucratic nature. As I have described, the implementation of audit culture in the museum is a significant (though significantly over-looked) manner through which contemporary museum work has become procedural. This has had profound effects on creativity and initiative in the museum. The effect of performance management regimes was not confined to the Outreach team, since a significant feature of audit culture in the museum was its pervasiveness, which in turn has led to a further differentiation of teams based on distinct targets and priorities:

> Too often I think museums tend to draw the line. And I think this is because Learning was constructed when *Renaissance* money came in and [then] there was money to set up the Outreach team (...). So Outreach were effectively the sister team to Learning but this artificial line [was drawn]: Learning for schools and Outreach to communities. In a way we haven't yet recovered from this.[13]

Organisational silos are a typical feature of modern bureaucracies. This compartmentalisation of teams according to work specialisations strongly influenced the construction of team-based staff identities at TWAM, based around departmental targets. Over time, these boundaries created the deep organisational silos that shape institutional life (see also Macdonald, 2002). On one level, these silos are visible in organisational charts, and in the layout of offices, 'we are all separated in our different offices. I think sometimes it feels a bit disjointed'.[14] Certainly, this was something I felt acutely as a researcher entering the museum's backrooms for the first time: teams set up on opposite corridors or different floors, marking out physically a separation that would then manifest time and again in informal discussions, formal meetings and my varied interactions with staff. The imagery of being 'disjointed' was a recurrent complaint, meaning that opportunities for programmes and projects to support one another were often missed. In the Outreach team's accounts, there was a narrative by which Outreach and History had once worked closely together, but in recent years, these exchanges had stopped as priorities had shifted in line with different targets and funder requirements pulling the teams in different directions. Paradoxically, there was a further separation of teams because Outreach and History had worked so closely together in the past. In this account (mostly from senior managers), the sharing of practice was so successful that it was deemed that the 'Outreach ways of working' in relation to community engagement was now embedded in the work of the curatorial teams. And so, there was no longer a need for interdisciplinary team working, or indeed, a need for the Outreach-led *People's Gallery*, so it was reverted to a curatorial-led temporary gallery. At this moment, the naming of practice as 'embedded' had for effect the dismantling of the structures that supported it. We are here returned to the feelings described to me by community engagement workers upon my arrival in the museum: they experience institutions as resistant to their work. The loss of this space in particular affected moral across the Outreach team because of its symbolic value, further cementing feelings that their work was neither understood nor valued.

Black lines

Outreach workers described the experience of doing community engagement work as often being faced with 'black lines', 'where things stop flowing'. Such black lines express the institutional resistance to community engagement work. For Sara Ahmed's diversity workers, this is the 'brick wall'. The images dovetail to describe the ways in which the institution can be experienced by practitioners as resistant: the institution becomes that which they come up against. Ahmed writes: 'The official desire to institutionalize diversity does not mean the institution is opened up; indeed, the wall might become all the more apparent, all the more a sign of immobility, the more the institution presents itself as opened. The wall gives physical form to what a number of practitioners describe as "institutional inertia", the lack of an institutional will to change' (2012: 26). The black lines reveal the habits and cultures of institutions that maintain the museum, despite its official commitment to community engagement (Chapter 3). As I will go on to describe, these black lines also reflect the logic of contribution, where certain forms and products of participation are preferred (Chapter 2). When the contributions do not fit with the museum's expectations, lines are drawn.

There are also other reasons why these black lines appear, sometimes about conflicting interests, for example, the pressures of income generation for private hire of museum venues versus community use of a space. These types of conflict are significant in so far that a decision one way can produce a barrier to community work. What I am more interested in revealing here, however, are tensions that arise when different interests try to accommodate community engagement work. These tensions are more complicated. They have to do with notions of professionalism as well as organisational processes and procedures, and the ways in which museum workers attempt to adjust but also protect different areas of museum work. In the following section, I identify four areas of tension in the museum that result in black lines. The four areas are related through short narratives from practice, snapshots of discrete events that reflect much wider questions within community engagement work: questions of knowledge and expertise; the notion of 'quality' in the museum; the need to manage the expectations of participants in community engagement projects; and ideas of choice and control. Neither area is easily resolved, but each reveals something more of the ambivalent nature of community engagement in the museum.

Knowledge and expertise

A first tangled site of tension and one that figures centrally in museum studies surrounds the issue of authority in museums, and how it intersects with knowledge and expertise (e.g. Adair et al., 2011). The singular view of the museum as the gatekeeper of knowledge has long been challenged, and community engagement has been part of the movement to share authority in the museum as well as a method of gaining better information about collections where curatorial knowledge is limited or expertise is partial. This is particularly the case when it is possible to identify an originating community linked to the objects or collection in question, or when a community has lived experience of a particular issue represented by the object or collections. Indeed, and beyond museum institutions, public participation is often cited as the emancipatory solution to expertise; however, it is often the case that participation is a site where expertise is also maintained in particular ways (Cooke and Kothari, 2001; see Chapter 2). In the museum, tensions emerge around from the different framings of 'knowledge' and how they are valued and validated, especially in gallery display. In the following account, an outreach worker describes a point at which things stopped flowing along these knowledge hierarchies, and where they came faced with a black line:

> A few years ago, I worked on the World Cultures gallery, whereby a gallery was already set up and the text was more or less done and I was asked to bring communities in to provide an interpretation for those objects in the gallery. We ended up looking at poetic form as a way of expressing what we felt about the objects in the gallery because the group didn't have all the knowledge about it, neither did the curator. So we looked at a more creative way of people expressing themselves which didn't have to be based on facts but were based on people's experiences in terms of interfacing with those objects: Where do they fit in? Why are they here? Is it world cultures or world history or local history? Because people living here now are always connected globally. And all those things came out in some of the sessions we did. Ultimately the poems included the five sections in the gallery like faith, those things that define communities and people. That was an example of how I would use something creative to have a free narrative, a lay person's narrative, but equally important.
>
> But that wasn't used in the gallery interpretation. Because it's not always at the level at which the museum asks for that interpretation. It was used I think in some postcards we made for the project.
>
> I think for the museum it always seems to be 'we need an interpretation for this' and sometimes that has come because the curatorial experience isn't there or the museum needs expertise from communities. I think sometimes it seems to be about object narratives and I think that's sometimes a bit too two-dimensional. I think people are looking for other routes too, they want a deeper understanding of the museum in terms of things they don't even know about.

Often times, the black line is about what goes on the wall; what interpretation from the community is made public (or not) in the final display. As it has been noted, within the power dynamics of the museum, editorial control often remains firmly within the museum's grasp (Fouseki, 2010; Lynch and Alberti, 2010). In this account, we come to see the ways in which hierarchies of knowledge play out in the museum: object knowledge or experiential/ emotional knowledge; expertise or experience; fact-based interpretation or creative response. Curatorial staff were interested in the kinds of community expertise (based here on group identity) that could complement the museum interpretation. Essentially, the museum was looking for the community to contribute factual information, for example, about how a specific pot was used. The poetry was classed as a creative response, an opinion or narrative, as opposed to knowledge per se. It is not seen as a relevant contribution in the context of the museum display in this instance. Within the logic of contribution, the form of interpretation, the knowledge and expertise to be contributed, is fixed in format, and it needs to conform to what the museum 'needs'. When it does not, community engagement workers and communities are faced with a black line.

In relation to this tangled site, another barrier described by Outreach was a 'professional reluctance' to share or relinquish authority to communities. For Outreach, this reluctance was interpreted as being linked to 'professional pride': it was felt that curatorial staff still held a very singular view of expertise derived from the scholarly study of collections. This sometimes transpired in my own conversations with curators, but always in a much more nuanced way, linked to the professional accountability of curators, their sense of duty and diligence towards information collected and documented about objects in the collection. In the Outreach team's opinion, this reluctance to engage with community engagement was linked to fear – a fear of the unknown (and the need to manage risk) or a fear of professional standards (i.e. quality) being dropped. This attitude could block the inclusion (and even the discussion of inclusion) of community work and community voices in exhibitions. This was particularly the case where community engagement work was 'bolted-on' at the end of an exhibition project where the narrative was already pre-set. As I observed in my own conversations with staff across the museum, these anxieties were complicated by another fear: the fear of redundancy, in both senses of the word. The challenge to expertise inferred in community engagement can be threatening to expertise, making curatorial knowledge redundant; but it was also felt as a direct threat to staff's employment. This fear of redundancy was further exacerbated within the climate of cuts to staffing budgets that characterised the austerity period of this research. A related concern that was sometimes voiced was that if the community and volunteers can do it, are museum professionals needed at all?

I think possibly people felt threatened because if 16- and 17-year olds can do it, you know, why have specialists?

And there is a lot of paperwork involved and fear in different teams about what community engagement means. We don't have time to get things out and send it to communities and then if Outreach have access [to museum objects] and does that mean the History team aren't needed anymore or....?

Resistance? Yes, and it will come from curators as they say 'if you want me to release all my knowledge whether it is in my head or in my history files beside my desk, you are undermining my value to the organisation.

Another manifestation of this fear, highlighted in the second quote, focused on issues around collection access, both physical access to the store and online access to the collection management catalogue (to which only the curatorial teams have full access). Outreach reported many instances of being faced with 'a flat out no' when attempting to access accessioned collections on behalf of their groups or to include them in co-curated displays, as a member of the Outreach team recalled: 'one of the communities was the Ethiopian community living up here in the West End and they asked "have you got a painting of this?" – it was some special moment in their history and it was at Sunderland Museum when I looked at it, but we couldn't have that painting because there was always an issue around conservation and how much it was going to cost. This also happened with a Sudanese object. It's very difficult to work in those conditions'. Collections access in the museum was bound up with layers of bureaucracy (collections management procedures and protocols), but equally, it was managed through unwritten rules and routine. Holding onto these unwritten rules is one way through which staff could remain 'specialists'. One Outreach staff commented:

It's all privy knowledge ... but it's not, it's stuff you can learn really easily – it's just you do this, this and this; but [the curators] would only answer questions but they wouldn't give suggestions – can we select these things, what do we do now? Do I book transport? Do you book transport? And they don't get back to you.

Again, this is not a straightforward reluctance on the part of curators, but rather, it is bound up with the bureaucratic cultures of organisation, particularly the deep organisational silos in the museum, the different professionals' sense of their workplace identities, the professional boundaries they draw up around work remits and specialist skills and the perceptions of their value to the institution. For community engagement workers, these black lines were felt emotionally, as feeling that they were not trusted by collection-based teams. I put this to curators I spoke to:

I don't think it's issues of trust really. I think it's a curator is trained to absolutely care about every little bit of care of that object and giving it over to somebody else who is not a curator is like giving up responsible care for that object ... which is how we have been trained really. But I think that mind-set means that objects aren't easily given to the community because they wouldn't be given to Outreach I think that is a bit of stumbling block.

The stumbling block here is not simply about trusting individuals, but rather about professional boundaries and professional understandings of roles, responsibilities and accountabilities. This presents a particular area of tension within the museum. My point here is not to reproduce lazy caricatures of curators, and it is beyond the scope of this work to further unpick curators' sense of their professional selves. What is apparent, however, is the sense through which the value and meaning of 'work' held in different teams distinctly shape the museum and staff experiences of their institutions. By drawing our attention into professional work-worlds, we can come to better understand conflict in museums as part of the making sense of museum work (e.g. custodianship, representation and participation), and more broadly, the making sense of the idea of the museum itself.

Quality

The narrative for Outreach was that community work is not valued in the museum because it is felt to be of lesser quality than museum production. Reflecting on the previous community gallery, one staff member made this sentiment clear: '*The People's Gallery* was the community space, with the paper mâché heads and a kind of narrow idea of a community exhibition and nobody cared about the space in the museum'. Most of the museum's venues do not have a dedicated community exhibition space (let us remember *The People's Gallery* has been taken over for other programming), and instead, work was often confined to the stairwell or the corridors:

> We were going to be in the exhibition space, but we were moved into the corridor so I had to say to my group 'Oh it's better in the corridor, more people walk there and will see it, and it's our little space'. I had to make it sound fabulous rather than 'you've been chucked out of the main exhibition and now you're in the corridor...

More than symbolically, then, community engagement is maintained at the periphery, 'in the special area over there'. In these moments, quality standards were often invoked to block community engagement display in certain museum space:

> The idea was that [the community] would produce things that would go into the exhibition and there was a bit of a wobble from [the venue] where they have a certain standard of things on display – and if the community produced something that wasn't up to their standard they would then say it couldn't be included.

From the institution's perspective, including community voices and choices troubles the museum's responsibility to maintain professional standards and problematises what can be accepted as quality. The institution must also consider 'public interest' or, to put this another way, the accountability of the museum voice. Only stories or art works compatible with public display can be told or can be shown for public consumption. Within the logic of contribution, the individual act of contributing – an object, a story, a narrative or interpretation – is also part of the process of transferring ownership to the museum, and in turn, part of the act of making that contribution 'public'.[15] The contribution is therefore understood in relation to the institutional demands for quality that govern how the contribution is received, valued and managed in the museum. Time and again, Outreach staff faced the 'black lines' when it came to include community-produced work in temporary or permanent galleries. At the same time, in the museum, there was no clear definition of quality or public interest and what they meant in terms of display. As such, it would often feel to Outreach that arbitration through these terms was in fact an argument in support of aesthetic taste or personal judgement. For many members of curatorial staff, the idea of quality was more intimately linked to a wider sense of professional accountability in their work, derived from upholding duties to a wider historical narrative or a standard of quality for accessible display. For Outreach, the main tensions around quality and public interest were that these were rarely part of wider discussions that might be influenced by their participants. They could also have more damaging effects when invoked last minute, as they often were, leading to an editorial take-over or cancellation and the disappointment of participants. A short story reveals these tensions:

> A youth group is doing a photography project with the Outreach team about life in their neighbourhood. Their photos are of desolate estates, of chicken wire and graffiti walls; the themes are raw and tough. The local councillor, who first suggested the project as part of wider project on neighbourhood renewal, is unsure; it's not what he had expected, and he doesn't like the way it portrays the neighbourhood it was meant to celebrate. It is also felt that this does not represent how the wider community feel about their neighbourhood. In the end, the pictures don't make it onto the walls in the museum as planned, and the youth group is moved on to another project.

There were other occasions recounted to me where participants' stories were edited beyond professional standards of text access and readability, and where quality and public interest were invoked for editorial control. The short story above reveals how the public role of the museum is negotiated with its specific work of inclusion, and the priority is often taken by the former. The story also reveals how the museum negotiates the dynamics of community engagement through distance and proximity: community engagement at proximity is about working with young people to tell their stories of their place; community engagement at a distance is concerned with balancing different perspectives and public interest, allowing for multiple stories, and attempts at representational equity.

While the Outreach team accepted that 'it's one of those things that not all groups produce something that's really amazing or really pretty', for them, a key aspect of community engagement work (at proximity) was to provide opportunities to celebrate participants' work through public display. They saw their own role within this as supporting participants to produce work and display of a standard that would inspire pride in communities as well as ensure their voices and stories were heard and seen in the museum. One staff member who previously worked principally in the *People's Gallery* spoke of their role as 'making things look good' for display in order to translate community ambitions into the spaces (and rules) of the museum. In this way, issues of quality were dealt with in practice through tweaks, work arounds and compromise in flexible ways that were inclusive of participants, and where staff expertise of production and display was a part of that which is co-produced. I return to some of these ideas in Chapter 6.

Managing expectations

In most of the conversations I had with staff in the museum (other than Outreach), the initial response to our discussions of community engagement (and even sometimes, it seemed, as a definition for it) was 'community engagement, it is about managing people's expectations'. There are particular effects to this comment, its recurrence, the length for which staff would talk about it and what this tells us about how community engagement is managed within organisational settings. One aspect of this conversation was around 'gatekeepers', which is often highlighted as a challenge in participatory work. There was a need to manage the more 'vociferous voices', as one curatorial staff put it: 'my initial concern would be that you would have those vocal individuals [who] would drive their own agenda and the key is what controls you put on that'. This view was shared across curatorial, collection and senior management teams. In other conversations, there was a certain pessimism about what community engagement could really achieve since the organisational procedures were felt so inflexible and what communities would surely ask for would be too difficult to deliver. Museum staff were very aware of the critique of tokenistic participation and 'false consensus' (Lynch, 2011b) and conscious not to be complicit or mislead participants. The key effect of this recurrent phrase, 'managing expectations', was to paralyse staff:

> [Staff] have an idea of what it means to be working with communities in their heads and it scares the bejezus out of them because they think 'oh God it's an extra piece of work' and 'if I don't agree with them, if they want to put something on a label and I don't want to put it on a label, do I have to put it on a label?' and I think there are a lot of misconceptions or worries about what it might mean.[16]

Staff sometimes became too anxious to even attempt engagement work as a result:

> When they are managing expectations, people feel if they get asked something by the community or suggested to them they feel like they have to do it, and so they would rather just not go there at all rather than having to say no.[17]

Within this rhetoric, the risk of disappointing participants outweighed the benefits of participation. What I found throughout the museum was that community engagement was discussed and operationalised through the bureaucratic structures of risk management. The issue of risk management is primarily one of managing certainty. Collaboration is an inherently uncertain process, especially when working with groups or communities outside of the museum and its norms. Attempting to embrace uncertainty is in direct conflict with the need for certainty built into the operating values of museums.[18] For example, in order to produce an exhibition, fixed points of certainty must be established: flow charts, Gantt charts with plans and procedures for object conservation, design and technical construction, to interpretation, mount and display. Staff who carry out these different functions typically do so across a number of programmes and therefore require allocated times to perform these functions on the project and manage their own workloads. This leaves little room for uncertainty or the messiness of participation with external groups (see Askins and Pain, 2011). Within this operational concern, community engagement is constructed at a distanced and disembodied scale as a variable to be managed alongside budgets, timetables and technical museographic tasks.

Another element of uncertainty is the community itself. Staff would often anticipate conflict with communities, and so planning for community engagement activities also became about anticipating risk. To take one short example, partway through my research, I attended the first meeting to develop a series of engagement activities around a portrait on loan from a national gallery. The aim of the community engagement activities was to engage the local diaspora community around this particular painting. Almost immediately, the meeting became centred on how to manage the community's expectations, even though they were not in the room; there was a long discussion about the need to use the national museum's branding and anticipating the conflicts that might arise from this. The absent community was imagined entirely through the need to manage its expectations rather than through any discussion of how to raise its aspirations or ambitions. Such a configuration is concomitant with the logic of contribution, where the contribution is framed by the museum's priorities and conventions. For example, in this senior staff's comment: 'before you start any community engagement, I think you have to be clear about what it is you want to achieve and what you are prepared to accept and not to accept'. There is of course a good sense of pragmatism here and, indeed, a more honest approach to the possibilities of co-production – but it also frames the process, from the very start, not in terms of an ethics of collaboration, but in terms of risk management where communities are viewed as antagonistic, and engagement is necessarily confrontational.[19] Framed in this way, managing expectations becomes the main way in which the idea of community engagement is operationalised in the museum. The effects are the loss of creativity, enthusiasm and confidence in this area of work.

Choice and control

I want to suggest that the response of 'managing expectations' is also linked to the prevalence of ideas of choice and control within the discourse of participation in the museum sector. As I discussed in Chapter 2, notions of choice and control are set within the logic of contribution and are central to the ladder of participation model. In the ladder of participation model, there is a hierarchy of participation that equates the greatest level of relinquishing of power with the most valuable forms of participation work for both individual participants and the institution. The top of the ladder focuses on decisions, and participation is understood as the ability to exercise choice and control in decision-making processes. These become the primary markers of a successful community engagement project. Attached to this model was a deep sense of anxiety felt by many museum professionals, which again could lead staff to disengage from this work:

> And we worry about are we doing it right? And can we do more? And how should we be doing it and are we getting the right people?[20]

> I think some of the officers felt that there would be pressure on them all the time to keep having to go higher and higher (...) but there is always that concern with some people that it becomes a stick to beat them with.[21]

> There seem to be a subconscious hierarchy that says - people expressing themselves = good; mediation = bad, or steering people = bad, and that somehow, it's wrong to steer projects.[22]

Across the museum, there was a sense that 'good' community engagement work was a matter of individual or group choices whereby the museum handed over control and did not intervene. Let us turn to another short story where these tensions come to the fore. As part of the 2012 Cultural Olympiad, the museum facilitated a youth-led exhibition project with the World Cultures collections, where the intention was for the young people to have (total) control. They were presented with a 'blank canvas' and the opportunity to direct every aspect of the project, supported by a mixed team including curators and youth workers. For the museum, this project was the most democratic (in their terms) form of co-production they had ever attempted. Another objective was to bring young people into the museum to challenge traditional practices. However, over the course of the project staff often spoke amongst themselves (and with me) about their concerns over some of the young people's choices, for example in terms of design and interpretation, and the ways in which they had chosen to represent cultures to which they did not belong. This anxiety focused in particular on the choice of the title for the exhibition: 'The Curious Case of …'. For the young people, this title connected with their experience interpreting objects 'forgotten' in museum stores. For the museum staff, there was a profound discomfort around its connotations, replicating Western imperialist views of world cultures as exotic. However, staff did not always feel that they were able to challenge the young people through the process of engagement as they worried that intervening would diminish the young people's experience of participation and their ability to exercise choice. In this project, the role of facilitator was imagined as enabling the young people to achieve their decisions, whatever they chose. However, this particular project was further complicated by ethical considerations linked to the use of World Cultures collections with a group that perhaps did not have direct legitimate claims to interpret these collections. By focusing on the young people's participation, staff did not feel able to tackle these questions, and we were all left wondering whether not taking a stand, the museum was effectively divesting itself of its responsibilities. The more fundamental question that emerges from this example concerns how participation itself is imagined: are participants involved because they have experiential knowledge, because they are able to communicate best to the audience, because they can affect institutional change or simply because they have volunteered to be involved? In each case, the museum 'intervening' may be more or less appropriate. Here, the strict focus on choice and control for a group of young people, who in fact, had little direct, legitimate claim to these particular collections, led to misrecognition of the stakes of participation and of the role of the museum as facilitator in community engagement work.[23]

Across the museum more generally, as I observed it, the discourse of choice and control had the particular effect of actually closing down opportunities for community engagement. By focusing narrowly on choice and control, decision-making had become an end in itself, an act of closure. The act of decision-making as the logical outcome of choice and control suggests a frame that emphasises closure that is counter-intuitive to community engagement as a more open-ended process. Furthermore, satisfying participants with 'choice' is not necessarily the same thing as providing opportunities for fulfilling engagement. In the museum, these were often narrow procedural conceptions of decisions focusing on the choice of objects and their place in a display. Set within the logic of contribution, participation is only oriented towards the museum and is firmly set within institutional frameworks. Since the museum wants contributions, the key for engagement is the decision that gets to said contribution, usually defined as a choice of object or interpretation (in other words, 'museum-type' decisions). While choices are often presented as open choices (often with the best intentions of being open), in effect, the choice often becomes about deciding between A and B, and on rare occasions, C and D. This type of choice operates as it would in the market, with participants as individual customer in a target group. This is not necessarily a meaningful type of engagement in a cultural space. Such models of engagement assume a knowledgeable and self-directing subject, capable of easily identifying and articulating their desires as choices that can be translated into the language of the institution (Clarke, 2007; Clarke et al., 2007). Critical scholars have discussed this in terms of the 'inequality of choice' since institutions rarely provide participants with the resources to make informed decisions (Vidler and Clarke, 2005). This is important to recognise in the context of community engagement work with groups that may have never before engaged with the museum and that may even feel excluded and marginalised from cultural spaces.

In the opening to this book, I expressed a doubt around the prevalence of choice and control as the central feature of community engagement in museums. This doubt is not so much about the principle, rather about how we think decisions should be made. I wish to suggest that in community engagement, the means (including the encounters between the museum and participants) are in fact much more important than the ends (the decision). It is about how decisions are made, not only who makes them. This argument is not new, but it needs revisiting precisely because of the persistence of choice and control in current debates about museum participation. In the Outreach team, I found other ways of looking at these concerns. For the team, while community decision-making mattered, it had to be supported: 'A blank canvas is the cruelest thing. If you go to communities with a blank page, they won't trust you because they will see it as if the museum is hiding its agenda – they need something for communities to hammer down and rebuild together'. The Outreach team would also talk about managing expectations, but in order to be much clearer about institutional processes and procedures, and what is possible within current museum structures. They would speak of raising aspirations and ambitions for groups who may have never before considered what the museum might offer them. Therefore, choices and opportunities for engagement were not always framed around objects, as tended to be the case in other teams' views of community engagement. In one sense, community engagement workers were more alert to their institutions as they often experienced their structures as resistant to their work – they come up against the black lines and the brick walls. The imagery of 'hammering down and rebuilding' is evocative of a way of working with communities that is less certain and more open to adjustments, fixes and work arounds, where good engagement work emerges out of collaborative attempts to adapt the museum to community interests. In the wider museum, the focus on choice and control was as an act of closure, whereby a decision is reached. Far less attention was paid to the wider processes that support engagement between the participants and the museum.

By suggesting that the acts of choice and control should not be the main or only focus of participation, I am cautious of how my argument may be interpreted. How can anyone seriously doubt that young people engaging in museums or the museum sharing control is a good thing? My purpose here is not to return patriarchal authority to the museum; nor am I writing against discourses of empowerment. I am not saying that participants making decisions and having control is unimportant. It does still matter, and in some cases, it is ethically imperative. And yet, I also want to argue that choice and control in the museum is not always as wonderful as it may seem to be. If I question current practice of participation in the museum, it is not to frustrate efforts to enable communities to contribute to the museum. I would like to find another logic to think through choice and control and the other areas of tension that I have presented above – knowledge, expertise, expectations and quality. I do this to respond to the work of community engagement workers that I observed on the ground and that were animated by different sets of concerns that need illuminating in order to present other ways of valuing community engagement work.

Institutional work

Across my time in the museum, it became clear to me that the community engagement work was as much about working with communities as it was about working with other museum professionals and working within (and against) operational structures. In order to 'do' the work of community engagement, professionals must also work 'on' their institutions (Ahmed, 2012). One of the key aspects of this practice is its 'institutional work', the attempts to move around black lines, to keep things flowing. Institutional work is defined most often as 'nearly invisible and often mundane (…) day-to-day adjustments through which institutions are created, maintained, and disrupted' (Lawrence et al., 2009b: 1). As one member of the Outreach team put it, much of their work is about 'thinking about how things are working, and how I can do things, and then how the system here works'. There were daily examples of how staff tried to manage the different areas of tensions I described, with more or less success. Community engagement could be 'bolted-on' at the end of an exhibition, but they would ensure that participants did not feel that way. When projects took another direction, like in the earlier example of the World Cultures Gallery, they would follow people's interest through other creative solutions, such as publishing postcards. They would negotiate more narrow approaches to engaging a community based on their specific cultural or ethnic identity, instead enabling participants to define the terms of their own involvement based on how their experiences and/or interests resonated with the objects. For Outreach, a central element of practice was to enable responsive projects:

> Because when there are guidelines and rules, when you go out and apply
> them in the real world, when we go out and work with communities,
> you have to negotiate them and bend them. Because what you are going

to find is that nobody will want to work with you at the end of the day. That is the nature of the work we do – it is about negotiation, it's about being positive, it is about being flexible.

This work of negotiation was both external with communities *and* internal within their institutions. Community engagement practitioners must negotiate moves between the margins and the core. I witnessed this strategic labour of internal advocacy every day: 'There is an element of when you come back in the organisation you have to fight for those communities, you have to represent those communities. There is this niche where you are when you are an Outreach Officer when you go out, you come back in, and you're like a mediator'. One team member spoke of this work as the work of translation within their institution. An example: one of the outreach workers was doing a photography project with a group from a mental health service. Inspired by an exhibition about local theatres in the museum, the group visited and photographed five of these theatres. Such was the quality of the work that the outreach worker felt that it should be framed and displayed, and its value as a social record should be recognised, since there were no records in the current collection. However, convincing the curator to include the photographs in an already set-up exhibition was not straightforward. The settlement was for the group to select a few photographs for digital display on a screen in the exhibition. The outreach worker pushed further. After weeks of conversations, the curator was convinced to accession the photographs, a process in which the group would also be involved.[24]

While seemingly mundane interactions within an organisation, stories such as these represent the work of 'doing' community engagement. This work happens as much in communities as it does in the museum in the day-to-day practice of negotiating and adjusting the museum. Each worker had their own style in seeking to affect change. For some, this was about acting as an irritant in order to coax internal collaboration: 'You've just got to keep asking the question until the point where you're irritating them. Because you're calling them everyday day, what's happened with this? (...) What can I do to help? What is the next procedure? You've got to keep reminding them and it's like you're the bottom of the pile because you've got no money behind you and you're the outreach community thing'. As work, these acts are on one level quite mundane (making phone calls and sending emails); they are not about paradigmatic shifts in practice, but they have an effect by setting a precedent or by simply keeping the 'community thing' on the agenda. As mediating acts, they are part of the daily institutional work of community engagement workers, the ways in which they work in and 'on' the museum. This purposeful work can be seen as the work of searching for and creating passage points within solidified institutional structures through tinkering and work arounds. Faced with black lines and brick walls, staff use a variety of tactics to influence institutional arrangements and staff attitudes in order to pursue their objectives and those of communities. One team member summarised this work of mediation and translation in the museum as a way to expand the creative possibilities for engagement work with communities:

> There are different strands to the way we can use what a museum does to work with people, and to involve them. And that has become more and more diverse over the years. I think there is a core group in museums who think this is about objects and about interpretation. I think that's an attitude and learned behaviour and I think Outreach fits somewhere between mediating between that and the museum and the communities. We are in between the museum and the community. You have to advocate on both parties: you have to bring what's important for communities into the museum, and then you have to go out with all the limitations that you may have from the museum when you work with communities. That sometimes drives you a bit nuts sometimes.

Institutional work takes its toll – it 'drives you a bit nuts sometimes'. As I described earlier, reflecting on the different structures that organised their work under the social inclusion agenda, the team also spoke of feeling exhausted by the frenetic pace of work and of the problems of working within project structures that prevented long-term partnership working. Simply put: 'we felt we could, and should, be achieving more in terms of social impact'. Other ways of working were needed.

The time of my research coincided with a number of significant changes for the UK museum sector. This brings us, in a sense, to the next part of the history of community engagement at TWAM. In May 2010, the New Labour government was replaced by a Conservative-led coalition and then a majority Conservative government from 2015. This marked two significant changes: first, the start of a long period of austerity politics and reductions in public expenditure, most notably local council contributions, following the 2008 economic crash; and second, a reverting of culture to a peripheral governmental concern, with significant cuts to museum funding in real terms (Gordon et al., 2015). As a local authority museum service, the impact of the cuts on TWAM has been significant. In November 2012, Newcastle City Council, one of the main funders of TWAM, cut its contribution to museums by 50% over three years. In March 2013, Sunderland City Council officially left the museum Joint Agreement to take on direct management of the museums in Sunderland as part of a cost-saving measure. Between 2009 and 2017, overall, TWAM budgets were reduced by about a third, leading to £4.3 million of savings and to consecutive cycles of cost reductions, restructures and job losses across all museum departments, including in the Outreach team. At the same time, a new set of opportunities arose: there was a 'transition' year in terms of *Renaissance* funding (2009–2010), followed by a shift from central government funding to Arts Council funding, and in this short time frame, policy directives and the requirements of data collection were temporarily suspended. It was possible, for a moment, to stop 'performing' community engagement. As one member of the team put it: 'it enabled us to get off the conveyor belt of projects'. Other changes also presented opportunities in the concurrent reform of the health sector. Mental health and wellbeing were becoming central concepts in cross-cutting UK policy areas (HM Government and Department for Health, 2011) and in local authority priorities. In England, the Health and Social Care Act of 2012 (and following on, the Care Act of 2014) transferred the responsibility for public health from the National Health Service to local authorities and opened up a significant re-organisation of the provision of health services by extending the variety of provider organisations to include public and private sector, charity, voluntary and/or social enterprise organisations – including the museum. Reflecting on the breadth of work under the social inclusion agenda, the team had over a decade's experience of working with care homes, mental health charities, people with a long-standing illness or impairments and a range of groups who could be considered marginalised, vulnerable or otherwise excluded. Anecdotally and in case studies, there were scores of examples of museum engagement contributing to people's wellbeing by developing their confidence and self-esteem. At the time that budget cuts and restructures were taking place across the museum service, it was imperative to find alternative funding sources to sustain community engagement work. At a council level, it was urgent to once again articulate the social value of the museum in a time of budget reductions. And perhaps more significantly for the team, it was crucial to find a more sustainable manner of working with communities and a more profound way of achieving impact. There was an opportunity to consolidate previous work and strengthen partnerships with health and social care providers to tap into the opportunities created by the changes in the health and social care reforms. There were opportunities to develop new approaches to measuring the impact of the team's work in terms of its health and wellbeing outcomes. And there was also a recognition, within council priorities, of the particular health challenges in the local area, including disproportionately higher levels of ill-health, disability, mental health issues and addiction issues in North East England.[25] Across these contexts, the team felt that the museum could, and should, respond. We might look to this as another aspect of the institutional work of community engagement practitioners, where they seek opportunities within external environments to position and support their work. It is within this context that the Outreach team has reconfigured its programmes of community engagement towards long-term partnership with health and social care organisations, including mental health charities, addiction recovery support services, care homes and hospitals, and through which the form of the museum as a space of social care is emerging. The next part of the book explores this.

Notes

1 Museum management is a well-discussed topic in terms of leadership, marketing and other distinct management areas (e.g. Sandell and Janes, 2007); what is perhaps still lacking is an approach to the museum as an organisation which recognises 'the procedural and mundane everyday inside the museum' (Morse et al., 2018: 113).

2 As a reminder, I am using community engagement workers to refer the Outreach team, and I do this more systematically as the book progresses to draw out the wider implication of the case of TWAM to community engagement work more broadly.

3 My research also included interviews conducted in 2012 with two previous directors and a number of past employees in the museum in order to gain a sense of the tradition of community engagement work in at TWAM

4 Social categories are often used in museum visitor research studies in the UK and are based on occupational groups, where C2 = skilled manual workers, D = semi-skilled and unskilled manual workers, E = people dependent on the state through sickness, unemployment, old age or other reasons.

5 Examples of pioneering curatorial-led project at the time included *Objects of Desire* (2000), which invited thousands of local people to select their favourite items from the museum collections that were then displayed in exhibitions, and *Making History* (1999–2001), the museum's first large-scale contemporary collecting project. It worked with 220 people from across Tyne and Wear who were asked to donate items that had been significant at one point in their lifetime, along with a personal testimony, collecting a total of 900 objects, including a paper weight in the shape of a side of bacon and a pair of swimming trunks. Throughout the mid-1990s, the curatorial teams also ran a number of small-scale exhibitions where community groups were invited to choose objects from the storerooms and create and display their own works inspired by their choices. *The People's Choice* series led to eight community displays using the art collections, followed *From the Vaults* which had 13 iterations, while *Clothes from the Closet* delved into the Fashion collection for eight versions. These temporary displays involved schools, a crime reduction charity, a creative writing group and adults in substance recovery.

6 In one way, the museum is exceptional as being part of a small group of museums that already pro-actively framed their work and their public value in this way. This also makes it a particularly significant case study from which to untangle community engagement more generally as an area of contemporary museum work.

7 During this period, several venues set up community consultation panels, such as the *People's Panel* and *Collective Minds* (a youth panel) at the Laing Art Gallery and the *Children's Panel* at Discovery Museum, to inform museum programming and events. Curatorial-led projects included, for example, *Memory Net* (2005), a web-based project which explored the lives of communities in the North East who have a connection to the sea, and *One in Four* (2006), a co-curated exhibition exploring experiences of living with a disability.

8 While early project like *From the Vaults* in the early 1990s had involved working with groups to make displays with objects from the stores, these were very much short-term projects, often displayed in a single case, in a corner of a gallery. As a former member of the team explained, these projects were not necessarily about influencing mainstream curating practice or developing alternative knowledge and understandings of the collection.

9 The form of community engagement was also shaped by the requirements of funders such as the Heritage Lottery Fund which placed objects at the centre of

community engagement. Indeed, as one former staff member recalled: 'participation at that time that wasn't the mantra [of HLF]. The focus then was objects, objects, objects – you've got to get more objects out.'

10 *Street Skate Style* (2006) was an outreach exhibition in collaboration with the Wallsend Skaters Group to create a documentary of their culture including footwear, clothing and skateboards. The objects displayed were accessioned into the permanent collections. *Punk79* (2006–2007) celebrated the 30th Anniversary of the Punk music revolution through the voices, artefacts and memorabilia of local band members, producers, writers and fans. The exhibition came about because of a suggestion made by members of the public. Over six months, a dozen volunteers helped to create an oral history archive by capturing the memories of local bands and fans. *HMP & Me* (2008) examined the daily life of people living and working in North East prisons. The exhibition displayed work produced during three projects in the prisons and displayed photographs, sculpture, screen prints, oral histories and personal items from the individuals involved. *Sound & Vision* (2008) was inspired by the science and industry collections relating to broadcasting and showcased art work, a film and a drama performance of 12 young refugees, which addressed issues regarding the media's representation of young people. *Mind the Gap* (2007–2009) explored the history of, and people's personal experiences of, mental health, distress and illness and aimed to challenge stigmas surrounding mental health issues. The project was delivered in partnership with the Northumberland, Tyne and Wear Service User and Carer network, which acted as a steering group. Another 20 community groups from across the region provided content for exhibition.

11 In the TWAM agreement with DCMS (until 2011), the negotiated budget was linked to targets set over a period of three years, focused almost entirely on numbers: for example, total number of visitors, number of C2, D and E visitors, number of under 16 visitors and revenue generated per visitor.

12 Strathern and Shore's work on accountability focuses on the University, rather than the museum, but as I have suggested previously through reference to Ahmed' work in the previous chapter, there are interesting parallels to draw out across these institutional contexts.

13 Learning team member interview.

14 History (curatorial) team member interview.

15 This idea of 'making public' is also discussed in relation to digital stories and what happens when they are accessioned in the museum (Graham et al., 2013).

16 Venue Manager interview.

17 Art Team member interview.

18 It is important here to note that these anxieties were also exacerbated in the context of budget cuts in which my research took place – tight budgets and old habits are a potent mix that work against experimental and uncertain work.

19 Indeed, for Lynch, there is a democratic imperative for engagement work to be agonistic, whereby the museum must work through conflict (2011a). However, as I found it in practice, the pervasive operationalisation of community engagement as a risk to manage had for effect the closing down of practice. In the following chapters, I show how a more synergistic take on community engagement (which Lynch writes against) is not necessarily patronising or exploitative when the practice of community engagement is viewed along other terms, such as care.

20 History (curatorial) team member interview.

21 Management team member interview.

22 History (curatorial) team member interview.

23 I have written more extensively about this case elsewhere (Morse, 2013; Morse et al., 2013).
24 It is significant to note that while community work is only rarely displayed, it is nearly never accessioned.
25 Health inequalities are such that the poorest adults in the North East England on average will die eight years earlier than the richest adults in the South of England (Marmot et al., 2010).

References

Adair B, Filene B and Koloski L (eds) (2011) *Letting Go?: Sharing Historical Authority in a User-Generated World.* Philadelphia, PA: Pew Center for Arts & Heritage.

Ahmed S (2012) *On Being Included: Racism and Diversity in Institutional Life.* Durham, NC and London: Duke University Press.

Askins K and Pain R (2011) Contact zones: Participation, materiality, and the messiness of interaction. *Environment and Planning D: Society and Space* 29(5): 803–821. doi: 10.1068/d11109.

Belfiore E (2002) Art as a means of alleviating social exclusion: Does it really work? A critique of instrumental cultural policies and social impact studies in the UK. *International Journal of Cultural Policy* 8(1): 91–106. doi: 10.1080/102866302900324658.

Belfiore E (2004) Auditing culture: The subsidised cultural sector in the New Public Management. *International Journal of Cultural Policy* 10(2): 183–202. doi: 10.1080/10286630042000255808.

Belfiore E (2012) 'Defensive instrumentalism' and the legacy of New Labour's cultural policies. *Cultural Trends* 21(2): 103–111. doi: 10.1080/09548963.2012.674750.

Bourdieu P and Darbel A (1990) *The Love of Art: European Art Museums and Their Public.* Stanford, CA: Stanford University Press.

Clarke J (2007) Unsettled Connections: Citizens, consumers and the reform of public services. *Journal of Consumer Culture* 7(2): 159–178. doi: 10.1177/1469540507077671.

Clarke J, Newman J, Smith N, et al. (2007) *Creating Citizen-Consumers: Changing Publics and Changing Public Services.* London: Sage Publications.

Coles A (2008) Instrumental death of a reductionist. *Cultural Trends* 17(4): 329–334. doi: 10.1080/09548960802615471.

Cooke B and Kothari U (eds) (2001) *Participation, the New Tyranny?* London: Zed Books.

DCMS (2000) *Centres for Social Change: Museums, Galleries and Archives for All.* London: Department for Culture, Media and Sport.

DCMS (2002) *People and Places: Social Inclusion Policy for the Built and Historic Environment.* London: Department for Culture, Media and Sport.

DCMS (2004) *Culture at the Heart of Regeneration.* London: Department for Culture, Media and Sport.

Fleming D (1999) A question of perception. *Museums Journal* 99(4): 29–31.

Fleming D (2002) Positioning the museum for social inclusion. In: Sandell R (ed.) *Museums, Society, Inequality.* London and New York: Routledge, pp. 213–224.

Fouseki K (2010) 'Community voices, curatorial choices': Community consultation for the 1807 exhibitions. *Museum and Society* 8(3): 180–192.

Gibson L (2008) In defence of instrumentality. *Cultural Trends* 17(4): 247–257. doi: 10.1080/09548960802615380.

Gordon C, Powell D and Stark P (2015) The coalition government 2010–2015: Lessons for future cultural policy. *Cultural Trends* 24(1): 51–55. doi: 10.1080/09548963.2014.1000585.

Graham H, Mason R and Nayling N (2013) The personal is still political: Museums, participation and copyright. *Museum and Society* 11(1): 105–121.

Gray C (2012) Museums policy: Structural invariants and political agency? Centre for Cultural Heritage Studies, Newcastle University.

Gray C (2014) 'Cabined, cribbed, confined, bound in' or 'we are not a government poodle': Structure and agency in museums and galleries. *Public Policy and Administration* 29(3): 185–203. doi: 10.1177/0952076713506450.

Gray C and McCall V (2018) Analysing the adjectival museum: Exploring the bureaucratic nature of museums and the implications for researchers and the research process. *Museum and Society* 16(2): 124–137. doi: 10.29311/mas.v16i2.2809.

HM Government and Department for Health (2011) *No Health without Mental Health: A Cross-Government Mental Health Outcomes Strategy for People of All Ages.* London: Department for Health.

Holden J (2004) *Creating Cultural Value: How Culture Has Become a Tool of Government Policy.* London: Demos.

Hooper-Greenhill E, Dodd J, Phillips M, et al. (2004) *What Did You Learn at the Museum Today? The Evaluation of the Impact of the Renaissance in the Regions Education Programme in the Three Phase 1 Hubs (August, September and October 2003).* Research Centre for Museums and Galleries. Available at: http://hdl.handle.net/2381/67 (accessed 7 October 2010).

Lang C, Reeve J and Woollard V (2006) The impact of government policy. In: Lang C, Reeve J, and Woollard V (eds) *The Responsive Museum: Working with Audiences in the Twenty-First Century.* Aldershot and Burlington, VT: Ashgate, pp. 19–29.

Lawrence TB, Suddaby R and Leca B (eds) (2009a) *Institutional Work: Actors and Agency in Institutional Studies of Organizations.* Cambridge: Cambridge University Press.

Lawrence TB, Suddaby R and Leca B (2009b) Introduction: Theorizing and studying institutional work. In: Lawrence TB, Suddaby R, and Leca B (eds) *Institutional Work: Actors and Agency in Institutional Studies of Organizations.* Cambridge: Cambridge University Press, pp. 1–28.

Lynch BT and Alberti SJMM (2010) Legacies of prejudice: Racism, co-production and radical trust in the museum. *Museum Management and Curatorship* 25(1): 13–35. doi: 10.1080/09647770903529061.

Macdonald S (2002) *Behind the Scenes at the Science Museum.* Oxford: Berg.

Marmot M, Allen J, Boyce T, et al. (2010) *Fair Society, Healthy Lives: The Marmot Review.* London: University College London. Available at: www.instituteofhealthequity.org/projects/fair-society-healthy-livesthe-marmot-review. (accessed 14 August 2019).

Mol A, Moser I and Pols J (eds) (2010) *Care in Practice: On Tinkering in Clinics, Homes and Farms.* Bielefeld, Germany: Transcript.

Morse N (2013) An interview with the young curators from 'Stories of the World'. *Journal of Museum Ethnography* 26: 32–52.

Morse N, Macpherson M and Robinson S (2013) Developing dialogue in co-produced exhibitions: Between rhetoric, intentions and realities. *Museum Management and Curatorship* 28(1): 91–106. doi: 10.1080/09647775.2012.754632.

Morse N, Rex B and Richardson SH (2018) Special issue editorial: Methodologies for researching the museum as organization. *Museum and Society* 16(2): 112–123. doi: 10.29311/mas.v16i2.2810.

Nisbett M (2013) New perspectives on instrumentalism: An empirical study of cultural diplomacy. *International Journal of Cultural Policy* 19(5): 557–575. doi: 10.1080/10286632.2012.704628.

Resource (2001) *Renaissance in the Regions: A New Vision for England's Museums.* Available at: www.museumsassociation.org/download?id=12190 (accessed 10 August 2012).

Sandell R (2003) Social inclusion, the museum and the dynamics of sectoral change. *Museum and Society* 1(1): 45–62.

Sandell R and Janes RR (eds) (2007) *Museum Management and Marketing.* Leicester readers in museum studies. London and New York: Routledge.

Selwood S (2002) What difference do museums make? Producing evidence on the impact of museums. *Critical Quarterly* 44(4): 65–81. doi: 10.1111/1467–8705.00457.

SEU (1998) *A Report to the Social Exclusion Unit.* London: Department for Culture, Media and Sport.

SEU (2001) *Preventing Social Exclusion.* London: Social Exclusion Unit.

Shore C (2008) Audit culture and illiberal governance: Universities and the politics of accountability. *Anthropological Theory* 8(3): 278–298.

Strathern M (2000) *Audit Cultures: Anthropological Studies in Accountability, Ethics and the Academy.* London: Routledge.

Tlili A (2008) Behind the policy mantra of the inclusive museum: Receptions of social exclusion and inclusion in museums and science centres. *Cultural Sociology* 2(1): 123–147. doi: https://doi.org/10.1177/1749975507086277.

Tlili A, Gewirtz S and Cribb A (2007) New Labour's socially responsible museum: Roles, functions and greater expectations. *Policy Studies* 28(3): 269–289. doi: 10.1080/01442870701437634.

TWM (1993) Annual report 1993. Tyne and Wear Museums.

Vidler E and Clarke J (2005) Creating citizen-consumers: New Labour and the Re-making of Public Services. *Public Policy and Administration* 20(2): 19–37. doi: 10.1177/095207670502000202.

West C and Smith CHF (2005) 'We are not a Government Poodle' – Museums and social inclusion under New Labour. *International Journal of Cultural Policy* 11(3): 275. doi: 10.1080/10286630500411259.

Part III

The emotional life of community engagement workers

5 Community engagement as care work

In the next two chapters, I want to focus on the emotional life of community engagement workers, in order to gain a deeper understanding of the experience of 'doing' of community engagement and its logics. The Outreach team at Tyne & Wear Archives & Museums (TWAM) define community engagement as setting 'the conditions for creative ways of working with people who maybe had never thought about museums and galleries as places where they belonged in, or could contribute to, [or] could offer them anything that could benefit them in their lives'. It is about creating opportunities for participants to explore their sense of self, their sense of place and belonging through collections. It is about establishing supported access to museums. It is about using art and culture to make a difference in people's lives. At the heart of this definition is the work of establishing relationships and enabling individuals' empowerment and flourishing through museum activities. Here, community engagement evokes a style, a mode, a way of working that exceeds the logic of contribution in museums that is generally adopted by other parts of the museum and the definition of community engagement at a distance (Chapter 2). In this part of the book, I want to deal with proximity in the dynamic of community engagement. This moves us away, for now, from the institutional life of community engagement workers to consider practice up close: what happens in community engagement sessions? What practices hold these activities together? How are the felt qualities of this work delivered? This chapter brings together discussions with community engagement workers[1] and snapshots of practice from my own time spent with the team, both within the museum and in community settings with participants in a range of different community projects, including mental health charities, addiction recovery support services, a dementia ward and a support group for people who have experienced a stroke. It centres on the emotional life of community engagement workers by paying close attention to what they do in practice, how they talk about the work that they do and the emotions attached to their work. From these perspectives, I will place care in the context of museum engagement work.

The language of care is most commonly associated with the world of health provision or the intimacy of parenting and private care.[2] Care is usually seen as it applies to doctors caring for patients in professional contexts, or care within families, such as children receiving parental care. This view of care is about direct forms of care involved in supporting another person who is unable to manage alone (including, for example, physical tasks such as bathing, feeding or shopping). For a long time, care has figured in the sciences as necessary practicalities and professional regulations, linked especially to medicalised care. But care also extends beyond practical support into the emotional realms of friendship and love. Care conjures a number of meanings such as 'affection, love, duty, well-being, responsibility and reciprocity' which are 'demonstrated by touch, action, emotion, bodily expression' (Phillips, 2007: 1). When we recognise care as central to daily life, there is a need to study it. Writing about care started in feminist work as a way of making visible practices that had previously been hidden in the private sphere of the homespace. Essentialised notions of parental care (and in particular motherly care) were re-presented as care work and 'domestic labour' to stress its importance as a public matter and as a way of adding value to it.[3] Nursing studies also began to talk about care, exploring caring in institutional settings. While highlighting how this work is conceptualised as 'women's work' (and within this, highlighting assumptions about women's innate ability to care), it also sought to strengthen nursing as a profession where caring work mattered, all the while recognising the importance of 'emotion work' in supporting patient care.[4] The complexity of care – as public and private, as professional and emotional work, as skill and disposition – continues to shape these discussions.[5]

Recently, the importance of care has begun to receive attention across several disciplines: sociology, geography, science and technology studies and ethics have started to talk about care.[6] Social scientists became concerned with the wider social effects of care, notably care provided by state institutions and their tendencies towards failures of care. Medical sociologists and disability scholars turned their attention to social power within professional care.[7] Across scholarship, the key question became: what constitutes 'good' care? This shifted attention from those who deliver care to those who receive care, so often positioned in precarious, passive or powerless roles. The important point here was to recover agency and to undo unidirectional views of care towards a co-productive engagement with caring relations. Writings about care across disciplines show that it can be a difficult term to use, and to further complicate matters, it has many critics.[8] Recently, geographers have begun to consider care in unusual yet ordinary places such as such as cafés, parks, community centres, art spaces and allotments.[9] This body of work examines the ways in which care is emotional and relational, involving both care providers and care recipients, and how it is located in formal and informal spaces and our everyday interactions within these spaces (Milligan et al., 2007). Across locations and disciplines, scholarship highlights commonalities *and* stresses the specificities of care, as something that is *done* rather than simply something to be bought or delivered or regulated (Mol et al., 2010).

Writing about care then covers a wide range of sites and attempts to give a language to practices and knowledge that have previously been unspoken.

To talk about care in the museum, I begin with David Conradson's (2003b: 508) conception of care as 'the proactive interest of one person in the well-being of another and as the articulation of that interest (or affective stance) in practical ways'. This stresses how care involves both an awareness of the situation of another, an emotional move towards addressing that situation, and the practical expression of that orientation in terms of assistance to meet another's need (Conradson, 2011: 455). Care is both an activity and a disposition (Tronto, 1993). While the community engagement workers in the museum did not always use the language commonly associated with care, the principles of their existing practice and the everyday relations of support they develop for participants are unmistakable as forms of caring activity. My concern here is with the specificities of care in the museum. As I have argued, community engagement practices in the museum are not recognised or carefully attended to (Chapter 3). It is therefore important to recover this domain of the contemporary museum and articulate this mode and way of working. By describing practices to do with care in the museum, all the while exploring what care for people is, my aim in this third part of the book is to outline *a logic of care* for the museum, inspired by Annemarie Mol's research in the clinic and the doctor's surgery.

To talk about care in the museum, I also start within geography to locate the museum as a space where care takes place. Ealasaid Munro (2013) first drew attention to the potential of the museum as a caring environment in her research on community exhibition work and their 'ethics of encounter'. Through the example of an intercultural exhibition project in a museum service in Scotland, she foregrounds the relationships that are forged within engagement sessions with diverse minority groups to examine how these relationships can be considered caring relationships. She highlights the work of museum staff in building participants' self-confidence, taking time to listen and talk to people, which she marks out as practices of care. Together with Munro, we have brought our research into conversation to expand this idea and present museums' community engagement programmes as spaces of care (Morse and Munro, 2015). Here, I want to advance our work on the 'museumness' of care (Morse and Munro, 2015: 18) in two ways to consider care across the varied practices of the museum. First, in this chapter, I locate practices of care at the particular crossover between the realm of the museum and the realm of formal care in the team's partnerships with health and social care organisations and their users, including hospitals, mental health organisations, addiction recovery services and care homes. My focus is to articulate museum work as care work at this crossing with professional care, as a distinct 'museum-like' form of care, with its own relational, affective and material dimensions. This places care in the museum within a sociomaterial frame, and within a small area of geographical research that has sought to examine the 'psycho-social relationships' that constitute care and the materials dimensions of the spaces in which these relations take place (Conradson, 2003a: 451).[10] It also places care firmly as a form of professional work, with specific skills and aptitudes. Second, I explore curatorial work as a form of care work, which I will do in the next chapter, following the work of the Outreach team during a community-focused exhibition. In each case, I articulate the logic of care that animates these modes of working.

Partnerships for care

Previously, I considered some of the agendas (internal and external) in the history of community engagement at TWAM (Chapter 4). In the seven years up to the time of writing, the work of community engagement at TWAM shifted towards partnership working across the health and social care sector. This is where I locate my first discussion of care in community engagement work. For the Outreach team at TWAM, partnerships with care organisations developed in a particular set of circumstances – changes in government, shifts in cultural and health policies and the deepening context of austerity across public services. These circumstances provided the team with the opportunity to re-assess their work: 'We wanted to get off the conveyor belt of projects'. The key issue for the team was the lack of sustainability of community engagement work linked to short-term funding, combined with 'scatter gun' and 'bolted-on' approaches, and a deficit model of engagement. Changed circumstances enabled the team to shift their practice from short-term projects to long-term partnerships and programmes with a smaller number of key organisations: 'We felt as a team that we could and should be achieving more in terms of social impacts'. Reflecting on the wider social context of the North East, local council priorities in a time of budget cuts, new opportunities around public health funding and the core purpose of their work in terms of contributing to people's sense of identity and their wellbeing, a new model of community engagement emerged:

> We didn't just want to get people connecting with collections, it has to be something bigger. If you think about the mission statement, it's all about people. It's about their self-worth. It's about their identity. It's about their place in the world. And that's the bigger thing we are aiming for.

This new model consolidated strategic partnerships with third sector mental health organisations, addiction recovery services, the justice system, care homes and NHS services (a dementia assessment unit and a forensic unit). The partnerships developed over several years and included many meetings and work-shadowing to gain deeper insights into the work of these organisations: 'We needed to slow down and needed to get to know more about our partners. We wanted to know what they stood for, what they were trying to achieve, what difference they were trying to make in people's lives?' For the team, these partnerships were built across organisations with common aims. Each organisation works with its service users by focusing on developing a sense of purpose and meaning, improving confidence and self-esteem, supporting wellbeing and good health and improving social networks. For these organisations, the practices of care centre on providing the right levels of intervention and support for service users towards recovery and gaining greater control of their lives. Across these organisations, meaningful social activities often feature as part of psychosocial approaches to person-centred care and group support (Kitwood, 1997; Ramon and Williams, 2005). Community programmes enable service users to develop their own support systems in the community, while for institutional care (e.g. dementia wards and forensic units), meaningful, creative activities are central to supporting mental wellbeing. The strategy of the Outreach team was to position the museum as part of these community programmes and use museum activities and collections to support service users through the development of new interests and creative engagements with culture: 'We wanted to really support people to enhance their own lives. Our Unique Selling Point is our collections, our buildings, our staff'. This approach to partnership brings the objectives and priorities of external care organisations into museum programmes:

> We [ask partners] what they might need and what things need to happen to make the conditions right for a project to flourish and for people to flourish in that project. We might get really different answers and that's fine. We can be very creative in the mechanism of how that happens. (…) The reasons why some of the people we work with are supported by their agencies, the service they are involved in, is because they have had a disconnect. I think what we are trying to do, and those organisations are trying to do, is help people to kind of cope with what life throws at you. One of the ways is doing really positive activities and positive experiences like peer socialising, and it might be building up [participants'] skills, their confidence, their self-esteem: all of those things are part of a package that helps people to either be abstinent or to be more stable, to take control of their lives. We are part of that. We are not saying that we help people solely to do that, but we are part of chain, *we are like a link in that chain.*

Together, these partnerships bring the museum and its engagement practice into the work of health and social care. They position the museum as a link in a chain of caring institutions by directly supporting the activities of health and social care organisations and their service users through museum activities. This is the first setting from which I want to look at the practices of care of community engagement workers and the work they do, 'to help people to cope with what life throws at you'.

Community engagement sessions as spaces of care

To talk about care in the museum, I want to start by looking at what happens during a community engagement session. In the text below, I weave snapshots of practice to focus on what geographers Milligan and Wiles call the 'micro-landscapes of care' (2010), which they understand as the every-day settings, social arrangements and work practices that accommodate the performance of care. The snapshots do not recount in full the details of the creative activities that took place during sessions or their outcomes, or the museum collections that were used, or even the exact locations of these events; instead, I focus on the felt quality of these moments to draw out a broader sense of care in the museum. The spaces of museums' community engagement work are manifold, but as a general point, activities usually take place in the museum (on gallery floors, in learning studios or store-rooms) or in community centres. After the work of consultation and prepa-ration, a project will usually take place over several months (usually three or four) with weekly sessions in a small group (8–15 participants). Many of the participants across the outreach projects are socially isolated and vul-nerable and have very low self-esteem. This can leave people feeling very apprehensive about entering new environments and trying new experiences. Often, participants have not set foot in a museum since a (usually unhappy) school visit, and museums are not part of their everyday lives. There is a shared sense that these cultural spaces are not for them, not welcoming of them. The first concern of staff is to provide a welcoming, safe and inclusive environment for participants. Demands for creating spaces where partic-ipants feel included are central to scores of contemporary museum schol-arship and cultural policy. Despite this, there has been little attention paid to what these spaces look like in practice, or the practices that enable and maintain feelings of inclusion. This extends beyond general conditions of access (ramps, audio loops, etc.) to a specific sense of access by mobilising tailored practices to create welcoming, safe and inclusive environments for different groups. While all three dimensions are deeply connected, undoing each enables us to explore their affective dimensions and to shine a light on the logic of care that animates museum engagement sessions.

Welcoming spaces

A first snapshot from practice:

> We are visiting 'Crossing the Tyne' at the museum, an exhibition about the bridges and tunnels that enable passage across the Tyne River. For many, it is their first visit to the museum. The group has met just once before, at the centre of the mental health charity. The Outreach Officer is showing us round, but it's not like the usual museum tours, informa-tion overload, facts, figures and dates. It is very informal, warm: like she is inviting the group into her home. She points out things she finds strange, or amusing, and tells an anecdote about how difficult it was for the curator to fit one of the bridge models into the case. Later, we con-gregate in the learning room and plan the next outing, where the group decide they will visit some of the places they have seen in the exhibition.

I had just joined the group, as a researcher, an outsider of sorts doing ethnographic work. I was quickly asked by different participants: would I be coming to the next outing to the Tyne tunnel? Later when I reflected with the Outreach staff about this session she explained: 'they are treating you in the same way that they themselves want to be treated. It's about making you welcome.'

Creating spaces that are welcoming is the first way by which care is manifest in museum engagement work. In the Crossing the Tyne exhibition visit, we see the museum worker acting as a welcoming host and attempting to make people feel 'at home' in the museum through her very personal tour, her use of humour and anecdotes. These modest acts of hospitality are all part of creating spaces that *feel* comfortable. They are part of a general caring disposition that is key to creating these atmospheres. Being friendly is one part of this. But more than this, it requires museum workers to negotiate the physical and social spaces of the museum as sites of exclusion. This is not always about physical or financial barriers (nearly all the venues are free); it is also about the complex effects of museums' long history of privilege, their accumulated years of exclusion and inherited advantage and their assimilationist demands requiring participants to change and behave in certain ways to fit into their institutions – a '"gentle, invisible violence, unrecognized as such, chosen as much as undergone"' (Bourdieu, 1990: 127). Museums are produced through certain rules, codes of conduct and atmospheres ('don't touch', 'don't run'), and they remain intimidating spaces for many. Creating a meaningful welcome is also about recognising these dynamics and about collective attempts to dismantle them. There was a strong awareness of this in the way that museum workers talked about the work that they do. For community engagement workers, this extended to negotiating the wider institution itself, on behalf of participants. Critically, this is not about changing participants to fit in; rather, it is about accepting people as they are and opening up the museum to welcome them, towards creating new spaces of the museum. The Assistant Outreach Officer later told me: 'now, they stomp into the museum learning room like they own the place – it's great!'.

Creating a welcome is also about attentiveness that extends to numerous aspects of the sessions, a minutia of activity less often described, but which, taken together, maintain this welcome. This begins with learning participants' names and remembering them. It is about starting sessions with cups of tea and coffee. This would often take up the first half hour of a two-hour session, sometimes longer, and occasionally most of the session, but this was seen as important for participants to settle, for everyone to have informal chats, 'do all the weather stuff', until people feel relaxed and comfortable. Taking and making time mattered to create welcoming environments for often apprehensive participants. Within this work, welcome is not a single opening act; rather, it is a feeling that is reproduced in every interaction with the group. These atmospheres are carried through each session. It is also a shared welcome. As the passage above suggests, the welcome that is shaped by museum staff can also be returned by participants themselves. While staff described the importance of opening welcomes, they also stressed the importance of endings. Each project would end with a celebration, marking out individual and collective achievements (more tea, and often cake as well), opportunities for feedback and exploring together what the next step might be. On some occasions, this could be another project with the group in the near future, or, for some participants who felt able, this could be moving on to supported volunteering within the museum service. For every participant, it is hoped that museums more generally are now places where they feel welcome.

Safe spaces

Creating safe spaces for participants was another way by which care was oriented within museum engagement sessions. Safe spaces are often defined as spaces where people can be themselves, spaces that are free from judgement and prejudice and where people can talk freely. At one level, creating safe spaces is about working in partnership with care professionals to ensure the safeguarding of vulnerable adults through clear policies and working guidelines (which are also about keeping staff safe). Within the team's model of working, sessions were always attended by a community worker or care professional from the partner organisation. This ensured that individuals were supported at the right level; it also recognised that museum staff do not have the skills or abilities for more specialised forms of support (I come back to this in a moment). Before embarking on a project, staff did not usually ask for information about participants such as their diagnosis or how long they have been accessing services. There are issues of confidentiality here, but also an ethics of practice. Staff accepted participants as people who are experiencing 'some kind of crisis in their life', 'some kind of disconnect' – they are individuals in different stages of recovery, with different access needs and that's all there really is to know. Most importantly, they are individuals with different interests and aspirations. Creating safe spaces is about the ordinary, everyday actions and attitudes towards participants. As one staff member commented: 'we create the right conditions (...) so that we are not in a situation where people are fearful or are made to feel stupid'. For many participants, taking part in creative activities on offer in museum sessions – crafts, photography, ceramic making, collage, textile making – did not come easily or naturally. Previous bad experiences (for example, from school), a lack of confidence in their abilities, anxious not to be embarrassed in front of a group – all these complex feelings made up many of the sessions I attended.

Several commentators have noted how museums have the potential to act as safe spaces, as they are nearly always non-stigmatising environments (Camic and Chatterjee, 2013; Wood, 2009). Indeed, the museum space is very different from the clinic. However, as I have mentioned before, the work of Outreach also took place in institutionalised spaces – the dementia unit, the forensic ward and the addiction recovery service. It is helpful to think of these spaces of care as not only geographically located in the museum but rather as spaces that are formed within a number of different activity rooms. A second snapshot from practice:

> We are meeting at the drug and alcohol misuse support centre, the Outreach worker, the centre worker and me. It's not a very 'easy' space: we have to be buzzed in, first at the front door, and then again at the top of the stairs where we sign in. Obviously, there are a lot of safety and confidential measures. We set up the activity, including MacBooks and other craft materials – this the fifth week of the project. The group are creating jewellery, bags and tee-shirts, using photos they have taken around the city as the design (hence the MacBooks – to manipulate the images that will be printed on the bags and tee-shirts). We have been here for about half an hour now, and still none of the participants have arrived. Last week, no one came. Because the participants are on this project as part of their court order, they haven't chosen to be here. Although they decided what activities to do with support from the museum worker, it is hard to sustain the enthusiasm. There is also little consistency in the group, as some people join at different times, and others leave halfway through.
>
> Eventually two people turn up. They are reluctant and dismissive at first. They don't take off their coats. I also feel like the three of us are crowding them a bit. Eventually though they begin to get back into the project. The Assistant Outreach Officer is encouraging, she reminds each individual what they have been working on; she asks them to tell me more about the pictures they have taken. She does this with each participant, taking her time. Slowly the atmosphere relaxes, tentatively. One participant starts to open up as he talks about the photos of graffiti he took around the city. By the end of session, we haven't 'produced' anything, or made much 'progress' on the project – but I'm not sure this really matters.

It becomes clear then that creating welcoming and safe spaces is not a 'one off': it is a practice that needs to be repeated and re-created every week with the same amount of care and attention. It is required to move across space and time through its constant re-iteration. As such, these are inherently fragile spaces. In the session described above, which was not atypical, the focus of the worker was creating those conditions where participants can again feel welcome and safe and able to take part in the creative activity on offer. This might take different amounts of time, depending on the session, or the people attending, or any number of circumstances – sometimes, it can take up the time of the whole session. The temporalities of engagement sessions also require flexibility. A project planned for 10 weeks might take longer, and timescales would always shift in the projects I attended. As one staff member put it: 'you can prepare something, and you might not use it, but so what? If people end up talking, then they didn't need it, it's just a plan B anyway'. This flexibility is utterly central to the work of community engagement; it also necessitates a certain attitude from staff to be able to live with this level of agility and to respond 'on your feet' with alternatives. It requires recognition that outputs (so central to the logic of contribution) do not always matter in that moment.

Inclusive spaces

Creating inclusive spaces is about developing museum programmes that are appropriate and support participation. The Outreach team frequently worked with vulnerable groups who had complex access requirements and therefore needed to develop environments that were accessible and adaptable to various social, psychological, physical and intellectual needs. This was done through practical arrangements (for example, holding the session at the same time every week to establish a routine for people with otherwise hectic lives) but also through a multitude of ordinary caring acts and through their attentiveness to group dynamics. A third snapshot:

> There is a sense of closeness between some members of this group, but it isn't obvious. Everyone in the group has experienced brain injury, as a result of a stroke or accident, or another health condition. In this project we have explored portraiture, through a visit to the art gallery, and we are currently working with a photographer to create individual portraits, stories of self and of recovery. Today some people are really chatty, but a couple of individuals tend to keep to themselves to themselves. One of them rarely talks to anyone else. Another one of the men often sits a bit further away from everyone when we are at a table, with his head down. But the Assistant Outreach Officer, who knows the participants well now, tells me 'they might not look interested, but actually most of the time they are, I can really tell: acting quite distant is just how they cope'. Perhaps this unobvious closeness is about it being a 'safe' space to be together, feeling included, whether people are having a good day or a bad day.

Being attentive to individuals is an affective stance through which staff come to understand the social dimensions of care. As one member of the team commented, 'the people we are working with, they are disconnected a lot of the time with life, and the community they are living with'. Part of the purpose of a group activity is to facilitate spaces of sociality. Indeed, following Conradson (2011: 454), 'care holds the possibility [...] of facilitating new ways of being together'. Some projects over time create strong bonds between participants, while others present an emergent sense of 'closeness', but not obviously. In institutional settings, such as the hospital, or in the substance misuse centres where attendance is compulsory as part of court orders, sustaining enthusiasm and a sense of a cohesive group could be particularly difficult. Many outreach projects are tentative spaces of relatedness where participants' levels of engagement may vary from session to session, and some days, they may be more or less comfortable or isolated within the group. These affective shifts highlight the ways in which participants experience museum engagement in different ways, and the effects that group dynamics can have on an individual's experience within a session. This snapshot also reminds us of the inevitable fragility of caring spaces. Many commentators have cautioned how quickly spaces of care can break down: a negative experience can mean a service user leaves and never returns. The endurance of spaces of care depends as much on the willingness of facilitators as the receptivity of participants (Conradson, 2003b). Munro (2013: 59) has also described the often-hectic nature of museum engagement: 'disruption in the pattern of care could cause the relationships being cultivated to change course, to regress, or in extreme cases, to fail'. It is thus important to also consider spaces of care and their potential for inclusion critically. At the level of practice, the spaces of care created in museums engagement sessions do not end distress or suffering, which are often very present for many participants. People in recovery have better and worse days, and these affect their experiences of community engagement. Just as staff do, it is important to be attentive to these more tentative spaces of relatedness, and the work and effort they require. This highlights the ways in which care is fundamentally a collective endeavour: it emerges from being together and holds the possibility of new ways of being together. For many participants, this came from knowing that others in the room had a shared lived experience. This meant that care was intersubjective: it was often found in the relations between participants. This could mean the group slowing down during a museum tour to make sure that no one was left behind (even when the outreach worker was rushing ahead), being patient when listening to one another, and recognising individual needs as also being part of the wider responsibilities of the group. This did not always occur across all projects, with some groups' membership being more transitory, and the occasional personality clashes. But often, the level of care and attentiveness demonstrated by museum staff was quickly seen in the relations and interactions between participants and between participants and other care staff. This sense of care as distributed, as a collective endeavour, was perhaps most noticeable in the team's work in hospitals and care homes, or with older adults living with dementia, where sessions would often include care partners, relatives or spouses:

> He is her full-time carer. In the museum sessions where they go together, they share in the activity, they do it together, both actively engaged in process – making Christmas cards this time, and there was singing the

previous week. They are doing the activity on a level, as two people, as a couple. Doing this creative activity together is so different to the being-together as carer/cared for (the daily washes, the cleaning and cooking). In these moments they seem to be together as a couple – she is no longer only someone living with dementia, and he, only her carer.

Spaces of care in community engagement programmes are fragile yet hopeful. They are perhaps best described as emergent spaces of care. Showing such fragilities and fractures highlights the importance of care as emotional and practical labour and the continuous need to 'work at' these spaces and relations of care.

Caring work

Looking closely at what happens within community engagement sessions makes apparent that these spaces are made up of a myriad of ordinary acts of care. Care work can therefore be said to be central to the museum's work of community engagement. Some of this work is very practical: contacting a group, meeting the workers, booking transport, calling ahead to check on last-minute requirements, organising handling objects and making cups of tea. But 'you can't just pick up the work of outreach', I am told. So, where does it start?

> A lot of it is about appearance and body language, and the hidden things, I guess. For example, in terms of body language: you deliver the greeting and the handshake that's culturally acceptable. Eye contact... but it's also in terms of dress: you go to a lot of place where if you wear a suit it's ridiculous. But you have to appear someone who is amenable and accessible and... somebody who's approachable really, and somebody who can get trusted, all these things.

> [Outreach worker:] Sometimes if I'm with somebody who has a Geordie accent[11], my Geordie accent tends to come out, I get more twanged... It's not even like a put-on thing, it's a kind of instinctual. And the banter as well - you always have a bit of banter.

> [Me:] If people were to hear that would they say you are being a bit fake? What's the quality that makes it not fake?

> [Outreach worker:] You have to be genuine. When we start doing outreach work, people can actually see through that, whether you believe in what you are saying or not. To me, if somebody feels comfortable with you, you're not changing who you are, your personality or your beliefs, all you're doing is making that person more comfortable.

> [Outreach worker:] You've got to establish a sense of: we get you.

> [Outreach worker:] I think we do an amazing job: we are constantly looking for signs and signifiers and getting a general idea for what the feel is when you get in a room all those things come together and your

behaviour responds to that in the way that you think is the best way. You make decisions and you don't even think about it.

[Outreach worker:] It's about courtesy, manners and a sensitivity towards how to treat human beings.

This snapshot of a discussion provides a first window onto the practice of engagement workers in their own words. Their practice starts with their bodies, their language, their dress and the way they present themselves to others outside the museum. The work of engagement therefore begins around this closest of spatial scales: of the body and feeling and their articulation through relations and interactions with others. Each can be reflected as a caring disposition: a way to establish a sense of connection, a starting point to build trust. It is described as an authentic disposition, as opposed to fake gesturing. But community engagement practitioners hasten to add, 'it's not about laying it on thick' – it is a carefully aware and sensitive practice. It is an attentive practice, where museum workers are constantly looking out for telling signs of people's mood, whether they are having a good day or a bad day, in what they say and in their body language, and responding to this in the most logical and appropriate manner. Over time, it becomes routine: 'you make decisions and you don't even think about it'. One member of staff described herself as a 'social chameleon': 'you don't change who you are, but you change your behaviour to fit the circumstances you are in'. Through museum sessions, community engagement workers build the emotional knowledge that enables them to observe and attend to each individual participant in the right way – a practice that is best described as a practice of care.

What is care? What does it mean to care and to practise care? Across scholarship, we find common answers. For Nel Noddings (1984), care is about the attitudes that underpin caring activities. In her view, close attention to the needs, feelings and desires of those cared for and a skill in understanding the situation from that person's position are central to care. Even before working out the action of care, empathy and involvement in another person's situation are required. For Selma Sevenhuijsen, care is 'an ability and willingness to "see" and to "hear" needs, and to take responsibility for these needs being met' (Sevenhuijsen, 1998: 83). Virginia Held (2006) and Joan Tronto (1993) both focus further on this responsibility. It is not only about feeling with another; care requires attentiveness and proactive activities responding to emotional cues (see also Conradson, 2003b; Munro, 2013). Care is a practice and a value (Held), a disposition and an activity (Tronto). It involves emotions, action and work, and it requires 'working at':

> caring relations seem to require substantial capacities on the part of those in them for being sensitive to feelings of others. (...) Mistaken interpretations are usually frequent on both sides, but in a good relationship there is a steady progress in mutual sensitivity and awareness.
>
> (Held, 2006: 53)

As the community engagement workers put it, they were 'constantly looking for signs and signifiers' in order to 'respond in the way that you think is the best way'. This marks out the work of community engagement staff as a form of affective labour in which mind and body, intellect and feeling are employed together. Staff spoke of this practice as 'coming from the heart'. Descriptions of sessions were often shot through with feelings of excitement and pride, but also empathetic upset or indignation at different peoples' situation when these were felt to be unjust. Discussions of their work were set in thickly emotional narratives. Focusing on the role of emotions tells us something important about the practices of the community engagement workers. While the museums and heritage studies literature has experienced what might be described as a turn to emotions and affect, the idea of 'affective labour' has not often been discussed (with Munro, 2014 as an exception). The concept of affective labour refers to the intense work of producing and managing emotions, such as listening, comforting, smiling or caring. Such ideas have origins in feminist scholarship that provides extensive analysis of the gendered dimensions of this work as 'women's work' (e.g. Barker, 2005; England, 2005; Hochschild, 1983). Much of this scholarship intersects with discussions of 'care work' to describe how this labour is located at the level of the body, but nonetheless produces affects that are immaterial, such as a feeling of ease, wellbeing or comfort, even a feeling of belonging and connectedness. Taking this work as a starting point, the concept of affective labour has been further developed by Michael Hardt and Antonio Negri as part of a wider discussion of 'immaterial labour' in late capitalism (2005). Broadly put, the concept of affective labour is used to describe work that is done by one person in order to elicit an emotional experience in another person, with the wider aim that such 'laboring practices produce collective subjectivities, produce sociality, and ultimately produce society itself' (Hardt, 1999: 89).[12] What is compelling here is how a broad conceptualisation of affective labour challenges narrow understandings of productive work to include immaterial labour – a relevant consideration in the case of the museum, where community engagement work is largely immaterial and not always recognised as productive within the bureaucratic and 'museographic' operating values of the institution (Chapter 3). My aim here is not to theorise affective labour in museum work per se; rather I proceed with the term in a broad and descriptive sense to illuminate data and in order to examine the affective, emotional and embodied ways in which museum engagement practitioners talk about their work. For now, my primary aim is to theorise engagement work as a *care work*. In doing so, I move between emotional and affective registers without carefully parsing this terminology, focusing instead on describing the logic that underpins this work, which I describe as the logic of care.

In each outreach session I attended, what was clear and what I have attempted to surface in the previous discussion of the spaces of community engagement sessions were the ways in which staff were constantly demonstrating a caring demeanour, through acts and speech. Staff would often refer to individual participants by their name, noticing how their mood might change across sessions (for better or for worse). For example, staff were always asking people 'how are you today?' and 'how are you feeling?'. Outreach sessions became as much about talking and listening as they were about the creative or heritage activities. This again marks out the subtlety of community engagement work. As a practice of care – as the articulation of a proactive interest in someone's wellbeing (after Conradson, 2003b) – this work is about the practice of noticing, of being attentive to people, and responding in appropriate ways. Staff notice posture, whether participants are chatty or quiet; they hear sadness in the tone of voice and excitement as people share their stories, inspired by a particular object or painting; they share cups of tea before the sessions start or after they have ended. Attentiveness is part of the dynamic of proximity of community engagement, and emotions permeate all aspects of the sessions. The importance of listening, 'really listening', 'active listening' and 'listening until the end of what someone is saying' was constantly described by museum staff as a key component of their work. Staff would then take time after the session to reflect on and discuss together their attempts to make the session 'work' for the group. In all this, I was struck by how deeply museum staff embedded their professional subjectivities in a deeply emotional commitment to other people. The affective work of caring was felt and enacted corporeally by staff, in their body language, facial expression, their accent and their dress. These were all aimed towards certain affects within the spaces of the community engagement sessions and beyond (see Bondi, 2005). These attentions were also part of staff becoming 'accessible', appearing 'amenable', 'approachable' and as 'somebody who can get trusted'. In part, this was about developing a sense of familiarity between staff and participants through small acts such as remembering people's name. More broadly, 'it's about courtesy, manners and a sensitivity towards how to treat human beings'. Humour (or 'banter' as mentioned in the snapshot) also plays a role here. Indeed, as Conradson (2003a) reminds, care can emerge through humour and play as much as through serious discussion. In all these different ways, we come to see how care is largely constructed by how museum professionals strive to present and comport themselves (Bondi, 2005). It is enacted and sustained through everyday practices, long-term commitments and through physical and affective labours.

The affective work of community engagement professionals is not simply about producing certain affects within museum sessions but it is also generative of specifically emotional moments for all involved. Set at the crossover between the museum and formal care, the care work of museum staff is more often that of emotional rather than physical support. Emotional support could be found in the ordinary acts of a museum worker as they encouraged a participant to try a new activity or helping them in a creative making task. But this emotional support also takes on a wider dimension. Working with vulnerable participants, staff framed the ways in which they responded to participants in terms of 'having people's best interest at heart' and often spoke of the sensitivities in negotiating this 'best interest' to alleviate the problems of people in a period of crisis or ill-health. Care is manifest in concrete situations. Sometimes, this was about recognising that remaining stable was part of someone's wellbeing and that small, fleeting moments of engagement were appropriate for that person; sometimes, it was about challenging someone to take risks and 'move forward', building up their confidence through creative activities; sometimes, it was about recognising how a person can live well within a chronic illness, working within the limitations and finding other ways to support participation; sometimes, it was about working very closely with other (health-) care professionals who can better support that individual. Many of these decisions came about from attending carefully to the way people feel within each session, with regular care every week over several months. The previous activities I have described and the actions of museum workers in creating safe, inclusive and welcoming spaces can be done without attentiveness and without an affective dimension, but it is likely that they will not be done well. We would find these sessions to be cold if they did not concern themselves with the work needed to ensure participants feel cared for. Instead, 'good' engagement work is characterised though affective and emotional registers and a mode of working with its own distinct logic – a logic of care.

Co-producing care

One of the important cautions in the literature on social inclusion is to highlight a tendency to categorise individuals as an illness or a problem to be fixed in a deficit model of community engagement (Levitas, 2005). Within the Outreach team's practice of community engagement, this view was strongly resisted. Museum activities were about activating people's abilities by supporting the development of new interests and the confidence to try creative activities. This is the starting point for care as a basis for action:

> We are building on people's skills that they already have. We aren't looking at the deficiencies, their needs, or what they don't know - we are looking at things that they do know. (...) They have a lot of that already in them, they have it in their head, their emotions. They don't need to feel intimidated. We want to meet people in a place where we are not educating them. We're doing something together where we are learning together.

As such, the aim of community engagement as a caring interaction is to find out and respond to the interests of participants and to work together to develop projects and activities. Going back to the definition of community engagement for the Outreach team (in Chapter 3), empowerment was key but its semantics were important: 'we don't empower people; people empower themselves to change their lives'. Their work focused on creating environments for creativity, enjoyment and learning that make a positive difference to people's lives and allow them to flourish. The purpose was to enable people to empower themselves to enhance or change their lives, using culture as a tool. This approach recognises the latent creativity in each participant: 'They have a lot of that already in them, they have it in their head, their emotions'. This approach shifts care away from patronising narratives of service users as passive recipients of care and, instead, frames care as supporting service users/patients as active participants in their own wellbeing and personal development. The relations of caring demonstrated by staff were not coming from a position of superiority, but rather a more modest claim of enabling the conditions which support the emergence of more creative versions of participants (see also Munro, 2013). In this way, the practices of staff are based not on a patronising form of helping; they are oriented in empathy, but also based in equality, respect and solidarity (see Darling, 2011).

Conradson (2003b) suggests that practices of care need to be examined through a focus on the social relations within specific spaces, and the subjectivities that emerge, or are made possible, within these relational environments. He argues: 'we may observe significant changes in subjectivities – our sense of self, who we are and feel able to be – across different spatial settings' (2003b: 509). These are spaces where people can be 'lifted' out of their day-to-day lives, their worries and concerns. Following this lead, Munro (2013: 56) suggests that the caring spaces in museums are best understood as 'those spaces that support the emergence of more positive selves, and encourage the crystallization of these more positive selves'. In feedback, participants nearly always spoke of enjoyment, laughter, having a 'nice time'; sometimes, new friendships and support networks were formed; anxiety, intrusive thoughts or chronic pain were kept at bay; a sense of pride (both individual and collective) was achieved from trying something new, learning new skills and harnessing creativity. This all indicated the emergence of more positive subjectivities through engagement with the museum activities. This sense of more positive selves was arguably made possible through acceptance, emotional support and the encouragement that were consistently displayed by museum staff towards participants, and how these affective stances created the conditions for collaborative spaces of care. In this way, care in museum engagement work was essentially co-produced. This point is significant because it takes us back into the heart of the discourses of participation in the museum. Thinking of engagement work as care work dislodges the logic of contribution to favour another logic, the logic of care, which is emotional and relational.

A central and long-standing aspect of the Outreach team's practice was co-production: working with participants to create bespoke projects that are directed by the interests of the group and individuals within that group.

Outreach staff were resisting tokenistic and contributory versions of community engagement; instead, their approach was focused on people's interests, and creating the conditions for the creative exploration of those interests in the museums. Significantly, projects were not problem or issue-based, for example, a mental health group doing a project about the stigmas associated with mental health (unless, of course, the group decide this is what they want to do, and this did happen on different occasions). Instead, staff encouraged participants to experiment with new activities. However, this does not mean that participants' needs or issues were side-lined or ignored: emotional support was woven through the engagement programmes through the ordinary caring acts and attentions of staff. Community engagement projects used museum collections as inspiration for creative responses, from object photography to portraiture to proggy mat making. The early stages of a project often included using handling boxes, visiting exhibitions and going 'behind the scenes'; then followed taster sessions, before deciding together on the creative activity. As one staff commented, taster sessions were important 'because if you ask them what they wanted it would be so cruel, because they don't know what you've got to offer'. Key to co-producing projects was an openness and flexibility on behalf of staff to the ideas of participants and making these possible. When this was not possible because of resources or safety issues (both relating to people and museum objects), the team would discuss this openly with participants and co-design alternatives.[13]

This form of 'managing expectations', anchored in a logic of care, is very different from managing the risk of conflict described in the previous chapter. Within the logic of care, decision-making is situated in relations: it is not always central, but rather it is part of wider practices that support the emergence of more positive selves and facilitate more positive ways of being together. In this logic, decision-making is about self-actualisation within a group; as one staff member put it, 'it is about people valuing themselves and knowing that they are valued by others'. In this context, the significance of staff's earlier reflection to me in 'they are treating you in the same way that they themselves want to be treated' is powerfully revealed. This shows participants as active co-producers of their own care, showing us (myself and the museum) what is really important by extending their own acceptance, generosity and support. Through the collection of ordinary, thoughtful and reciprocated acts, we can perhaps finally arrive at a sense of 'you get us' and 'we get you'. Recognising these correspondences, as forms of collective care, I suggest, is key to better understanding the different ways in which participants engage in and participate with the museum.

The materialities of care

Up to now, I have focused on the relational and affective dimensions of care between staff and participants and between participants. But, of course, there are also materials. Care in the museum is distinctive because it involves museum objects, heritage and culture more broadly. Across the varied types of engagement projects I attended over the course of the research, what became apparent was the importance of the materialities that were entangled in care; in particular, the materialities that make up the creative experiences of participants. Central to engagement work is the opportunity for participants to engage in meaningful, creative activities in which a whole range of materials are enrolled, including artefacts (handling objects and replicas) but also a raft of creative and arts materials (felt, paints, clay, beads, cameras, cups of tea, and on one occasion, a herb garden). The next two snapshots reveal some of these objects in action:

> The museum worker takes the museum objects out of her trolley one my one. She then crouches down next to one of the hospital residents in the dementia ward, who is sat in an armchair. The woman raises from a half-slumber. Gently, the museum worker then guides the women's hands together and places the object – a glass baby's milk bottle - into her open palms. There is first silence, then a quiet 'What is it?' as the resident begins to turn the bottle over in her hands. The museum worker stays crouched on the floor beside her as the resident continues to turn over the object, as if caught in a reverie, until, she suddenly recognises it, and breaks into a smile and a half chuckle.
>
> ---
>
> The group is involved in a portraiture project. The idea is that at the end of the project a photographer will take their portraits with objects that represent them. Across the first few weeks, we have been meeting at the stroke support community drop-in centre, and we have looked through a number of object handling boxes from the museum collection as a starting point to think through our relations with objects. One in particular made a strong impression: the box containing the life of a WWI soldier. Different objects seemed to hold different participants' attention: a whistle, a letter or a medal. Inspired by these boxes, participants have brought in a variety of objects from home that represent them. They include old records, comic books, an extensive coin collection, picture of a dog and family albums. We sit around the table, surrounded by these objects, picking them up and putting them down, passing them along, telling and sharing stories.

The engagement between people and objects goes to the heart of material culture approaches to museum studies (Dudley, 2010a).[14] This approach draws attention to the very 'thingness' of museum objects and their capacities to provoke a range of immediate reactions – emotional, sensory and visceral. In museum engagement sessions, like the snapshots above, engagement with objects was at first sensory and emotional, then creative and sometimes part of reminiscence. Participants were encouraged to make their own connections, either personal or using their imagination, and to use collections as inspiration within a creative project – for example, photography, creative writing or creative conversations. 'Facts' were rarely the most important way of engaging with objects. Their physicality was the starting point for stories, inspiration and imagination. Objects were also used to spark connections with other personal objects, as in the second snapshot. Or a group might take inspiration from objects on display in the galleries as the starting point for a creative project, like the earlier example of the photography projects about bridges around the city.

Across a range of interdisciplinary literature, the powerful affective qualities of materials have been noted (Miller, 2008; Pye, 2008), alongside the involvement of 'things' in care practices (Buse et al., 2018; Mol et al., 2010). Within the 'museums in health' literature, the focus has been on evidencing the links between material engagements, 'touch' and their impacts on wellbeing, memory and emotions (see Camic et al., 2017; Chatterjee, 2008; Chatterjee and Noble, 2013; Solway et al., 2015). Research within a humanities vein (and to some extent museum evaluation) has highlighted how engaging with collections and creating personal connections with objects offer opportunities for people to express themselves in powerful and restorative ways (Dodd and Jones, 2014; Froggett et al., 2011). Within this work, there has also been attention to the specific role of museum engagements in terms of mental health, addiction recovery, dementia and hospital care and combating social isolation (e.g. Ander et al., 2013; Camic et al., 2015; Lanceley et al., 2012; Morse et al., 2015; Thomson and Chatterjee, 2016). Alongside museum objects, as I mentioned, are creative processes and arts materials, which have also been considered for their sensory and affective modalities and their contribution to wellbeing (Clift and Camic, 2015; Stickley and Clift, 2017). The common feature across these diverse disciplinary perspectives is that museum objects and creative materials have powerful affective and emotional qualities, and through these qualities, they can support the emergence of more positive selves.

In talking about materialities of care in the context of community engagement as I am now, I am eschewing details and the focus on 'impact' to make a wider argument about museum workers' practices of care.[15] At the same time, I want to argue that there is something *specific* about these practices of care in the museum in terms of the ways in which different materialities are entangled in practices of care. In turn, these materialities make visible the ordinary and tacit aspects of museum workers' care practices: they become the starting point, the anchor for conversations and the conduit for practices and relations of care. Going back to Conradson, through care practices, we can observe changes in 'our sense of self, who we are and feel able to be' (2003b: 509). Museum objects enabled participants to reflect on sense of place, history and their own position in relation to these. Objects were woven into the creative materialities of the projects (the photographs, the portraits and the ceramics) and their association with a personal sense of achievement and sense of pride. While projects were co-designed as a group, sessions often took the shape of group activities with individual creative endeavours: for example, each participant taking their own photographs or creating their own portrait. The productive acts of creating and making were seen as important for participants to access their own sense of potential: 'I never knew I could do this' was a sentiment often repeated in sessions. The influence of engagement sessions could, over time, become transformative: for example, a participant creating a digital story about her personal journey of recovery from addiction; or a person gaining employment after a photography project helped him develop the confidence to feel able to return to the workplace. For many others, the influence was more modest, creating momentary spaces that lifted someone's mood. This more modest capacity is nonetheless significant when viewed from participants' perspectives, when holding negative thoughts at bay and feeling positive are all part of what makes a 'good' day, as opposed to a bad one. The routine of the creative engagements with the museum, once a week, was also significant as a point of reference for participants with often isolated and sometimes chaotic lives. The materialities of community engagement sessions supported social interactions in a way that also supported the co-production of care between museum workers and the participants and amongst participants. In many instances, creative 'making' enabled conversations, interaction and connections. For example, a participant offering advice or showing another participant how to manipulate clay, or pointing out certain surfaces on a museum artefact, or how to use a camera, and another participant accepting this help. Noticing these tentative interactions is important, since for many participants in these vulnerable groups, feeling positive and comfortable with others, or accepting and offering help, are all signs of the emergence of more positive selves. In museum projects where a space of care was more fully realised (even if temporarily), museum objects and creative materials could provide opportunities to reflect on identity and sense of place and lead to recovering or re-establishing a sense of narrative where these may have become lost or fragmented as a result of different personal challenges (for instance, a stroke) in either substantive or more modest ways.

Arguably, these different materialities can only become important if they are supported by a caring process. While museum objects hold affective qualities, it would also be possible to use them without care. Engagement with objects and creative activities requires support, both practical and emotional, so that, as the Outreach team put it earlier, 'so we are not in a situation where people are fearful or are made to feel stupid'. The distinct nature of care in the museum is that it is also a practice of 'caring through things' (Puig de la Bellacasa, 2011) – museum objects and creative materials. For staff, it was also important that the pieces created were displayed, either in the museum or when this was not possible, in the partner organisation's spaces. This highlights yet another dimension of care in the museum: care is about celebrating achievements, and doing so publicly – museums are, after all, about representation and display. There was a very clear impact on participants in seeing themselves and their work recognised and celebrated.

Caring professionals

By looking up close at engagement practice, we can discern 'museum-like' forms of care, with their own relational, affective and material dimensions. The shape of care in the museum is about providing emotional support through encouragement, listening and kindness; and providing practical support by offering opportunities to develop skills, confidence and interests as well as always being sensitive to access and other practical needs. To talk about care work in the museum invites us to recognise care as an orientation and an embodied, relational and emotional practice with social and materials dimensions. It is an attentive and gentle practice: care describes the concern of museum staff to provide a welcoming environment for participants when they enter the exhibition spaces. Care describes the ways in which participants are supported to participate in creative activities and conversation in the substance misuse centre. Care describes the intimate moment of delicately touching hands and objects on the dementia ward. Care describes the desire to make a connection and recover our sense of selves post-stroke. Care also describes the ways in which community engagement workers respond to each of these settings; how they choose what is appropriate or logical to do in response to participants. We might, as I have suggested, productively think of these actions as part of a specific logic – a logic of care in community engagement. Through a close examination of the 'doing' of community engagement, we come to recognise this logic in action, and we come to recognise the abilities of community engagement practitioners. It is not simply a skill, but it is also talent, intuition and insight: the ability to sense what is needed, when and what form it should take. It is a quality acquired through experience and commitment. It is about creating spaces that feel warm, comfortable and safe, supporting individuals emotionally and using museum materialities to create connections. As per Conradson's definition, care work in the museum is both a disposition *and* practical-material actions based on particular skill sets.

In TWAM, two equally problematic tendencies were noted: community engagement is possible because of either a natural *disposition* that only certain people have, and therefore only certain people can do, or it is a series of straightforward *tasks* that anyone can learn and undertake (Chapter 3). As a caring practice, community engagement work must be understood as *both* a skill and a disposition; as creative competencies and embodied knowledge; as technical work and affective labour. The two tendencies uncovered in the museum both undervalue community engagement practice in different ways through its attribution as unskilled work. What the accounts above make unmistakably clear are the distinct skills required to do community engagement work. In the previous chapter, I argued that, currently, community engagement work goes unrecognised within institutional structures. In particular, the intimate, emotional and relational dimensions of community engagement do not easily fit within the managerial frameworks that measure performance and efficiency in museums. Within such frameworks, community engagement is subjected to rules and regulations whereby its relational dimension is reduced to 'ticking boxes', and its emotional dimension is translated into 'managing expectations'. Thinking through care challenges these understandings. In the final chapter of this book, I attempt to resolve some of these tensions by presenting how the logic of care can be applied to the whole museum, and how it might connect subjective and institutional practices and concerns.

Care work is a central part of the emotional life of community engagement workers. It is underpinned by an understanding of community engagement at proximity, and as part of the fundamental social responsibility of the museum: as a duty of care towards its community (Chapter 3). There is an ethical imperative in museum work that is directly affirmed by community engagement practitioners, linking their work firmly into the museum mission: 'because if you look at our mission statement it's all about communities and identity and it's a fairly obvious thing to be doing – any people with any background – you are helping them and supporting them with their wellbeing'. This 'duty of care' is reflected in the geographies of their partnerships with health and social care partners, as strategic partnerships for care in their close community, responding to local public health challenges. Developing these long-term partnerships was central to a new way of working that was felt could have a more significant social impact. Considering the previous ways in which the team had operated, and the impact of regimes of performance management and audit culture on staff (Chapter 4), there was also a clear sense in our discussions that staff located renewed job satisfaction in a commitment to care for other people. There was also a sense by which their professional subjectivities themselves were constituted through registers of feeling and care – for instance, talking about having 'people's best interest at heart' and articulating their practice a 'sensitivity towards how to treat human beings'. When staff described their work, there was a belief that the work that they do could make a difference, through art and through culture, all the while working in partnership with other (formal) care professionals to extend care in a meaningful way. Across the team, and from their varied backgrounds (let us here remind ourselves that the team built up over the years included staff with backgrounds in nursing, youth work, community development and artists working alongside individuals with a background in museums practice), staff were also negotiating evolving professional subjectivities in the dynamic context of their partnership work.[16] This included continuously pursuing opportunities for a broad range of training delivered by external organisations (e.g. dementia training, emotional resilience training, dealing with challenging behaviours training,

counselling introduction sessions and work shadowing care workers and social workers). These approaches all influenced the way staff continued to
understand and develop their practice within health and social care settings.

Perhaps, the most significant aspect of this negotiation was through demarcation in a very clear manner:

> We are not social workers. We have a lot of skills that community de-
> velopment workers and social workers have but that is not what we are
> employed to do. It's very important that we are not seen by participants
> as being able to offer those skills. And that is why we always work in
> partnership with staff from other organisations.

This sense was further articulated in a 2018 report of their work:

> We don't claim to 'cure' people, we don't claim to be experts in commu-
> nity development practice or health promotion. We do however work
> within a model of practice that views cultural and heritage organi-
> sations as having a responsibility to collaborate with experts across
> multiple sectors to be part of a solution by enhancing community pro-
> fessionals' working practices, so they see museum resources as useful
> and relevant.
>
> (Not So Grim Up North Research Team, 2018)[17]

This discursive framing of their work in support of other professional
domains is important since there are tensions that run through the notion of social work as it has been applied to museums (Silverman, 2010).
Externally, the phrase 'social work' sometimes holds negative connotations, repositioning museums work well beyond its traditional purview.
The term brings forward questions over whether museums – and museum
professionals – are really equipped to support vulnerable individuals
and whether misguided efforts might cause more harm, either directly
or through diverting resources away from other specialised services (see
Silverman, 2010: 3–4). The argument here is that social work is not the
work of culture. Similar concerns are raised when talking about therapeutic work in the museum (Lanceley et al., 2012; Silverman, 2003).[18] It was
also important for the team to unambiguously distinguish the boundaries
of their work in terms of how far they felt they could emotionally support
participants, and the need to recognise where and when more formal care
was required. Such a discursive framing is about negotiating and articulating the 'museumness' of care. Care work is part of a professional approach
and vocational disposition to museum engagement work. It is a professional expertise that is constructed in both established skills – creative
engagement through objects – and new ones, developed through partnerships with health and social care workers and recipients. This work can
have therapeutic outcomes, but as staff make clear, it is not therapy. The

ideas and the practice that support care in formal therapy environments influence the team through their close partnerships and exchanges with care professionals, but their work is first and foremost about culture and creativity. This language and ways of thinking about the aims of engagement work (for instance, in terms of self-actualisation or personal growth or wellbeing 'outcomes') would permeate the language of engagement workers but always as a way of framing how museum activities can support the wider aims of these organisations (or as part of evaluation). As such, there was a constant process of both alignment and differentiation.[19] These distinctions are key when talking about care in the museum.

In my discussion over this chapter, I first situated the emotional life of community engagement workers within the context of the engagement sessions, across its different geographies, both inside and outside of the museum. But this emotional life is not contained in those spaces, since it returns with them to the workplace. It is clear that community engagement work was also felt as an emotional demand on staff, and they recounted many events when they had become upset in response to the suffering of others, or angered in the face of the injustices experienced by many, or where they had felt unprepared in a session where a participant might have disclosed particularly difficult emotions (feelings I also shared during my time with the team). The manager of the Outreach team was acutely sensitive to the potential personal tolls of the emotional strain and stress of community engagement work from her own experiences. As such, the team were encouraged to discuss their feelings and difficulties during individual catch-up meetings as well as seeking other support when required. This highlights the very crucial importance of addressing the emotional impact of this caring work. Within her own work on community engagement in a Scottish context, Munro (2014: 50) highlights the danger when staff are unsupported in this work, whereby 'the personal costs attached to their caring' can lead to stress and burnout. In the case of TWAM, there was support built into this work in so far as the practice of care was shaped in partnership with formal care professionals and supported through training, internal debriefing processes and supervision. However, both cases bring forward an important point: emotions saturate care work. Vulnerable participants bring with them a range of complex and difficult emotions to museum projects, and museum professionals must respond and deal with their own emotions within these sessions as well as put systems in place for their self-care. It also highlights the challenges surrounding the logic of care, and how we might apply it to the museum and to museum practice. Care as work brings emotions and relations into focus as central to the work that is done by community engagement practitioners, and with it, a particular set of problematics. In the final part of the book, I return to some of these considerations. For now, and in the next chapter, I want to consider the logic of care further and through another aspect of community engagement work, in the context of a community exhibition.

Notes

1 This included story-telling and participatory workshops with the Outreach team to elicit the qualities of their work by describing and writing about their experiences with participants and breaking down what happens in practice in a detailed and emotion-centred way to uncover 'hidden' or unspoken practices. My own engagement with museum sessions was recorded in field diaries.

2 I give a number of references here as footnotes rather than in text. There is much to read in these areas, and these footnotes do not review the literature but rather give a sense of areas of thought that have influenced the direction of my thinking. The aim is to point out some broad areas for the reader to pursue. Key references that have shaped the particular argument in this book are referred to in text. I also come back to several of these sources more directly in the final chapter.

3 While domestic work is crucial to the reproduction of daily life in many Western cities, it is often poorly rewarded and regarded (Anderson, 2000; Ehrenreich and Hochschild, 2003); see also England and Folbre on the 'costs' of caring (1999).

4 For nursing studies, see James on emotional labour in hospices (1992), McQueen on emotional intelligence in nursing (2004) and Theodosius on emotional labour in healthcare (2008).

5 Emotion work and emotional labour are concepts associated with Arlie Russell Hochschild (1983). See also England for review of theories of care work (2005).

6 In STS, Mol et al. (2010) have explored care in terms of parents for children, farmers for their stock, care for people who are old or who are disabled. In ethics, there is a burgeoning literature on theorising and expanding the concept of care as a broad framework for making moral, political and policy decisions (Held, 2006; Kittay, 1999; Sevenhuijsen, 1998; Tronto, 1993). Sociologists have also shown an interest in care from a social policy angle (Hankivsky, 2004; Twigg, 2002; Ungerson, 1990).

7 For references about care in disability scholarship, see Fine and Glendinning (2005) and Kröger (2009).

8 For critiques of an ethics of care, see Crigger (1997) for example.

9 Geographers are becoming more attuned to the relations of care that are taking place within a growing myriad of 'ordinary' spaces of care in particular in community contexts including cafes (Warner et al., 2013), parks (Laws, 2009), community gardens (Knigge, 2009; Milligan et al., 2004) and arts spaces (Hall, 2013; Parr, 2008).

10 In geography, one key focus of many studies has been on understanding the specific, variant spatial characteristics that create spaces of care (for example, the layout of a room, see Conradson, 2003b; Parr, 2000). What is distinctive about the work of TWAM is the multiplicity of sites of engagement – from galleries to museum back rooms and stores; to community spaces such as libraries, community centres and the institutional settings of the hospital ward. Another distinctive element is the range of collections used (notably in a local authority museum like TWAM that holds varied collections from art to social history and science and technology). To account for these multiplicities, I focus on what holds all this diverse work together in terms of practice and highlight the importance of the materialities of care in a more generalised way.

11 'Geordie' refers to people living in the North East.

12 For instance, in media and cultural studies, affective labour has often been discussed in the context of studies of fandom to explain meaningful activity that does not result in a direct financial profit, but rather produces a sense of community and belonging for those who share a common interest (see Gregg and Seigworth, 2010).

13 This could take on a very practical dimension as staff would often bring in external artists or creative practitioners to support a particular activity that the group might have identified as being of interest – such as ceramics or textile making. While the team had a broad range of creative skills, they would also work in partnership when funding was available.

14 Drawing on anthropological traditions and phenomenology, this approach examines how objects carry meanings *and* feelings, so as to shift the focus back onto the materialities of objects which had become lost in some quarters of museum studies given over to a broader focus on museum experience and concerns over interpretation (see also Dudley, 2010b).

15 I have also parsed distinct disciplinary traditions – though it should of course be recognised that each would take us in very different directions of focus. My focus in this chapter (and in the book more generally) is on the practices of care as discussed in feminist philosophy and social geography.

16 See Paquette (2012) on the construction and negotiation of professional identity for those working in the arts, heritage and culture industries, with a particular focus on cultural policy.

17 The Not So Grim Up North report was based on a three-year research project involving TWAM and in which I acted as postdoctoral researcher. The focus was on measuring the impact of museum activities on health and wellbeing outcomes for participants using quantitative measures and qualitative research.

18 This opinion is rarely found in published materials, but was one that I heard frequently in professionals conferences at the time; however, it should also be noted that as the area of 'museums in health' continues to grow, these opinions are increasingly being challenged in UK context.

19 I have attempted this too in my readings across the literature in order to frame this work in writing. For instance, in Conradson's work, the language of care is developed within psychotherapy, but refracted through social geography, while Virginia Held's work examines care from a feminist and moral philosophy tradition.

References

Ander E, Thomson LJ, Blair K, et al. (2013) Using museum objects to improve wellbeing in mental health service users and neurological rehabilitation clients. *The British Journal of Occupational Therapy* 76(5): 208–216. doi: 10.4276/030802213X 13679275042645.

Anderson B (2000) *Doing the Dirty Work?: The Global Politics of Domestic Labour.* London and New York: Palgrave Macmillan.

Barker DK (2005) Beyond women and economics: Rereading 'women's work'. *Signs* 30(4): 2189–2209. doi: 10.1086/429261.

Bondi L (2005) Making connections and thinking through emotions: Between geography and psychotherapy. *Transactions of the Institute of British Geographers* 30(4): 433–448.

Bourdieu P (1990) *The Logic of Practice*. Palo Alto, CA: Stanford University Press.

Buse C, Martin D and Nettleton S (2018) Conceptualising 'materialities of care': Making visible mundane material culture in health and social care contexts. *Sociology of Health & Illness* 40(2): 243–255. doi: 10.1111/1467–9566.12663.

Camic PM and Chatterjee HJ (2013) Museums and art galleries as partners for public health interventions. *Perspectives in Public Health* 133(1): 66–71. doi: 10.1177/1757913912468523.

Camic PM, Baker EL and Tischler V (2015) Theorizing how art gallery interventions impact people with dementia and their caregivers. *The Gerontologist*: Online First. doi: 10.1093/geront/gnv063.

Camic PM, Hulbert S and Kimmel J (2017) Museum object handling: A health-promoting community-based activity for dementia care. *Journal of Health Psychology* 24(6): 787–798. doi: 10.1177/1359105316685899.

Chatterjee HJ (ed.) (2008) *Touch in Museums: Policy and Practice in Object Handling*. Oxford: Berg.

Chatterjee HJ and Noble G (2013) *Museums, Health and Well-Being*. Farnham: Ashgate.

Clift S and Camic P (eds) (2015) *Oxford Textbook of Creative Arts, Health, and Wellbeing International Perspectives on Practice, Policy and Research*. Oxford: Oxford University Press.

Conradson D (2003a) Geographies of care: Spaces, practices, experiences. *Social & Cultural Geography* 4(4): 451–454. doi: 10.1080/1464936032000137894.

Conradson D (2003b) Spaces of care in the city: The place of a community drop-in centre. *Social & Cultural Geography* 4(4): 507–525. doi: 10.1080/1464936032000137939.

Conradson D (2011) Care and caring. In: Del Casino VJ, Thomas ME, Cloke P, et al. (eds) *A Companion to Social Geography*. Chichester, West Sussex and Malden, MA: Wiley-Blackwell, pp. 454–472.

Crigger NJ (1997) The trouble with caring: A review of eight arguments against an ethic of care. *Journal of Professional Nursing* 13(4): 217–221. doi: 10.1016/S8755-7223(97)80091-9.

Darling J (2011) Giving space: Care, generosity and belonging in a UK asylum drop-in centre. *Geoforum* 42(4): 408–417. doi: 10.1016/j.geoforum.2011.02.004.

Dodd J and Jones C (2014) *Mind, Body, Spirit: How Museums Impact Health and Wellbeing*. Report, 1 June. Research Centre for Museums and Galleries (RCMG), University of Leicester. Available at: https://lra.le.ac.uk/handle/2381/31690 (accessed 15 March 2018).

Dudley SH (ed.) (2010a) *Museum Materialities: Objects, Engagements, Interpretations*. London: Routledge.

Dudley SH (2010b) Museum materialities: Objects, sense and feeling. In: Dudley SH (ed.) *Museum Materialities: Objects, Engagements, Interpretations*. London: Routledge, pp. 1–17.

Ehrenreich B and Hochschild AR (2003) *Global Woman: Nannies, Maids and Sex Workers in the New Economy*. London: Granta Books.

England P (2005) Emerging theories of care work. *Annual Review of Sociology* 31(1): 381–399. doi: 10.1146/annurev.soc.31.041304.122317.

England P and Folbre N (1999) The cost of caring. *The ANNALS of the American Academy of Political and Social Science* 561(1): 39–51. doi: 10.1177/000271629956100103.

Fine M and Glendinning C (2005) Dependence, independence or inter-dependence? Revisiting the concepts of 'care' and 'dependency'. *Ageing and Society* 25(4): 601–621. doi: 10.1017/S0144686X05003600.

Froggett L, Farrier A and Poursanidou K (2011) *Who Cares? Museums, Health and Wellbeing. A study of the Renaissance North West Programme*. Preston: University of Central Lancashire. Available at: http://www.healthandculture.org.uk/publications-case-studies/publications/who-cares-museums-health-and-wellbeing/ (access 1 July 2018).

Gregg M and Seigworth GJ (eds) (2010) *The Affect Theory Reader*. Durham, NC: Duke University Press.

Hall E (2013) Making and gifting belonging: Creative arts and people with learning disabilities. *Environment and Planning A* 45(2): 244–262. doi: 10.1068/a44629.

Hankivsky O (2004) *Social Policy and the Ethic of Care*. Vancouver: UBC Press.

Hardt M (1999) Affective labor. *Boundary* 26(2): 89–100.

Hardt M and Negri A (2005) *Multitude: War and Democracy in the Age of Empire*. London: Routledge.

Held V (2006) *The Ethics of Care: Personal, Political, and Global*. New York: Oxford University Press.

Hochschild AR (1983) *The Managed Heart: Commercialization of Human Feeling*. 2nd edition. Berkeley: University of California Press.

Kittay EF (1999) *Love's Labor: Essays on Women, Equality and Dependency*. New York: Routledge.

Kitwood TM (1997) *Dementia Reconsidered: The Person Comes First*. Maidenhead: Open University Press.

Knigge L (2009) Intersections between public and private: community gardens, community service and geographies of care in the US City of Buffalo, NY. *Geographica Helvetica* 64(1): 45–52. doi: https://doi.org/10.5194/gh-64-45-2009.

Kröger T (2009) Care research and disability studies: Nothing in common? *Critical Social Policy* 29(3): 398–420. doi: 10.1177/0261018309105177.

Lanceley A, Noble G, Johnson M, et al. (2012) Investigating the therapeutic potential of a heritage-object focused intervention: A qualitative study. *Journal of Health Psychology* 17(6): 809–820. doi: 10.1177/1359105311426625.

Laws J (2009) Reworking therapeutic landscapes: The spatiality of an 'alternative' self-help group. *Social Science & Medicine* 69(12). Part Special Issue: New approaches to researching patient safety: 1827–1833. doi: 10.1016/j.socscimed.2009.09.034.

Levitas R (2005) *The Inclusive Society? Social Exclusion and New Labour*. 2nd edition. Basingstoke: Macmillan.

McQueen AC (2004) Emotional intelligence in nursing work. *Journal of Advanced Nursing* 47(1): 101–108.

Miller D (2008) *The Comfort of Things*. Cambridge, MA: Polity.

Milligan C and Wiles J (2010) Landscapes of care. *Progress in Human Geography* 34(6): 736–754. doi: 10.1177/0309132510364556.

Milligan C, Gatrell A and Bingley A (2004) 'Cultivating health': Therapeutic landscapes and older people in northern England. *Social Science & Medicine* 58(9): 1781–1793. doi: 10.1016/S0277–9536(03)00397-6.

Milligan C, Atkinson S, Skinner M, et al. (2007) Geographies of care: A commentary. *New Zealand Geographer* 63(2): 135–140. doi: 10.1111/j.1745-7939.2007.00101.x.

Mol A, Moser I and Pols J (eds) (2010) *Care in Practice: On Tinkering in Clinics, Homes and Farms*. MatteRealities/VerKörperungen 8. Bielefeld: Transcript.

Morse N and Munro E (2015) Museums' community engagement schemes, austerity and practices of care in two local museum services. *Social & Cultural Geography*. Online First: 357–378. doi: 10.1080/14649365.2015.1089583.

Morse N, Thomson LJM, Brown Z, et al. (2015) Effects of creative museum outreach sessions on measures of confidence, sociability and well-being for mental health and addiction recovery service-users. *Arts & Health* 7(3): 231–246. doi: 10.1080/17533015.2015.1061570.

Munro E (2013) 'People just need to feel important, like someone is listening': Recognising museums' community engagement programmes as spaces of care. *Geoforum* 48: 54–62. doi: 10.1016/j.geoforum.2013.04.008.

Munro E (2014) Doing emotion work in museums: Reconceptualising the role of community engagement practitioners. *Museum and Society* 12(1): 44–60.

Noddings N (1984) *Caring, a Feminine Approach to Ethics & Moral Education*. Berkeley: University of California Press.

Not So Grim Up North Research Team (2018) *Not So Grim Up North: Investigating the Health and Wellbeing Impacts of Museum and Gallery Activities for People Living with Dementia, Stroke Survivors, and Mental Health Service-Users*. Available at: http://www.healthandculture.org.uk/not-so-grim-up-north/research-publications/ (accessed 1 August 2019).

Paquette PJ (ed.) (2012) *Cultural Policy, Work and Identity: The Creation, Renewal and Negotiation of Professional Subjectivities*. Farnham: Ashgate.

Parr H (2000) Interpreting the 'hidden social geographies' of mental health: Ethnographies of inclusion and exclusion in semi-institutional places. *Health & Place* 6(3): 225–237. doi: 10.1016/S1353–8292(00)00025-3.

Parr H (2008) *Mental Health and Social Space: Towards Inclusionary Geographies?* RGS-IBG Book Series. Oxford: Blackwell.

Phillips J (2007) *Care*. Key concepts. Cambridge, MA: Polity.

Puig de la Bellacasa M (2011) Matters of care in technoscience: Assembling neglected things. *Social Studies of Science* 41(1): 85–106. doi: 10.1177/0306312710380301.

Pye E (2008) *The Power of Touch: Handling Objects in Museum and Heritage Context*. London and New York: Routledge.

Ramon S and Williams JE (eds) (2005) *Mental Health at the Crossroads: The Promise of the Psychosocial Approach*. Aldershot: Ashgate.

Sevenhuijsen S (1998) *Citizenship and the Ethics of Care: Feminist Considerations on Justice, Morality and Politics*. London: Routledge.

Silverman LH (2003) The therapeutic potential of museums as pathways to inclusion. In: Sandell R (ed.) *Museums, Society, Inequality*. London: Routledge, pp. 89–103.

Silverman LH (2010) *The Social Work of Museums*. New York: Routledge.

Solway R, Camic PM, Thomson LJ, et al. (2015) Material objects and psychological theory: A conceptual literature review. *Arts & Health* 0(0): 1–20. doi: 10.1080/17533015.2014.998010.

Stickley T and Clift S (2017) *Arts, Health and Wellbeing: A Theoretical Inquiry for Practice*. Cambridge: Cambridge Scholars Publishing.

Theodosius C (2008) *Emotional Labour in Health Care: The Unmanaged Heart of Nursing*. London: Routledge. doi: 10.4324/9780203894958.

Thomson LJ and Chatterjee HJ (2016) Well-being with objects: Evaluating a museum object-handling intervention for older adults in health care settings. *Journal of Applied Gerontology* 35(3): 349–362. doi: 10.1177/0733464814558267.

Tronto JC (1993) *Moral Boundaries: A Political Argument for an Ethic of Care*. New York and London: Routledge.

Twigg J (2002) *Bathing: The Body and Community Care*. London: Routledge.

Ungerson C (1990) *Gender and Caring: Work and Welfare in Britain and Scandinavia*. New York: Harvester Wheatsheaf.

Warner J, Talbot D and Bennison G (2013) The cafe as affective community space: Reconceptualizing care and emotional labour in everyday life. *Critical Social Policy* 33(2): 305–324. doi: 10.1177/0261018312449811.

Wood C (2009) *Museums of the Mind: Mental Health, Emotional Wellbeing, and Museums*. Bude: Culture: Unlimited. Available at: http://cultureunlimited.org/ pdfs/museums (accessed 20 January 2013).

6   Curatorial work and care

In the previous chapter, I located my descriptions and my concerns up close on community engagement sessions with excluded or marginalised groups. Such events represent a key facet of contemporary museum work. The second facet of community engagement work focuses more directly on issues of representation and display and is often referred to as community 'co-production'. While this second area requires different 'types' of work, I will go on to show that this practice is animated by the same logic of care that I described in the community engagement sessions with vulnerable adults. In this second area of work, however, the term 'community' takes on a much more expansive sense as diverse groups defined by common interests, cultures or geographies. The aim of engagement with communities is more directly focused on exhibition production and telling new stories of, and with, communities, using the museum's modalities of display. This is the aspect of community engagement work that most closely intersects with another area of museum practice, that of curatorial work. Today, curatorial work is no longer defined only by its relationships to objects; it is also defined by relationships to visitors and by relationships to the communities represented in collections (Kreps, 2003; Witcomb, 2003). Despite this expansion of the curatorial role into collaborative areas, it is still positioned as a distinct domain of professional work (i.e. not engagement work), as the example of TWAM shows in the strong demarcation of teams and their labour. Within TWAM, curators primarily defined their role in terms of the practice of social history, where people's stories are just as important as objects, and involving people in telling their own stories is crucial (and ethically necessary) to the wider relevance of the museum. I argued that these engagement practices of curators are based on a logic of contribution, where collaborative work enables 'better' knowledge and the pluralising and democratising of content in the museum (Chapter 2). In this chapter, I focus on the curatorial-like work of the Outreach team in the West End of the city. I want to examine how we might reconsider curatorial work more broadly through the logic of care in light of the practices of the team in the West End and an Outreach-led exhibition. My description of practice is in two broad movements: taking the museum out into the West End and bringing the West End back into the museum.[1] Across these moves, out of, then into the museum, I continue with my concern to understand the work of community engagement as a set of skills and as a disposition enmeshed in a logic of care in order to articulate and value the subtlety and nuance of community engagement work.

The chapter describes practices that were developed as new ways of working at a time when the team was rethinking and consolidating its work (Chapter 4). At the heart of the new approach was a conscious move away from the previous 'conveyor belt' of projects that had prevented long-term, embedded work with communities. The new approach was to locate the museum in its neighbourhood. This model of working was described as 'mapping the community': a process of going out and finding out about the organisations and community groups that were already active in the neighbouring area. Throughout this chapter, I examine how this way of working produced what I will term networks of engagement, connecting the museum into the community. In the logic of contribution, outreach work of this type is focused on going out to collect stories and objects to bring back into the museum. The relationship is ultimately about coming back to the centre, with the museum as the focal point. In a logic of care, the curatorial process shifts attention away from the museum to ways of working together, and the relations and settings in which stories and objects come to be shared. The logic of care focuses on networks of engagement that are distributed: the museum is just one point within a larger network of organisations, of people, things and ideas. There is no centre, and as such, no centrifugal move towards it. In networks, there is no single direction. Networks are rarely coherent. They might have multiple centres. They are marked by the diversity of their relations. As both a concept and a metaphor, the network presents a more compelling description of museum-community relationships that goes beyond a focus on linear relationships of contribution. Approaching the museum through ideas of networks in which people, things and ideas are assembled has gained ground in museum studies (Bennett et al., 2017; Byrne et al., 2011; Harrison et al., 2013; Horwood, 2019; Latour and Weibel, 2005; Macdonald, 2009; Macdonald and Basu, 2007; Schorch, 2017; Tolia-Kelly et al., 2016) and geography (Anderson and McFarlane, 2011; Anderson et al., 2012). A key tenet of this work is to forefront a view of museums as collectives (or 'meshworks') in which human and non-humans – staff, artefacts, funding bids, display cases and collections management software – are held together in provisional and contingent wholes. These ideas have particular resonance, such as the museum materialities entangled in the practices of care in my previous chapter. However, and as always in this book, my first concern is with practice, and perhaps, more precisely, with the practical work of assembling as it is performed by museum professionals.[2] Things and materialities are part of my accounts, but it is an account that privileges a discussion of the 'doing' of community engagement from a staff-centred perspective.

Talking of networks of engagement offers a concept that enables me to describe and analyse the work of the team in the West End, and it also prefigures a methodological concern. To look at how things are assembled in networks focuses our attention on 'following the story' (Latour, 1987) and using the 'thick description' (Geerzt, 1988) of the ethnography tradition. In terms of community engagement, this means following much longer stories that do not simply describe the moments of decision-making involved in creating an output (such as a community-led or co-produced display) or the time-bound impact of engagement of participants. Instead, it requires us to take a more open view of how, where and when relations are created. In other accounts of museums, parts of the story are hidden from view (for example, projects abandoned, altered texts and multiple preparatory meetings) and others are given prominence (the final interpretation plan, the joint decision and the final display). In considering networks of engagement, it is necessary to examine relations and events that are not necessarily or obviously directed towards the functioning of museums, but that might still be significant to others involved. Methodologically, then, it requires research that decentres the museum. As such, this chapter spends time both in and out of the museum in an attempt to follow the work of community engagement practitioners in shaping networks of engagement in the West End. Within these networks, one exhibition, *West End Stories*, becomes a focal point. However, it should not be viewed as an end point or even a central event; rather, its purpose is to enable me to narrate practice from a particular vantage point.

Another feature of the network is to question the constitutive nature of community (Schorch, 2017). In the network view, communities and museums are necessarily co-constitutive: communities assemble the museum as much as they are assembled by the community (Bennett, 1998: 205). In my account, I am most interested in the ways in which the museum assembles community; as such, my account is necessarily partial. By focusing on the proactive work of the Outreach team in the community, I consider how the practice of community engagement can also be understood as the practice of assembling community, and I draw further attention to the skills and disposition of this labour – work that is marked out by its logic of care. As this account unfolds, we will find that the community was not directly involved in curating the *West End Stories* exhibition. At the same time, it would not serve us well to describe the exhibition in opposition to, or as a failure of co-production. By focusing on the practices and relationships that led to the final display, we might instead consider the exhibition as a shared accomplishment, albeit one that is 'curated' and ultimately contestable, but which nonetheless reflects collaboration. Within this frame, we can reconsider the idea of curatorial work in museums along different lines and within a logic of care.

Mapping the West End

> I felt the work I was doing was very much driven by what the museum wants and ok, I work for the museums, but I felt there was a real tension with what the museum thinks and wants in terms of community engagement and what I think is important because I work on the ground, and it's about... you hear things and see things and meet people and then you get ideas about things.[3]

Previous ways of working in TWAM, framed within the logic of contribution and directed through bureaucratic structures and performance management, had led to targets, short-termism and a 'bolt-on' form of engagement, directed by museum and funder agendas (Chapter 4). The team's work in the West End at this time of the research developed as a response to these tensions. The team was looking for ways for each museum venue in the service to become more rooted within the local communities at their doorstep, and more responsive to their needs and interests; to respond to those things seen and heard on the ground, working with a whole community in all its complexity, rather than through the targeted approach that had characterised previous years. The team identified the West End as the Discovery Museum's (one of the main sites of the wider museum service) 'most immediately local community' as well as an area from which people do not come to the museum, despite its proximity. This was also about returning to a much older practice, as the first Outreach post in 1992 was linked to a regeneration fund for the West End.

The West End tells a particular story of urban change and community action over several decades.[4] Once a prosperous area linked to heavy industry and ships building in the late nineteenth and early twentieth century, it later shifted dramatically into decline and unemployment. At the time of writing, it contains some of the most deprived wards in the region. This decline is mapped onto the urban landscape and the area's story of large-scale demolition, slum clearances, displacements and dispersal, then new builds, privatisation schemes and regeneration programmes that have so far largely failed to reach their aims, in particular their rhetoric of community engagement (Robinson, 2005). Since the 2008 recession and subsequent austerity, regeneration programmes have mostly ground to a halt; whole areas that were once residential are now left empty and desolate. At the same time, the West End has a parallel history of community action and activism, including neighbourhood-based organisations, pensioners' associations, credit unions and women's action groups (Green, 2017). Many of these smaller organisations are still active in the community today. The West End has become the most diverse area of Newcastle, with many migrants coming into the ward. The West End, then, is a complex area with multiple stories that cannot be easily summarised. It is an area with multiple social issues, but it is also an area with a long tradition of collective action driven by people who believe in 'community' and value it.

Over the course of 2012–2013, two Outreach Officers began a process that they described as 'mapping communities' in the West End:

> It's not a project, it's an approach – it involves research and mapping of the area; finding out what resources exist there; what kinds of projects are live; what the capacity issues are there in terms of what people are working on. It's about gaps which exist as well. It's about looking and supporting.

The approach in the West End is best described as asset-based community development (Kretzmann and McKnight, 1993; Mathie and Cunningham, 2003), a process that focuses on community capacities rather than needs and identifies the different associations that build strong communities in order to 'begin to assemble their strengths into new combinations, new structures of opportunity, new sources of income and control, and new possibilities for production' (Kretzmann and McKnight, 1993: 6). The work of beginning to assemble community is my focus here. Over a period of a year, the two Outreach staff members met community groups and organisations in the West End to find out about their work. As they stated, 'we were going out to communities without a set museum agenda'. These were not only heritage or cultural organisations; they included a good neighbourhood project, a radio station, a women's support network, an activist film archive group, a knitting club and community organisations providing support for older people and their care partners. The 'mapping' approach focused on researching the capacities of individuals, groups and organisations, their skills, talent and interests as well as the current issues they faced, many linked to the local impact of austerity. They looked at how the community organised its own support through community spaces that have developed through small-scale initiatives; identifying formal and informal networks and how the community links to these and how they link to each other; and identifying community representatives and leaders. This was not always straightforward work, as the team's approach was at times met with cynicism or suspicion from small local organisations. Indeed, the West End is an area that has been overwhelmed by institutional regeneration interventions and consultations that have left communities disappointed and disillusioned. One member of the team commented, 'people are weary of big organisations coming into the area. They have no local knowledge, they parachute projects in (many of which are not welcome), they come and then go because agendas change, funding disappears'. There was a feeling across the community of a large cultural gap between the museum and the West End. For the Outreach team, the aim was to convey to communities a different impression of the museum and what they could (and should) expect from it. To this end, staff sought to develop new kinds of relationships with individuals, groups and communities, on two levels. First, it was about showing communities how the museum could become a resource for them to use. Second, it was about providing in-kind support to local groups and activities. Both levels can be read as attempts to bring the museum out into the community. What became clear for Outreach in the work of mapping was that the West End has dozens of groups and organisations that are researching, collecting, archiving and actively producing local history and heritage, without directly engaging with the museum around the corner. However, as one resident and community worker suggested: 'there are lots of arts and cultural things going on, but it tends to happen in portacabins and backrooms – the West End doesn't have a high-quality venue'. The aim of the team then was to examine how the museum could support activities in the area in a meaningful way:

> There are programmes already existing out there, local history groups, and there are resources that are in the museum that we can use, the archives, for example, and I just took those out and without much effort really you are supporting things that are happening out there.

Over the year, the team brought out handling collections into community spaces and took different groups into the museum for behind the scenes tours as well as raising awareness of the museums' free events and activities. Taking the museum out was not only simply about collections or visits to the museum, however, but also about sharing the different skills and expertise of museum staff: 'not to replicate what's out there but maybe to hone into more ways of supporting communities and community work'. For example, staff assisted groups such as the West End Picture Library, an entirely volunteer-led archive, with specialist advice on cataloguing and preserving their collections, and provided support for funding bids that other associations were putting together (without necessarily involving the museum as a costed partner). They also organised local heritage walks and talks in partnership with local groups. Over time, the approach consolidated into a programme of satellite exhibitions in the community,[5] supporting community groups with the technical expertise and time to develop their own exhibitions and repurposing several museum-grade display cases that could be toured across to venues in the West End. One such exhibition brought together a collection of photographs spanning 60 years of weddings in one of the local churches. Pictures from 180 weddings were collected as part of a local history community project led by the St James' Heritage Centre that called on local residents to share their memories, with photographs sent in from as far afield as Canada and New Zealand. The first community display took place in the church annex, hundreds of images fully covering the three walls of the buildings, sellotaped to sheets of paper, huddled together, creating a large photo album documenting six decades of marriage custom, fashion, hairstyles and love stories. Several months later, the museum team supported a second exhibition, with the outreach team collecting oral histories from eight of the couples in the photographs. A small display, *Wedding Tales*, was produced, with a budget of £400 from the museum to cover other associated costs. A museum bookcase cabinet was borrowed and installed at St James' to display keepsakes, wedding invitations, garlands and a floral display on loan by local residents. The museum provided pictures frames, a dress stand and headphones for the oral histories and produced an introduction panel. Outreach staff installed the space. This second iteration *looked* like a museum exhibition – quite different from the DIY aesthetic of the first display.

My point here isn't really to comment on the merits of either display. What is more significant is to recognise the process of collaboration. For St James' Heritage Centre, they were interested in getting some of the museum *out* into the West End – not necessarily the actual artefacts and objects, but the narratives and stories that the museum held about their neighbourhood. Working with the museum would also enable them, they felt, to lift the standards of their display: 'it just raises people's aspiration for what this could be (…) the idea that [the community] could have a mini museum right here on their doorstep would be fantastic'.[6] For St James', this quality was important to increase the collective local pride in the area and its history.

Networks of engagement

> We've started to establish links with people and we don't actually know what's going to happen from those links.

In the events and encounters that took place in the West End over those two years, there is no singular moment that can be clearly defined as 'engagement'. Instead, these events and encounters were constituted and sustained as networks of engagement that temporarily brought together people, objects, interests and organisations. For Outreach, crafting these connections was not just about linking groups up to the museum (in a unidirectional way); they also saw their role as 'joining the dots', as they put it, and connecting with different groups across the community. The team's model of 'mapping the community' aimed to develop a way of inserting the museum's community engagement professionals into already existing networks of cultural associations, local initiatives and community projects. As one member of the Outreach team commented, different resources came together in these networks: 'we share our skills with people and at the same time we learn about the way they get their communities engaged and involved and that's where I see the future of some of this work'. This was a slow-paced, experimental and sustained work of building links within community – the kind of 'creative labour of collaboration' that geographers Mar and Anderson (2012: 1) have highlighted for its capacities for 'entangling people, places, material artefacts, and ways of working and thinking'. The creative quality of this work lies in its responsiveness and flexibility: listening to community interests, needs and concerns and imagining how the museum can be brought out in a manner that is supportive and appropriate. One of the

Outreach workers described this practice as getting to know the local community through the very mundane acts of being present in the community:

> In this new way of working I have been attending a lot of community events, being in their areas, in their territory, without actually selling any of the goods of the museum – for example, involvement in an exhibition. I am there as a presence, I'm introducing myself to people, I am taking part in their activity and it's that kind of developing trust and visibility even before you get into a discussion about what we do and what they do, in this kind of silent engagement way.

In this way of working, the aim was for the Outreach staff – and by extension, the museum – to participate in the lives of communities. This included taking part in a range of community activities not necessarily focused on history or heritage. This idea of 'silent engagement' has a strong resonance with the notion of affective labour aimed at producing new forms of social networks (Hardt, 1999: 89). As affective labour, it is mostly 'immaterial' and refers to the intense work of producing feelings of trust, through acts such as listening, smiling, being a presence in the community. Outreach staff often spoke to me about the importance of first meetings with community groups and presenting themselves in a manner from which to foster trust:

> I've got subtle things like that. So, for example in my first meeting, I would always accept a drink - tea, coffee, especially the first meeting. I guess it's something that they are offering you - and that is one stabiliser isn't it? Something that says you aren't just going to be in and out.
>
> I always acknowledge the existence of the building or the venue... saying 'oh so this is where you are?' or 'have you got another centre somewhere else?' or even just notice something. Or I will say 'it feels warm in here' or just something like that.

Taking part in community activities, sharing a drink, noticing and commenting on aspects of the building and mentioning staff's own feeling of comfort in community spaces were all active practices through which staff demonstrated their interest in getting to know external organisations. They are recognisable as the mundane and ordinary acts of care (Chapter 5), and more widely, acts that demonstrate 'caring about' a place and its community. This creative labour of collaboration was also oriented towards action: 'caring about' was articulated in practical ways to support community interests. Such practices are rarely considered in current accounts of community engagement practice; and yet, they are fundamental to understanding how this practice operates, were it succeeds and where it might fail. Within the logic of contribution that characterises current participatory practice (Chapter 2), building relationships with communities is aimed towards exchange – a contribution to the museum (an object, a story, etc.). In the logic of care, these relations are ongoing, without the expectation of a return. This approach reverses the terms of museum engagement: going out without a museum agenda, meeting communities in their own spaces, creating associations for their own sake and making connections around community interests and knowledge. In this reversal, engagement is less about communities contributing to the museum (objects, oral histories, etc.), and rather more about the museum providing in-kind support to activities in the community, making its collections, staff, skills and resources available to the community, and shifting the terms of engagement towards community agendas. In the logic of care, the relationship is less a means to an end and rather a means in itself. For St James', a partnership could help bring the museum and its skills out to the community. For the Outreach team, working with St James' aligned with their efforts to make the museum more rooted in its local communities. Taking the wedding exhibition as one moment in the network, we can view this display as emerging through the creative process of entanglement, sharing resources and technical–curatorial expertise towards a joint project. The idea came from the community, and the role of the museum was to support the community by producing a 'high quality' display, which was important to St James'. The different agencies that shaped the networks of engagement emerged at the intersection of these interests, intentions and circumstances.

Networks of engagement are constituted through the relationships among their members. They can take any direction; they have no centre; they are constantly changing and are necessarily uncertain. Such a view stands in sharp contrast with current conceptualisations of participation within a logic of contribution, where outreach work of this type is focused on going out to collect stories and objects to bring back into the museum, and the relationship is ultimately about a return to the centre. Networks of engagement are formed through practices oriented in the logic of care about place and about community. Still, within the conceptualisation of the network of engagement, 'community' proves an elusive idea. Locating 'the community', as if it were shaped by determinate groups who share a singular connection to a place, is, as is by now well-known, analytically and empirically problematic (a concern shared by museum workers). A community is not a separate entity to be acted on, as many scholars have pointed out; rather, it is better conceptualised as an entity that is produced across different spaces and practices. I turn my attention to this next to consider how community itself emerged from the practices of museum's engagement workers, including the curatorial process that led to an exhibition.

Assembling community

West End Stories is the second exhibition to come out of the Outreach team's model of working. The ambition for *West End Stories* was to 'scale up' the work initiated by *Wedding Tales* and to bring elements of community practice back into the museum. Empirically and analytically, it provides an opportunity to examine in more detail the process of assembling community and the curatorial approach of community engagement workers. I start with the exhibition and trace back some of the events through which it came together. My purpose in starting with the exhibition is not to re-privilege the work of display; rather, the aim is to reveal the exhibition as an event within much longer networks of engagement. The details presented here are drawn from my own reading of the exhibition and accounts by staff.

West End Stories

What's so special about the West End?

Newcastle's West End has more than one story. These stories are important when you think about what has shaped the world we live in today: the industrial revolution, war, political change, the migration and movement of people and globalisation.

Helps us tell a story about Newcastle's West End.

This text is the introductory panel to the *West End Stories* exhibition, held in the old *People's Gallery* in February–June 2013 (Figures 6.1–6.5). The printed panel ends with a link to a Facebook group where visitors were invited to share their own stories about the area. Beyond this panel, there was no other substantial text in the exhibition, only object labels, which were most often descriptive text taken directly from the museum catalogue. The exhibition mixed photographs with museum objects and film, all of which have a connection to the West End. There was no timeline or set narrative; it did not follow conventional modes of display through chronology. Photographs from the 1950s were juxtaposed next to Roman spoons, next to a glass toilet box in the shape of a house and opposite, a handwritten note from a Japanese businessman to a military engineering group. In one case, there was a women's dressing jacket, with a label that read: 'This jacket belonged to Miss Elizabeth Robinson, a nurse from Benwell who died of malaria in a military hospital in Bazra, Mesopotamia (now Iraq) in 1919'. Next to it hung the portrait of a man who owned a site that manufactured ceramic ware in the West End. In the following case, there was a large box of unopened jam jars from 1962. Further along, we could find a decorative jug from 1870, with (as we learn from the label) 'a portrait of Tyneside rower James Renforth on the font', and next to it, a model of a naval gun. Around the corner was a wall displaying a small library of reports produced by the Community Development Projects (CPDs), the research teams funded through a government neighbourhood renewal project as part of the UK anti-poverty initiatives in the 1970s, one of which focused on the West End. Over several walls across the exhibition spaces were flat screen TVs showing a series of films on a time-differed loop. Many of the films were specially commissioned for the exhibition, including personal stories of residents currently living in the

West End as well as an interview with the Keeper of Archaeology where he interpreted some of the Roman objects displayed in the gallery. At the other end of the exhibition were three screens with archival films from a community project called Archives For Change. The archival film loops replicated the exhibition's juxtapositions through a collision of three sets of images: from recent buildings demolitions to interviews with community activists to women walking down a West End street in the 1950s.

Oblique narratives begin to emerge from the possibilities of these multiple juxtapositions. There was an overarching story about complexity, about change and permanence, about the connections between people and place. However, the exhibition refused to tell a single story from an authoritative viewpoint; it expressed narratives by opening up new kinds of connections that are suggestive of relationships across time and between material forms. There was an ambition to disassemble the temporal frame of the museum by mixing up events so that there are no clear beginnings or ends. At the same time, as it dismantled chronology, the space was punctuated with representations of different landmarks that relocate place in the gallery – for example, through a large model of the area, and in the centre of the room, a case filled with knitted and crocheted recreations of buildings from the West End on loan from local Knit and Natter group. The narratives that emerged were less about a linear story to be decoded in a didactic manner; instead, they resonated within more social and emotional registers. These

Figure 6.1 Detail from *West End Stories*, Discovery Museum, Newcastle, UK, April 2013. Decorative jug, 1870, next to a model of a naval gun, about 1930.
Source: Author.

Figure 6.2 Detail from *West End Stories*, Discovery Museum, Newcastle, UK, April 2013. Three screens showing footage from Archives for Change.
Source: Author.

Figure 6.3 Detail from *West End Stories*, Discovery Museum, Newcastle, UK, April 2013. Box of unopened jam jars, 1926.
Source: Author.

Figure 6.4 Detail from *West End Stories*, Discovery Museum, Newcastle, UK, April
2013. Reports from the Community Development Projects in background.
Source: Author.

Figure 6.5 Detail from *West End Stories*, Discovery Museum, Newcastle, UK,
April 2013. Knitted figures from the West End.
Source: Author.

were narratives created through the different ways in which objects and images talk to one another – fragmented narratives that reflect the changing qualities of place. 'Community' was reflected through the objects, images and stories across the exhibition but also in an open-ended manner. In a sense, community was brought into being within the space of the exhibition, where it was given shape and meaning through the interactions between the space and its visitors (the form and shape of which could not be predicted).

At one level, the exhibition can be read as an experiment.[7] Through its modes of display, *West End Stories* resisted essentialising the relationship between place and community. It was open to interpretation and appeared unscripted, its producers multiple and unspecified. Another way of reading the exhibition is as a sole-authored project. It was not 'co-produced' or 'co-created' in the sense demanded by participatory discourses. Rather, it was a 'curated' product in the sense that the Outreach officer in charge arranged the loans from other organisations and community groups and decided on objects and their final arrangements in cases; he chose the interpretive labels; he advised on lighting, framing and mounts. He wrote the introductory panel. And yet, to only consider these curatorial acts in terms of authorship or decision-making eludes the other important ways in which the exhibition was held together, and the other logics that led to its final form. By tracing back through the associations that led to the display, and the relationships that continue to hold it together, it is possible to have a different reading of the exhibition, as an event assembled in a much longer process of working in the West End. This enables us to consider curatorial work as part of the practice of community engagement itself, as a distributed process of accumulated knowledge and reciprocal exchanges with many constituencies, groups and organisations.

When I asked the Outreach officer to consider how the exhibition was produced, he reflected:

> This I wouldn't say per se that it is a co-produced exhibition. I think it has been to a degree but it's not the fact of people selecting objects. I mean people have produced work that we've included in here, and they've put it in the exhibition. (...) I got a chance to get the women in who'd done all [the knitting], and they came in like artists, just like you would if it was a contemporary art exhibition and they installed it. I was supportive, and we had Conservation in to pin stuff in as well, and it was given as much care as I don't know, the reified object-special-museum-kind-of-thing.

Early on, a decision was taken not to directly involve community members in the exhibition production due to very practical considerations of time and staff capacity:

> We'd only gone out and started meeting people a year and a half ago and to rush through getting some kind of token idea of co-production, I'd rather even not do it than do it in a token way. (...) But this is like a small thing that's part of bigger things.

Mindful of these circumstances then, there was a consideration not to rush through into a model of working that could not be realised. For the Outreach team, it was exactly this process of crafting informal, everyday relationships over a long period of time that felt different to the previous practices of the museum, which had been described as 'scatter-gun' and rushed opportunities that did not always present the best conditions for collaborative modes of working. There were opportunities to include community work, but the overall output would be curated by museum staff:

> This is my work, this is me being involved in this, I am of this stuff as essentially some kind of curator, but I feel that the partnerships that we've had with people, with groups outside the museum, for me, have been genuine in putting these together. There's been genuine informal conversations – and a genuine partnership where they've understood what I'm trying to do. And what *we're* trying to do. (...) I needed to meet people and I needed to understand the area a bit more and I needed to be talking with people.

Here, I find Yúdice's (2003) notion of 'col*labor*ation' useful for thinking through the processes and practice through which we eventually arrived at the exhibition. Situating his research around an international arts festival on the US–Mexico border, he underscored labour to 'emphasize that two or more parties that undertake a task or contribute to it are doing work' (2003: 213). In particular, he highlights the range of cultural labour that takes place in mailing lists, chat, newsletters and so on that together shape the knowledge and culture of events, but that are rarely acknowledged (or remunerated, as is his point). In our case, and in the museum, the concept acknowledges the many people who provided the stories, knowledge and emotions that shaped the content of the exhibition, but whose labour (and knowledge) is often invisible or ignored in accounts of curatorial processes. The idea of the network of engagement links strongly with this notion of col*labor*ation as distributed work with multiple actors. While the exhibition might on some level be single-authored at the point of installation, at the same time, the forms of display and narratives were influenced across a long timeframe and through multiple interactions.

> From over the last year of just being in the West End and doing a temporary exhibition with them and consulting with them in a very informal way about what they would want out of this. One of the main things they said was don't tell a story about the West End: don't have this kind of paternal, big organisation museum voice telling 'the' story of the West End.
> There's a traditional story that's told about the West End: the different factories, the kind of 'remember when nostalgia crowd'. But it's also an area that's changed enormously, and now has a bad reputation with

the slum clearances and gentrification ... but it's also an area with a rich and diverse heritage.

We were just looking at the West End and wanted to show interesting sides of it and not tell a singular story.

The West End is a place of constant flux, and it tells a particular story of urban change and community action. The exhibition aimed not to tell 'a' or 'the' story of the West End, but instead attempted to hold together all these different ideas and people that make up this place through time and through space. As a 'performative' exhibition (after Latour and Weibel, 2005), *West End Stories* sought to maintain the complexity, diversity and emergent nature of place and community through display. Mary Bouquet describes the process of moving from concepts to exhibition design as 'a three dimensional, visual process of meaning making' (2001: 195). In a similar way, the process of making of *West End Stories* was a process of 'translating' ideas into a 'composite artefact' that would then take on certain representational powers (ibid.). Looking at the details of the Outreach officer's practice over that year – a practice of repeated encounters with community – we can begin to see the many people, conversations, local events, newsletters and so on, and how this varied knowledge, stories and affects shaped the exhibition. Through conversations, activities, visits between organisations and 'just being there', the museum (via the Outreach officer) became to some extent (if momentarily) part of the West End as a complex, changing place as well as being part of the community as it emerged in these processes and practices. The final curatorial act was based on a situated and embodied reasoning (more than discursive intent), where choices were influenced by the process of col*labor*ation and framed in a common interest. This view highlights the very interdependence of the knowledge/stories/emotions that informed the display, and so the exhibition can no longer be seen as straightforwardly sole-authored. Indeed, the very idea of authorship is opened up in this reading.

As the Outreach officer reflected:

> The community: there's people who are involved in heritage groups, doing volunteer stuff, there's groups working with different kinds of people, whether it's young mothers or Asian people, or people with learning difficulties, or just anyone, Dad's groups, whatever – there's those groups and you could sort of say 'that's the community' or there's just everybody who lives in the West End, is that the community? And then there's a different demographics in between that. This [exhibition] was part of us working with them.

In this way, we can read the curatorial act as an attempt to translate or extend the networks of engagement into a composite artefact: a process of assembling community through the curatorial practice of display. In this view, 'community' is assembled and produced in the networks of engagement themselves, the fabric of which is assembled in the partnerships of collaborators who variously participate, and which is temporarily given form and shape in the exhibition space. The dynamic networks that make up the West End become interpretively assembled through the relations between people, objects and curatorial practices. In a sense, it doesn't aim to be representative; rather, it chooses to remain open, as a 'work in progress', as a way to capture the changing nature of place and community in the area. Throughout this book, I have suggested that the work of community engagement workers is largely misunderstood, and as such, it goes unrecognised in the professional working structures of the museums. In the discussion of the community engagement practices in the West End, and the final exhibition, the particular skills and disposition of this work of col*labor*ation come to the fore. In the example of *West End Stories*, the curatorial practice can be understood as bound up with the practice of community engagement: a practice of getting to know and understand the West End that is slow, attentive, caring work. It follows, then, that we should reconsider the curatorial act through the concepts of care and its logics. In the next section, I outline the implications of care thinking in relation to curating and the questions of authorship in order to trouble some of the commonly held views about 'community exhibitions' in the museum.

Curatorial practice as care

The verb 'to care' shares its etymological root with 'to curate' (Latin: curare – to take care of). Safeguarding and stewardship are the basis of this care, with curators as the keepers of collections. It is by now well established that the role of the curator extends from the technical and custodial care of objects to care for the aesthetic and/or intellectual and/or emotional experience of museum audiences (Witcomb, 2003). There are also long-standing demands to extend this role further to the communities represented in museum collections, especially minority and indigenous communities (Ames, 1992; Clifford, 1997; Kreps, 2003). And yet, talking about care of people in relation to curatorial work has hardly figured at all.

Through the example of the West End, I have argued that we need to recognise the work of community engagement workers as part of wider practices of care: where care is defined as the proactive interest of one person (the museum) in the wellbeing of another (the community) and as the articulation of that interest (or affective stance) in practical ways (pace Conradson, 2003a; Chapter 5). *West End Stories*, as an exhibition, can be read as an extension of these practices of community engagement, realised as a composite artefact of these relationships of care. To view the curatorial process through a logic of care calls on us to view curatorial work across a much longer timeframe and acknowledge the range of diverse relations that shape and influence this practice. In this perspective, curatorial work is a relational, material and affective practice that combines care for objects with care for people. When I asked whether he had curated the exhibition, the Outreach officer replied:

> Well what's curating? It's like to care for something. [People say I] should be a community curator but I like working with people and this is just a little part of things that I want us, the museum, to do in the West End. (...) Some people who see themselves as curators think you need some kind of privy knowledge to put objects next to each other, and I don't think you do. This exhibition is about people, about an area, about the West End.

To talk of curating as care extends the curatorial work to taking care of people, of a community, of a neighbourhood, and highlights the importance of all the work that happens before and after exhibitions. The act of display is then better understood as only a moment within a longer process of engaged curatorial practice. Within the logic of care, the role of the curator and the skills and dispositions required for this work are different; or perhaps more expansive. It extends the practice of taking care of objects to taking care of people, and the nature of such relationships as more than gathering people's knowledge or personal objects (their contributions) to a longer commitment and proactive interest in other people's interests. This work is experimental, flexible and mindful of its circumstances. The craft of curating a display combines the curator's knowledge of collections with the knowledge/stories/emotions of communities. This echoes Schorch's idea of curatorial practice as 'an interpretive or hermeneutic method through which the relationships between objects, communities and knowledge becomes assembled, disassembled and reassembled' (2017: 37).[8] In the logic of care, curatorial work is reconnected to the practice of community engagement, and the museum and its materially bounded work environment is extended beyond institutional boundaries.

What is interesting to consider now is how this relational, material and affective work in the community – the work of care – is translated back into the wider structures of the institution; in our case, we might consider how *West End Stories* was perceived in the museum. At the very beginning of the mapping exercise, the Outreach team had booked up the exhibition space three years in advance (the first slot available), without knowing what the exhibition would be, or whether indeed, there would be an exhibition in the traditional sense.[9] As the work in the West End moved back into the museum with the exhibition, it required Outreach staff to re-align their practice with the structures of the organisation, through a certain level of formalising relations, through interpretation plans, loan agreements and memorandums. It also required negotiating a number of tensions in relation to the institutional understandings of community engagement, in particular their links to ideas of quality, choice and control (Chapter 4). I include a long interview extract here to explore some of these tensions:

When the managers come in here and they are introducing people they describe it as like a community exhibition and by then they've not really had a look at it. And when they are going through, they realise it looks like quite a high-end sort of thing – [and they are thinking] 'oh but I thought this is like a community exhibition' ...

When I was talking [the venue manager] through what this was going to look like she was a bit shocked. One of the questions she asked me was:

'Are these things that participants have selected?'

And I went 'no'.

And she was like 'What!?' Because [senior managers'] idea is that this is Outreach so they'll be some kind of token 'this has been selected by Joe Blogs for this reason'.

And she said 'What about the themes of the exhibition?'

And I kind of said 'The themes aren't stated. This is about the West End'.

'So, you haven't divided it into themes? So, we've just got the objects labels? So, it's just a traditional museum exhibition with random objects?'

And I thought: I haven't just picked these out of a tombola...They're not explicit themes, it's not laid out like 'this is the Asian corner', 'this is the gay corner', 'this is the new West End', 'this is the old West End', but it's just the interesting connections between things whether that's through just aesthetics of what they mean... what can happen a lot is a timeline, a chronology. There's graphic panel which say 'this is what this means', 'this is what that means', and it very paternalistic. There are stories here and narratives but they are more open.

This long interview extract reflects some of the sites of tensions that animate the museum that I have presented in this book. They express the different meanings and purposes of community engagement – as either focused on notions of community 'choice' and 'control' (within the logic of contribution), or as a more embedded, long-term and open view of engagement and its possible outcomes. The extract also highlights some of the practical areas that needed to be negotiated when community engagement as a relational practice was translated into the museum, in particular around interpretation and modes of display. It reveals the tension over the perceived quality – and value – of this work. As I have previously discussed, in a logic of care, the work of community engagement practitioners is also to work within and against their institutions when bringing community projects back into the museum.

In current discussions of museum participation, the focus is on issues of power that are to be resolved by sharing more authority (Lynch and Alberti, 2010; Smith and Waterton, 2009). The relations between the museum and the community are often less than equitable, and in critical accounts of museum collaboration, issues of power are the key concern: the museum co-opts and coerces, and the community is disempowered. In this critical tradition, *West End Stories* might be critiqued for a lack of active involvement of communities in the final exhibition stages. And yet, to suggest that the exhibition was ultimately led by the museum's agenda only and sustained through 'false consensus' (Lynch, 2011) eludes the col*labora*tions that took place, and the ways in which community was influential and emergent in the process. It also problematically erases care as a significant force in these col*labora*tions. In the logic of contribution, the key concerns are authorship, decision-making and control, which are often located at the level of an individual (or group). In the logic of care, engagement is relational and takes place in networks of multiple interest and circumstances where agency can be seen as collectively (if unevenly) distributed since care is a shared accomplishment. When the accomplishment is attributed solely to the curator alone, something is lost, the collective event is traduced. In the logic of care, issues of authorship, decision-making and control are looked at differently. The question is no longer 'how much' control and 'where' is it located in the tug and pull between the museum (at the centre) and the communities (at the periphery), but rather the question becomes about the meaning and quality of relations across the network, extending some legitimacy for museum staff to do the actual work of display, against some of the more negative narratives of co-option. In the example of *West End Stories*, the agency of the creative curatorial act is intimately and inseparably connected to a longer care-ful engagement with the West End. At the same time, as a curatorial act, it acknowledges the role of the institution and institutional power as part of these interactions, as the Outreach workers reflected:

> There is me in this [exhibition], and community, but there's also the museum.

A key feature of current writing on care is to move away from only locating care in the close pair to a focus on how care itself is multidimensional and is produced in everyday interactions as well as extending over space (Barnes, 2015; Milligan and Wiles, 2010). Such a perspective is helpful in drawing attention to how other forms of participation influence and shape museum work. This shifts our understanding of 'co-production' in museum settings away from ladders and spectrums of participation to the multiple scales and settings of interactions and their effects/affects. In the case of *West End Stories*, the results of working through a logic of care led to an exhibition where open narratives could be derived that better avoided nostalgic or essentialising representations of place and community. In the longer-term work of the team in the community, we come to recognise the significant work of community engagement practitioners in bringing the museum out and enrolling it in wider networks of engagements in the West End, enabling the museum to participate in the lives of communities and extending wider geographies of care into its close neighbourhood.

Notes

1 The materials used in this chapter are drawn from ethnographic observations and my time spent with the team, alongside interviews and my own analysis of two exhibitions.

2 There is a range of ways of 'thinking assemblage'. My approach to the concept and metaphor of networks of engagement derives more readily from grounded, ethnographic perspectives.

3 All the interviews in this chapter were conducted between 2012 and 2013 with TWAM Outreach workers.

4 The history of community action in the West End is documented in a community film archive project 'Archives for Change' – http://archiveforchange.org/ (see also Green and Chapman, 1992). Their website captures the history of the area: 'Archive for Change was set up by three filmmakers and local community organisations with the aim of gathering and showcasing films that tell the complex story of this area from the point of view of those who have lived through these many changes, in order to highlight, preserve and celebrate the stories of those who have made the West End the unique place that it is. Stories like those of women who organised creches, credit unions and housing campaigns to defend their estates from poverty and unemployment of the amateur photographers who developed their art by taking to the streets and documenting the demolition and rebuilding of their neighbourhoods during the city's various redevelopment schemes, and stories of life now, in a landscape of constant change'.

5 This programme was later called 'the Network programme' following discussions between myself and the team around the thinking that informs this chapter.

6 St James' worker interview.

7 Ideas about exhibitions as experiments have animated museum studies for some time. Macdonald and Basu (2007) suggest that exhibitions offer formats for experiments when they mix together different concerns that are often considered separate in an effort to create new kinds of social relations. As experiments, such exhibitions differ from the traditional format where the display attempts to communicate information or particular experiences for visitors. Instead, they are produced as messy and complex 'assemblages' that offer 'spaces of encounter', the effects of which are necessarily uncertain (Macdonald and Basu, 2007: 14). Latour and Weibel (2005) describe these kinds of exhibition experiments as 'assembly of assemblies', where the desired outcome of the exhibition is not seeking neat convergence of purpose or meaning.

8 Schorch is writing in the context of curatorial practices across the Pacific. This difference in context is important, and throughout this book, I have been clear and careful to situate my discussion in a UK context, and more generally within social history curatorship.

9 Booking a gallery as a blank space was unprecedented, and this did not sit comfortably in the museum. Such uncertainty is difficult to resolve and accommodate within the certainty-driven world of museums where detailed exhibitions programmes are set up to five years in advance, and work plans, procedures and Gantt charts are the certainty tools through which staff perform and manage their work (Chapter 5).

References

Ames MM (1992) *Cannibal Tours and Glass Boxes: The Anthropology of Museums.* Vancouver: UBC Press.

Anderson B and McFarlane C (2011) Assemblage and geography. *Area* 43(2): 124–127. doi: 10.1111/j.1475-4762.2011.01004.x.

Anderson B, Kearnes M, McFarlane C, et al. (2012) On assemblages and geography. *Dialogues in Human Geography* 2(2): 171–189. doi: 10.1177/2043820612449261.

Barnes M (2015) Beyond the dyad: exploring the multidimensionality of care. In: Barnes M, Brannelly T, Ward L and Ward N. (eds) *Ethics of Care: Critical Advances in International Perspective*. Bristol: Policy Press, pp. 31–44.

Bennett T (1998) *Culture: A Reformer's Science*. London and Thousand Oaks, CA: Sage Publications.

Bennett T, Cameron F, Dias N, et al. (2017) *Collecting, Ordering, Governing: Anthropology, Museums, and Liberal Government*. Cambridge, MA: Duke University Press.

Bouquet M (2001) The art of exhibition-making as a problem of translation. In: Bouquet M (ed.) *Academic Anthropology and the Museum: Back to the Future*. New York: Berghahn Books, pp. 177–197.

Byrne S, Clarke A, Harrison R, et al. (eds) (2011) *Unpacking the Collection: Networks of Material and Social Agency In the Museum*. New York: Springer.

Clifford J (1997) *Routes: Travel and Translation in the Late Twentieth Century*. Cambridge, MA and London: Harvard University Press.

Geerzt C (1988) *Works and Lives: Anthropologist as Author*. Palo Alto, CA: Stanford University Press.

Green J (2017) Action–research in context: Revisiting the 1970s Benwell Community Development Project. *Community Development Journal* 52(2): 269–289. doi: 10.1093/cdj/bsx003.

Green J and Chapman A (1992) The British Community Development Project: Lessons for today. *Community Development Journal* 27(3): 242–258.

Hardt M (1999) Affective labor. *Boundary* 26(2): 89–100.

Harrison R, Byrne S and Clarke A (eds) (2013) *Reassembling the Collection: Ethnographic Museums and Indigenous Agency*. Santa Fe, NM: SAR Press.

Horwood M (2019) *Sharing Authority in the Museum: Distributed Objects, Reassembled Relationships*. Abingdon and New York: Routledge.

Kreps C (2003) Curatorship as social practice. *Curator: The Museum Journal* 46(3): 311–323. doi: 10.1111/j.2151–6952.2003.tb00097.x.

Kretzmann J and McKnight J (1993) *Building Communities from Inside Out: A Path toward Finding and Mobilizing a Community's Assets*. Evanston, IL: Centre for Urban Affairs and Policy Research, Northwestern University.

Latour B (1987) *Science in Action: How to Follow Scientists and Engineers through Society*. Cambridge, MA: Harvard University Press.

Latour B and Weibel P (eds) (2005) *Making Things Public: Atmospheres of Democracy*. Cambridge, MA: MIT.

Lynch BT (2011) *'Whose Cake Is It Anyway?' A Collaborative Investigation into Engagement and Participation in 12 Museums and Galleries in the UK*. London: Paul Hamlyn Foundation.

Lynch BT and Alberti SJMM (2010) Legacies of prejudice: Racism, co-production and radical trust in the museum. *Museum Management and Curatorship* 25(1): 13–35. doi: 10.1080/09647770903529061.

Macdonald S (2009) Reassembling Nuremberg, reassembling heritage. *Journal of Cultural Economy* 2(1–2): 117–134. doi: 10.1080/17530350903064121.

Macdonald S and Basu P (2007) Introduction: Experiments in exhibition. In: Macdonald S and Basu P (eds) *Exhibition Experiments*. Oxford: Blackwell, pp. 1–24.

Mar P and Anderson K (2012) Urban curating the 'interspaces' of art collaboration in Western Sydney. *Space and Culture* 15(4): 330–343. doi: 10.1177/1206331212460623.

Mathie A and Cunningham G (2003) From clients to citizens: Asset-based Community Development as a strategy for community-driven development. *Development in Practice* 13(5): 474–486. doi: 10.1080/0961452032000125857.

Milligan C and Wiles J (2010) Landscapes of care. *Progress in Human Geography* 34(6): 736–754. doi: 10.1177/0309132510364556.

Robinson F (2005) Regenerating the West End of Newcastle: What went wrong? *Northern Economic Review* 36: 15–42.

Schorch P (2017) Assembling communities: Curatorial practices, material cultures, and meanings. In Onciul B, Stefano ML and Hawke S (eds) *Engaging Heritage – Engaging Communities*. Martlesham: Boydell & Brewer, pp. 31–46.

Smith L and Waterton E (2009) *Heritage, Communities and Archaeology*. London: Gerald Duckworth & Co.

Tolia-Kelly DP, Waterton E and Watson S (2016) *Heritage, Affect and Emotion: Politics, Practices and Infrastructures*. Abingdon and New York: Routledge.

Witcomb A (2003) *Re-Imagining the Museum: Beyond the Mausoleum*. London: Routledge.

Yúdice G (2003) *The Expediency of Culture: Uses of Culture in the Global Era*. Durham, NC: Duke University Press.

Part IV
Social care in the museum

7　The museum as a space of social care

The idea of care surfaced in this book is about the proactive interest in the needs of another, and the provision of what is necessary to meet these needs. What would the idea of care look like if applied to the whole museum? What are the possibilities of care for expanding the contemporary social role of the museum? In this final chapter, I weave together arguments and ideas explored across the book to answer these two questions. I begin by offering a different perspective on the current logic of contribution in museums' participatory practice, as presented in Chapter 2, by outlining a logic of care in community engagement. I then consider what the notion of care would look like if we applied it to other areas of museum practice, focusing on management, front-of-house and curatorship. In doing so, I review and address the different barriers to community engagement work – as a form of care work – that I identified during my research and suggest some ways forward. As the close analysis of the case study of Tyne & Wear Archives & Museums (TWAM) makes clear, community engagement workers often experience institutions as resistant to their work – existing care practices are currently embedded in unsatisfactory contexts. In Chapters 4–6, I described the institutional work of community engagement workers as they aim to ensure community needs and concerns are brought back into the museum. Care practices are a matter of negotiating institutional arrangements and organisational structures on the way to transforming the museum. The museum as a space of social care that I describe in this final chapter is perhaps 'yet-to-be-realised' completely (see Chapter 2) but we can find instances of this museum in the varied practices of the community engagement staff at TWAM that I have followed throughout this book. Drawing all this work together enables me to describe the museum as a space of social care more fully and its wider capacities and potentialities.

Arriving at the end of this book as we have, we can begin to envisage the possible shape and purpose of the museum as a space of social care. Moving beyond TWAM and drawing in examples from other museums and art galleries, in this final chapter, I expand the terms of my argument to explore what a framework for social care can offer contemporary museum practice. The concept of 'social care' serves to connect the discrete caring practices of community engagement workers to the wider social role of the museum. While my main concern across this book was to examine every-day practice 'close up' to understand its logics, the discussion of social care in this final part offers a framework for thinking through the new role of the museum within wider landscapes of formal care and beyond, linking current community engagement work to the growing area of practice in health and wellbeing, and to wider concerns of museum practice and ethics. I propose social care as a wider orientation in the museum that holds the capacity to transform the institution's ability to create value for society in the twenty-first century. Social care provides a deeper focus on individuals and groups who experience marginalisation or disadvantage *and* considers the public function of the museum more fundamentally. To present a theory of social care in the museum, I draw explicitly on an ethics of care as a feminist philosophical perspective (following Virginia Held, Joan Tronto and Marian Barnes, amongst others) and from research in geography. The articulation of the museum as a space of social care completes this book.

The logic of care in the museum

In this book, I have examined care in the practices of outreach workers within community engagement sessions inside the museum with small groups and in the work they do off-site, assembling communities in their lo-calities through their participation in networks of engagement. My aim was to describe care in a precise way, as it takes form in museum work of engage-ment. I argued that care in the museum takes on distinct relational, material and affective dimensions involving museum objects and creative activities. I also argued that care is fundamental to museum participatory practice: without care, attempts to broaden access to a wider range of people in mu-seums are likely to fail. If care is not attended to, if it is not talked about and if it is not recognised as work, as a purposeful effort and a mindful stance, then the felt qualities of community engagement risk being eroded – we risk taking the 'heart' out of engagement with museums.

The practice of care in the museum is about providing emotional support through listening, encouragement, compassion and kindness, and providing practical support by offering opportunities to develop creative skills, con-fidence and interests, while all the time being sensitive to access and other practical needs. These practices support spaces of care in the museum that are made up of a multitude of ordinary yet sensitive caring acts, such as tak-ing time to share cups of tea, making small talk and listening, gently holding a person's hand and generally being friendly and approachable. Spaces of care in the museum also function through opportunities to socialise and relate with others and through engagement with museum materialities. In their most powerful form, they enable participants to reconnect with their sense of identity and their creative selves. The 'museumness' of care is differ-ent to the formal care that individuals might be accessing; it is about using museum objects and spaces, and culture more widely, as one respondent put it, to 'help people to cope with what life throws at you'. Museum staff are active in these caring activities, but spaces of care are essentially shared accomplishments with participants because care is relational. Care practices also extend beyond the intimate settings of community engagement sessions into wider networks of engagement in the community through the sustained practices of outreach, linking the museum into its locality.

Through this close examination of engagement work, we come to recognise the abilities needed for 'good' community engagement. As I noted at the start of the book, throughout, I have sought to understand the mode and style of this complex arena that might describe its 'good work' (rather than a focus on 'best practice'). Following Annemarie Mol, it is the logic of care that needs to be first understood to distil what makes 'good care' and therefore, good community engagement work. While Mol's work is based in the diabetes clinic, she anticipates the wider applications of her argument, but she also notes that 'when transported to other sites and situations, the logic of care (...) will have to be translated' (2010: 105). In the museum, the logic of care is translated into the practices of community engagement workers, and in my own attempts to articulate it in textual form. Community engagement is not simply a skill but it is also talent, intuition and insight: the ability to sense what is needed, when and what form it should take. It is a quality acquired through experience and commitment. This further situates emotions at the centre of the museum and museum practice. For the museum professionals involved, care is work as well as an emotion or intention. It is an affective stance and practical competence, a form of museum work that has its own logic: a logic of care. The logic of care articulated in this book originates from the specific sites and situations of my research. Even so, the implications of care are much wider.

The logic of care is presented as an alternative to the logic of contribution that currently dominates practice and scholarship in museum studies. In Chapter 2, I outlined a prevalent logic of contribution, where community engagement (and participation more generally) is conceptualised as a form of contribution to the museum (an object, a story, a bequest, visitor responses, etc.). The logic of contribution cuts across a number of theoretical positions for community engagement practice that constitute the participatory turn in museum studies. One particular feature of community engagement in the museum, I argued, is its ambivalence, most notably its constitutive dynamic of distance and proximity, holding together the public function of the museum (in relation to a broadly undifferentiated community) *and* its specific inclusion work with defined groups. The case of TWAM elucidates the ambivalence of community engagement, as a capacious term that encompasses all manner of activity. This ambivalence, I suggested, is an inherent feature of the contemporary museum.

The ambivalence of community engagement also shapes the potential and promise of community engagement practice. In the logic of contribution, community engagement promises the democratising and pluralising of museum spaces and practices and the possibility to disrupt existing power structures through empowering participants. However, it is first and foremost an institutional logic that reflects the political rationality of the museum (after Bennett, 1995). Contribution is set within the museum's invitation, where the contribution is primarily for the benefit of the museum (better knowledge, more relevant displays, more diverse audiences, etc.). Ultimately, participation is bound up with securing the legitimacy of the museum, and it returns its institutional form improved, but mostly intact. The critical scholarship on participation in museums has been crucial in naming the uneven power dynamics that continue to shape museum participation and its potential negative effects on participants. It also reveals the invisible power and the 'habits of mind' that undermine well-meaning intentions. My research at TWAM shows how the mundane, bureaucratic features of the museum-as-organisation also get in the way of this work. I also argued that the institution's commitment to community engagement is a non-performative speech act, which while seeming to commit the whole organisation to this work, in practice, it remains the responsibility of certain teams. The importance of the critical work on participation is that it diagnoses the problem of engagement: while invoking ideas of choice and control, participation often ends up as little more than tokenism or 'empowerment-lite', and it is kept at the margins through project-based work. However, the critique of participation is also optimistic for a modified participatory practice that might better accommodate participant choice and control and bring participation into the centre of the museum. I question this conceptual approach, since, as I argued in Chapter 2, the proposed solution is shaped within the same logic of contribution. This suggests a critical impasse, whereby the literature is caught in a critique-contest cycle (Graham, 2012). But in order to understand why this matters, we need to look at practice and the different ways in which activities work and do not work in particular sites and situations, or where they work, but only partially. From here, other logics come to the fore: other ways of explaining the rationale of practice that respond to what is appropriate and logical to do in the varied contexts of community engagement work. For instance, what is required in community engagement sessions with social care service users and patients and how to respond during a community exhibitions process. Within each of these particular sites and situations described in the book, participant choice and control were important, but there were also all manner of other ways of relating taking place and other factors at play. Together, these make up what I describe as the logic of care.

The starting point of the logic of care reverses the starting point of the logic of contribution: the question is no longer 'what can the community do for the museum?'. Rather it becomes 'what can the museum do for the community?' While this might appear deceptively simple, this requires ontological, epistemological and political shifts in our approach to community engagement in the museum. The first shift required is a focus on relations as central to community engagement. In the logic of care, contributions to the museum may be part of the process (indeed, and especially, individuals giving stories and objects to the museum and being heard when they have been excluded *is* immensely powerful), but it is just one aspect of what is going on. To be clear, the logic of care translated into the museum is not a direct opposite of the logic of contribution, but rather an alternative. Indeed, there is still an important materiality to care in the museum: stories and objects, including objects held by the museum or contributed by participants, have an important role to play in relations of care. They offer powerful points of connections both for ourselves and towards others. As Chapter 5 made clear, there is a distinctive materiality to the 'museumness' of care. The logic of care includes objects (as contributions) but draws our attention firmly onto relational matters.

The logic of care presupposes that we all need care. Care is important because it is part of everyday life – we have all received care at different points in our lives and at times we have been called upon to care for others. This entanglement needs to be recognised. In current discussions of participation in the logic of contribution, the focus is on the principles of choice and control: you choose what you contribute and you control your involvement. In this logic, power is treated as a resource that can be redistributed in a way that is singular and unidirectional. Typically, once a choice is made, that is usually when the relationship ends. There is reciprocity involved, but this is defined primarily in the relations organised around the contribution. The logic of care encompasses more: it is an ongoing process of to and fro. It exceeds reciprocity. 'Choice' and 'control' are aspects only of relations amongst a range of emotional engagements, affective encounters and forms of mutual support. My first concern here is nearly prosaic: without care, I have argued, attempts to include a wider range of people in museums are likely to fail. Recognising community engagement as care work is therefore critical. While all the different acts of care I described across this book may seem simple and diffuse, as Parr et al. (2004: 406) suggest, they 'demonstrate the reality of inclusion' and the acts and actions through which we come to feel included. In the logic of care, choice and control are no longer the defining facts of participation. Annemarie Mol is clear here: in her view, the logic of care 'is not preoccupied with our will, and what we may opt for, but concentrates on what we do' (Mol, 2010: 8). What matters then are the kinds of activities and relationships we engage with, as participants and as museum professionals. This in turn requires that we consider not just the forms of participation (such as in the 'ladder of participation' model) but also the content, product, processes, materialities, relationships and emotional dimensions of community engagement. Within a logic of care, we come to view participatory accomplishments in more distributed terms. Expectations are nurtured in proactive caring relations, where different kinds of expertise and knowledges (in the plural) are recognised, and outputs are established on collaborative terms.

A second consideration when talking about care in the museum requires that we reconsider the 'welfare model' critique of participation set forward by Lynch, especially in the context of the programmes that I described in Chapter 5. This argument suggests that engagement practices have been dominated by a disabling language and patronising practice of 'doing to' or 'on behalf of' participants. However, if we take a view of care as a shared accomplishment in which care-recipients are active in shaping relations of care, as I put forward in Chapter 5, we can hold onto this important critique, without necessarily abandoning the notion of welfare in the public museum. My point here is that care and empowerment are not always opposed, and caring is not always simply paternalistic, where care-givers assume that they know better than care-receivers what they need. This would not be good care. However, the logic of care must also be sensitive to the dangers of paternalism and tokenism. Indeed, this is often an accusation that writers of care come up against. The ideal of care cannot ignore the ways in which caring is also used to exert power through force or manipulation. This discussion has been central to debates between feminists and disability activists (Bondi, 2008; Kröger, 2009; Watson et al., 2004). These debates emphasise the importance of emotions to caring relationships by calling attention to the ways in which power is itself embedded in emotions and affective relations (Lawson, 2007). In the case of the museum, the logic of care still requires scrutiny of uneven power structures in the museum (historical and contemporary) and the power relations that animate participation work, including the ways in which emotional connections are themselves sites of power. Examining the complexity of caring relations allows us to more deeply understand the operation of power across a range of scales and sites without dismissing care altogether, as feminist philosopher Virginia Held makes clear:

> When we focus on relations, we can come to see how to shape good caring relations so that differences in power will not be pernicious and so that the vulnerable are empowered. Good caring relations can involve not only mutual recognition of moral equality but practices that avoid subtle as well as blatant coercion where it is disrespectful and inconsiderate. We can foster trust and mutuality in place of benevolent domination. Caring persons may often need to exercise power, but they will also understand how best to do so and especially how to avoid doing so in ways that become violent and damaging.
>
> (Held, 2006: 56)

The logic of care is not opposed to independence, choice and control (following Held, we might instead think of its opposite as neglect). While we tend to associate dependence with powerlessness and independence with power, these associations can be misleading. Care instead underlines interdependence as a fundamental human condition. Care also recognises that certain communities and people are more vulnerable than others. However, care does not promote a dependency relationship between people but talks about maintaining a relationship of interdependence and mutual efforts, opportunities and benefits. As the geographers Milligan and Wiles suggest, 'care-givers do not simply do things for people; they also support them with encouragement, personal attention, and communication in ways that endorse a *mutual* sense of identity and self worth' (2010: 738 emphasis in original). In the example of TWAM, this interdependence was clear in the way staff think about and talk about their practice, and how mutual efforts shape their sense of professional identity and the value of their work in relation to ideas of care, community and the wider social role of the museum. Care and welfare therefore have a place in the museum.

Next, the orientation to care in the museum requires that we reconsider how we value and recognise community engagement work in the museum. In the logic of contribution, the idea of professional skills is focused on taking care of the contribution (in whatever form); as such, it tends to recognise and privilege those traditional museum skills of care and custodianship of culture (material and/or intangible). In the logic of care, 'taking care' is much more expansive and encompasses people, relationships and contributions. The skills that are valued are those that facilitate and support caring relations and the creation and maintenance of spaces of care. The logic of care takes shape through the affective labour of museum workers and the emotional dimensions of community engagement sessions. In fact, the logic of care insists on the centrality of relations and emotions for 'doing' community engagement work. By deciding what is appropriate or logical to do in each site and situation, care is manifest in the museum as a shared accomplishment that is often fragile and fleeting. As a museum practice, it is persistent and deeply involved. It is the ongoing work of producing and sustaining spaces of care in the museum where people are supported and are enabled to connect with culture and heritage. These differences mark it out from the logic of contribution where the museum worker is usually presented as a neutral facilitator who must divest their control, and where the participant is positioned as a self-directing subject. In the logic of care, a proactive and attentive engagement in the wellbeing of participants is required, and interdependencies are highlighted. In the logic of care, participants are not the 'target group' as they sometimes are in the logic of contribution; rather they are partners in the practices of care and the practices that make the museum. Such a proactive engagement in relations of care can help challenge aspects of the invisible power at play in the museum as diagnosed by Lynch (2011a, 2011b). This can (and should) mean that 'habits of mind' – that shape museum work in terms of what is inevitable, usual or expected – are less easily returned to, since caring is a matter of 'attentive experimentation' (Mol et al., 2010: 2) in specific sites and situations.

Finally, the logic of contribution reflects the periphery/centre dynamic that animates museum studies, aiming to move participation from the margins to the core of the organisation. The logic of care takes a different view:

as a practice, it moves in and out of the museum. In Chapter 6, I considered the practices surrounding a community-focused exhibition. In the logic of contribution, engagement work of this type is typically focused on going out to collect stories and objects to bring back into the museum. The relationship is ultimately about coming back to the centre, with the museum as the focal point. When this work is framed as 'co-production', the key concerns are authorship, decision-making and control, with the community as an agential and external actor working at the museum's 'core'. In the logic of care, the networks of engagement are more distributed: the museum is just one point within a larger network of organisations, people, things and ideas. Within such a network, agency (and by extension the capacity to act and make decisions) is understood as distributed between the multiple interests and circumstances of diverse actors. In this view, 'community' is assembled and produced in the networks of engagement themselves. This opens up other ways of conceptualising curatorial acts in the museum as another significant aspect of community engagement practice (though, admittedly, not always recognised institutionally as such). The case of *West End Stories* reveals a deep and genuine care for community, investing large amounts of time over sustained periods, engaging in a range of activities, many of which directly served the community rather than the museum. The logic of care implies this more attentive, time-consuming and care-ful involvement of the museum in the lives of communities. This is a different orientation to the logic of contribution, which would focus more narrowly on bringing the community (usually defined as targeted groups) into the museum and its institutional functions.

Crucially, care provides a different way of thinking in the museum. Then, let us look at the first question of this final chapter: what would the idea of care look like if applied to the whole museum?

Care in organisations

One of the aims of this book was to consider the institutional life of community engagement workers: how they experience their institutions as resistant and their institutional work in negotiating this resistance. It is therefore fitting to consider how we might apply care across the organisational settings of the museum, drawing on the logic of care that was surfaced in earlier chapters, in an effort to address some of the barriers to participatory work. To do so, it is useful to turn to the work of Joan Tronto (2010), who has examined care in institutional contexts. Much research has focused on the caring that goes on in state institutions, such as healthcare institutions, and the *failures* of care in institution that are, or have become, increasingly faceless, hierarchical and bureaucratic; where profit drives relations with those who are cared for. Tronto argues that it is possible to use the principles of caring as a means of resisting a wider 'uncaring' institutional culture. Her starting point is to acknowledge that institutional caring requires attention to be paid to three key areas: purpose (a shared awareness of the ends of care to shape a common purpose); power (recognition and dialogue around relations of power inside and outside of the organisation) and 'particularity/plurality' (the 'attention to human activities as particular and admitting of other possible ways of doing them and to diverse humans having diverse preferences about how needs might be met' (2010: 162)). During my research for this book, I found instances of an institutional culture that was resistant to community engagement work. While not 'uncaring', neither was it always care-ful. Furthermore, the museum is (and always has been) an institution where there are many frictions and competing demands. To consider how we might apply ideas of care across the museum, I look at three further areas of contemporary museum: management, front-of-house and curatorship (furthering ideas presented in Chapter 6). In each case, I ask what would care look like if applied to each area of work. Though not exhaustive of all museum functions,[1] as key areas of museum work, they provide an opportunity to outline the implications of care across the institution of the museum.

Caring management

For management, taking forward ideas of care would mean understanding the process of caring across the organisation. This would begin with addressing the institutional commitment to community engagement. As I discussed in Chapter 3, current institutional commitments are predominantly non-performative: 'they do not bring about the effects they name' (Ahmed, 2012: 17). Caring relations are marked out by the responsibility to act: it is not enough to name this commitment, since to name only does not invoke commitment to action. In my discussion, I suggested that different teams understand community engagement in accordance to their own working practices and specialised domains, engaging with this practice either at a distance or in a proximate way. The non-performative nature of institutional commitment in the museum is further complicated by these multiple understandings of community engagement and *the effects they ought to have* because the effects that it names are multiple and directed towards different purposes – either for the public, visitors or specific groups. Community engagement occupies an ambivalent place in museum practice, holding together the museum's public function and its specific work of inclusion. Furthermore, community engagement (and participation more widely) is currently formulated within a logic of contribution, with the benefits aimed first towards the museum. While my study focused on a sole institution, these issues apply to different types of museums in different international contexts. There is therefore a role for managers in museums of different size with different collections to surface this ambivalence and the different understandings of community engagement across their teams, not necessarily to resolve these or collapse them into a single definition, but rather to work through these differences across teams towards a more clearly defined common goal; in Tronto's term, towards a shared purpose. This would also mean working through the different scales of this work to create closer correspondences between immediate relationships with communities and relations at a distance with the more abstract notion of the 'public'.

Another problem I identified during my research was the dual conceptualisation of community engagement in the museum as both an overarching ethos ('everything we do') and the set responsibility of a single specific team. There is, therefore, an important responsibility for managers to be clear about whose role it is to do community engagement, and how, across different areas of museum work. While I believe that a focus on caring relations could (in fact should) be applied across all museum work, it does not necessarily follow that all staff will be engaged in this work equally or that all staff will become directly involved in 'front line' community engagement work. Key for managers are the skills of dealing with complexity to help resolve conflicts (even if only temporarily) across the different functions of the museum as they arise in the articulation of a common purpose focused around care. To this end, they will need and reflect on particularity/plurality as it emerges in museum work: how the institution understands its caring responsibilities and how these are allocated; what it is trying to achieve for communities and society, in the short term and in the future; how it balances the needs of current and future stakeholders, and the interests of close and more distant communities, and which demands are taken as legitimate; how it negotiates demands within itself, for example, pressures around income generation. As Tronto makes clear, no caring institution 'can function well without (...) a *political space* within which this essential part of caring can occur' (2010: 168 emphasis in original). It follows that for Tronto, a practical requirement is that hierarchies are flattened in caring institutions. While she recognises, as I do, that this is perhaps easier said than done, it is likely to result in a better organisation of the contradictory demands on museums. For managers, this would mean bringing together more often groups of staff from across teams and seniority levels, and where appropriate, community members, to raise questions about the conflicting functions and contested demands on museums, and about how to best meet the needs of the people they serve. There is an interesting parallel here in terms of formal care institutions, where good care relies on multidisciplinary teams working together – nurses, occupational therapists, doctors, specialists, patients and family members coming together to provide a holistic approach to needs. Using this model in the museum to create deliberative spaces to address purpose, power and particularity/plurality, in order to resolve conflicting demands within the institution and among organisational actors and wider constituents, will better the chances of implementing care across the institution.

This brings us to the role of managers in addressing the institutional structures and cultures that currently block community engagement work: the 'black lines' faced by community engagement practitioners. In my research, several areas of tensions were identified, some structural, such as the short-termism of engagement work and its 'bolt-on' approach in exhibition programming. Others are more complex, such the effects of audit culture, organisational silos, the wider impasses around hierarchies of expertise and notions of quality in museum work, and the dominant narratives of participation as a risk area where expectations need to be managed. There are other ways to examine and resolve these tensions if we approach them through the logic of care. Again, creating more spaces for a variety of staff to discuss these tensions can lead to better resolution towards a more caring balance in the museum and a way to begin to overcome some organisational silos. This in turn requires that care is considered seriously as a way of working. Indeed, placing care in the institution is a requirement not only to care for community needs; workers also need to feel cared for. This must begin with recognising and valuing care practices and affective labour in the museum. Moving care into the routines of the museum is not an easy task, but one which I believe is worth doing. As I described in Chapter 4, community engagement work does not fit well within current operating structures, and as such, it is misunderstood and undervalued. The emotional and practical work of caring is not visible as 'immaterial labour', and it is not recognised in either a professional 'museographic' context or in the administrative structures of the organisation. There is an important role for managers to formally value this work as professional museum work and to recognise the skills and knowledges it requires; how these skills can be nurtured through professional development that engages more directly with staff identities, values and ambitions; how they are acknowledged in administrative structures such as job descriptions, appraisals and annual reviews; as well as rewarding contributions that are not solely linked to targets or income generation but are more relational (and potentially immaterial) in nature. There is also a need to recognise the different types of resources and time (significant amounts of time) required for this work, linked to its inherent uncertainty, as well as a need for different approaches to evaluating its effectiveness since it is always work in progress. This is not an argument against any form of organisational oversight or management, since care needs to be evaluated to be recognised as good care. However, current modes of performance management need to be revised to better reflect and capture this work. To this end, managers need to be more attentive and responsive to the ambitions and concerns of their teams. As one Outreach team member put it:

> they need to outreach to the organisation. Senior management kind of need to work with us like we work with community groups: we ask questions, we come to their place, we drink coffee, we discuss stuff, we have conversations, we collaborate, we use mutual language.

Managers need to develop their own practices of attentiveness to ensure that they better understand the more ethical core of engagement work, as well as understanding the arrangements that are required to sustain such ways of working, and to consider practical solutions within the current structures of organisations in order to translate these into real support. Staff need to feel that management have their 'best interest at heart' and to see this reflected in decision-making.

Taking care of staff is also about recognising the need to nurture an appropriate level of professional autonomy to ensure that organisations are vibrant and innovative and that staff derive job satisfaction. This may require greater levels of trust, for example, when staff spend time outside of the museum. In their discussion of managing complexity in museums, Janes and Sandell (2007: 5) make an important call for minimising hierarchical structures and promoting creativity through self-organisation: 'this requires that managers respect and nurture the so-called informal leaders – those individuals who exercise influence and authority by virtue of their competence and commitment, and not because of any formal position in the hierarchy'. Trust underpins care in a relational sense. From a management perspective, it also needs to be linked to courage to allow organisational members to experiment and it requires the exercise of 'lenient judgments' where these experimentations fail (von Krogh, 1998). In the context of community engagement work, supporting this form of autonomy and informal leadership is key to enabling collective decisions made outside of the museum with the community to come back into the institution.

To talk about care in museum work, in the second part of this book, I spoke about the emotional life of community engagement workers. If we recognise and understand caring work as affective labour, and we recognise the often extremely emotional contexts in which community engagement practitioners are working with marginalised and vulnerable groups, we need to take into account the emotional impact of this work on museum professionals, and the work that they do to manage their emotions. For managers, there are serious considerations here in relation to the provision of care in the institution in terms of appropriate supervision and support. Finally, there is an urgency in all this discussion of care. The research presented in this book took place against a backdrop of cut-backs and staff restructures in the context of austerity. In the UK, at the time of writing, there is little indication that this trend is reversing, while globally, funding for culture is rarely guaranteed. Employment in the museum sector remains highly competitive and often precarious. Management needs to recognise the profound effects of austerity and precarity on staff. Under these conditions, a commitment to care across the institution, into the routines of the organisation, and its relations with external partners, needs to be consciously developed and proactively implemented on the way to transforming the museum.

Other caring professional roles: front-of-house and curatorial staff

I want to now consider briefly two further areas of museum work. Front-of-house are a key staff group that can support the creation of caring institutions by virtue of their particular position at the 'face' of the institution. This is done on a first level by welcoming visitors, acknowledging them and showing appreciation for their visit. It requires front-of-house to demonstrate warmth and responsive friendless to make visitors feel that they are being taken into account and that they are not being judged upon entering the museum. This is of course part of 'customer service' but it is also about the proactive and persistent work of creating safe, welcoming and inclusive spaces for all who come to the museum. As I discussed in Chapter 5, spaces of care are inherently fragile accomplishments that need to be worked at and reworked every day. As the first person visitors meet when entering the museum, this first impression of care (or lack thereof) is important to all that follows. Much research has highlighted how the museum experience starts before the arrival and continues well after the visit (Falk and Dierking, 1992). The entrance to the museum is a singular and symbolic space, the physicality of which marks out certain rule-settings: 'museum thresholds are places were trust and expectations are built, protocols established and affordances noted' (Parry et al., 2018: 2–3). Within these thresholds, there is also the potential for caring practices. Without care at the entrance of the museum, it is likely that for a number of visitors, a first impression of the museum as an uncaring institution might have long-lasting effects in cementing a feeling that they do not belong or are not welcome in these cultural spaces. Front-of-house significantly contribute to the success of a visit, whether it be for entertainment, education or both. They help (or hinder) the rest of the museum experience. As such, the impact of their role is fundamental, and it can powerfully be re-asserted and re-valued organisationally through the idea of care. Some museums around the world do pay close attention to this role. Leeds Museums and Galleries in the UK is one example, where the work of welcome from their front-of-house staff is institutionally recognised and was externally acknowledged in 2018 through a 'Family Friendly' award from the charity Kids in Museums. There will likely be numerous other examples from practice. However, it is notable that front-of-house are a professional group that is rarely written about in academic contexts. Their significant role as the face of the institution and their professional skills deserve closer consideration for better understanding the wider social role of the museum.

A final group I want to consider is those staff members with curatorial roles. In Chapter 6, I argued that the logic of care extends care for objects in the museums to caring about ways of working together and caring for the relations and settings in which stories and objects come to be shared. As I noted in the previous chapter, care is central to the work of curating. Indeed, it derives its etymology from the Latin 'curare', which means 'to take care'. What I am also proposing is a thinking through care in a more expansive sense – bringing together care for objects and care for ideas, stories, people and places. This provides a much broader sense of care from which to discuss the contemporary work of museums of curatorship. However, we need to recognise that curatorial staff work differently with communities and for different reasons (see Chapter 2 on the different traditions of community engagement). At the same time, there are many opportunities for curatorial staff and community engagement workers to work more collaboratively to support each other's work. In a practical sense, curatorial staff will need to provide more collections access and support for outreach projects, and outreach staff will need to enable more direct connections with community groups. This can lead to a more mutual rather than adversarial ways of working between teams, which can support new cultures of participatory museum practice that break out of current organisational silos. There are also implications of care in terms of the preparation, execution and follow-through of curatorial projects. Setting this work in a logic of care rather than a logic of contribution would require curatorial staff being more open to communities about a whole variety of museum processes, for example, how the museum will take care of an object, what it will be used for, what information will go around it, when the opening will be, what will happen afterwards and where possible, keeping in touch over time (see also Graham et al., 2013 on the notion of 'courtesy' in museum-community relations). It will also require being clear about the terms of the collaboration and where there are restrictions, towards more informed and co-equal forms of exchange. It might also require curatorial staff spending more time outside of the museum to become involved alongside community engagement practitioners in more distributed networks of engagement in local or distant communities. There are of course examples of curatorial practice that follows these principles (see Kreps, 2003). But what is notable from my close study of TWAM, and bringing together wider studies of museum cultures in the UK (Lynch, 2011b), is that there are significant divides between curatorial and outreach roles and their approaches to community engagement that lead to significant tensions within organisations. My aim is not to pit curatorial work against community engagement work, but rather to bring them closer together, either as more blurred roles or as more directly connected teams where specific skill sets are recognised and equally valued. The approach to multidisciplinary team working may well depend on the museum itself, since I am not implying that all museum workers need necessarily take on community engagement roles; rather, there needs to be more structural connections between these different teams to enable externally facing care work.

Across different roles such as front-of-house and curatorial, the development of a logic of care that I am here advocating will necessarily take different orientations in relation to the other tasks, priorities and skills associated with these areas of museum work. If logics are contingent and context-specific, and the knowledges relevant to care practices are particular to specific, local situations (Mol et al., 2010), we need to consider what holds care together in a wider sense so that we are able to recognise it as 'good care' (and recognise when it is not). So, in this next part, I fold the logic of care into a wider *ethics of care* to situate care as both a set of prac-tices *and* a system of values that can be embedded across the museum. As Mol makes clear, ideas of care 'do not separate out ethical from other norms (be they professional, technical, economical or practical)' (Mol et al., 2010: 13). Turning to the work on ethics of care is therefore imperative to examine how care might be used to transform the museum, first from an organisa-tional perspective, and second, in a museological sense.

Ethics of care

To talk about a 'logic' of care is to look at how care is done in everyday prac-tices and in everyday spaces. It is not about defining care as a fixed thing, but rather it is about articulating the practices that underpin forms of caring, in my case, in the context of care for people in the museum. Caring practices are the starting point for an *ethics of care*.

The ethics of care is both normative and contextual. It involves reason-ing from the particular. Local solutions to specific situations need to be de-veloped to work towards 'good' care: 'the good is not something to pass judgment on, in general terms and from the outside, but something to *do*, in practice, as care goes on' (Mol et al., 2010: 13 emphasis in original). Sara Ruddick describes this link between the practice of care and its ethics:

> the 'ethics' of care is provoked by the habits and challenges of the work, makes sense of its aims, and spurs and reflects upon the self-understanding of workers. The ethics also extends beyond the activities from which it arises, generating a stance (or standpoint) towards 'nature', human rela-tionships and social institutions.
>
> (Ruddick, 1998: 21)

Scholarship on the ethics of care has now moved beyond its original for-mulations in the private realms of care between two people (usually mother and child) as represented in the foundational works of Nel Noddings (1984) and Carol Gilligan (1982) and has become a much broader feminist moral philosophy with relevance to the organisation and reproduction of pub-lic life and public ethics more generally (Barnes, 2006; Held, 2006; Kittay, 1999; Slote, 2007; Tronto, 1993, 2013). The basis of this work is the recog-nition of the value of caring relations in private contexts as having a direct importance to all human life. An ethics of care starts with a conception of 'persons as relational and interdependent, morally and epistemologically' rather than self-sufficient and independent (Held, 2006: 13). Individuals ex-ist in complex social networks where care is central to these networks: 'the self can only exist through and with others, and vice versa' (Sevenhuijsen, 2000: 9). For all of us, there are periods of our lives when circumstances mean that we need the care and support of others (families and profession-als) to help with our everyday lives. For some of us, the need for regular, skilled care is a precious necessity. Other times, we will be called upon to care for someone else. More fundamentally, we need relationships with others throughout our lives to grow, learn and experience wellbeing. Care involves meeting our needs and those of others; it takes shape in the acknowledgement of this dependence.

Following Virginia Held, to clarify care, we need to attend to and clarify caring relations. Such a perspective requires that we recognise our interdependencies and calls on us to take responsibility for these relations. The ethics of care is based in this relational ontology. An often-quoted definition for care and its relations is found in the work of Joan Tronto and Berenice Fisher (1990: 40; Tronto, 1993: 103), who describe care broadly as:

> a species activity that includes everything we do to maintain, continue, and repair our 'world' so that we can live in it as well as possible. That world includes our bodies, our selves, and our environment, all of which we seek to interweave in a complex, life-sustaining web.

Tronto describes caring across four phases: *caring about, caring for, care giving* and *care receiving*. This frames care practices across four elements: attentiveness (being attentive to the needs of others), responsibility (arising from the recognition of meeting these needs), competence (carrying through the intention to provide care) and responsiveness (recognising the experience of the care receiver in order to know that care has taken place and recognising our own vulnerabilities) (see also Tronto, 1993, 1995, 2013). This also underlines the significance of care as co-constituted by care-giver and care-receiver, resonating with social disability studies that demand that the agency of care-recipients is recognised (Fine and Glendinning, 2005). All four elements of care are evident across the museum settings I have described in this book, and we could go back and look at my discussion through these ideas: *caring about*, the attentiveness to different group needs and welcoming participants over the museum threshold; *caring for*, taking the responsibility to make sure needs are met, for instance, ensuring people feel they are in safe spaces free of stigma; *care giving*, where staff use creative activities to lift peoples' mood and develop the competence and necessary resources to support specific needs through partnerships with formal care service workers; *care receiving*, developing bespoke programmes that respond to people's interests and gathering feedback during sessions and the end of a project. The work of the Outreach team in the West End, as a more diffuse programme of work, also points to a wider sense of 'caring about' a community. This signals the much broader significance of care beyond interpersonal activities. Care ethics can help us to think this through.

Within an ethics of care perspective, 'care' goes beyond the activities of care to describe a wider set of attitudes and virtues at the centre of a serious moral philosophy so that 'a caring person will cultivate mutuality in the interdependencies of personal, political, economic, and global contexts' (Held, 2006: 53). Care is therefore a practice and a value:

> As a practice, [care] shows us how to respond to needs and why we should. It builds trust and mutual concern and connectedness between persons. It is not a series of individual actions, but a practice that develops, along with its appropriate attitudes. It has attributes and standards that can be described, but more important that can be recommended and that should be continually improved as adequate care comes closer to being good care (...) In addition to being a practice, care is also a value. Caring persons and caring attitudes should be valued, and we can organize many evaluations of how persons are interrelated around a constellation of moral considerations associated with care or its absence. ...The values of caring are especially exemplified in caring relations, rather than in persons as individuals. (...) The ethics of care build relations of care and concern and mutual responsiveness to need on both the personal and wider social level. (...) The ethics of care provides a way of thinking about and evaluating both the more immediate and the more distant human relations with which to develop morally acceptable societies.
>
> (Held, 2006: 42–43)

Through Held, we can see the wider significance of care ethics. While the majority of research in this area has examined interpersonal and gendered care relations, an equally important body of work has considered the value of care ethics within institutions in the applied contexts of social work and nursing and in wider social policy (Haylett, 2003; Sevenhuijsen, 2003, 2000; Tronto, 2010). This opens up the possibilities to situate care ethics in the museum and in cultural policy. Furthermore, by drawing attention to our reciprocal relations with and reliance on others, the ethics of care also extends to a critical argument for reconfiguring democratic politics. One of the wider debates surrounding care ethics has been around the significance of care to justice, where they are often positioned in conflict. But rather than viewing justice as oppositional to care, in the ethics of care, relations between individuals and groups are the source of ethical enquiry. Care ethics does not reject justice, but instead focuses on individual as well as collective responsibilities to care as the sources of justice with implications beyond the interpersonal, blurring the distinctions between the private and the public (for example Barnes, 2006; Held, 2006; Tronto, 2013). This is relevant to the discussion in museums, since the participatory turn in which so much community engagement work has taken shape has focused on wider discussion of democratic politics. In her more recent work, Tronto (2013) adds a fifth dimension to her elements of care: *caring with*, from which the conditions for trust and solidarity in a public and global sense emerge over time through caring practices. 'Caring with' brings forward the broader significance of care as a practice of communal solidarity that is core to Tronto's vision of a caring democracy. This powerfully asserts that care is much more than a parochial concern: it applies to national, international and global relations. Political aspirations for a fairer and more just world should be based on a recognition of our reciprocal attachments to others and our responsibility to respond. At this scale, 'caring with' is a sociopolitical vision where the distribution of care becomes a public concern, with caring responsibilities held by individuals, the state and various institutions – potentially, then, the museum – working together to provide the foundation for democracy.

Throughout this book, I have taken a particular spatial lens to consider the community engagement work of the museum in terms of the spaces of its engagement work. Geographers, and particularly feminist geographers, have productively developed the ethics of care by giving close attention to encounters between people in place in order to outline the ways in which care (or its lack) produces its own geographies, from the highly place-specific to the global (Barnett, 2005; Lawson, 2007; McEwan and Goodman, 2010; Milligan and Wiles, 2010; Popke, 2006; Smith, 1998). Ideas from geography, in particular the sub-field known as 'geographies of care', have already informed much of the discussion in this book up to this point. Here, I turn to geography's particular interest in the connections between people, place and care to identify some additional avenues. First, is geographers' engagement with the notion of 'landscapes of care', which encompasses the spatial manifestations of care across interconnected scales including 'the institutional, the domestic, the familial, the community, the public, the voluntary and the private as well as transitions within and between them' (Milligan and Wiles, 2010: 738). This has broadened our understandings of where care takes place to include the museum (Morse and Munro, 2015). Second, is a thinking through proximity and distance in relation to care, both spatially and in social terms; what Milligan and Wiles (2010) frame as 'caring for' and 'caring about'. The former implies proximate and specific subjects, while the latter is a more general commitment with less concrete attachments. It refers to an emotional ontology '[that] might also include the generalized relational and affective elements of *being caring*' (Milligan and Wiles, 2010: 741 emphasis in original) across different sites and different scales. Milligan and Wiles use these terms to trouble the dynamics of distance/proximity as an exclusive dynamic. They argue that it is also possible to care at a distance (and conversely, not to care at an interpersonal level). These different scales of care can be used to further articulate the off-site outreach work of community engagement practitioners (see Chapter 6) as part of a more general commitment to caring for place. The geographies of care discussion of care ethics further draws our attention to the connections between the personal, local, national, global and even planetary scales, drawing in many of the concerns from feminist political science, such as the above-mentioned work of Joan Tronto. In this way, moving our attention from practice to ethics as moral philosophy and socio-political vision with a focus on place (local and global), we can begin to see more clearly the potential of care thinking to a whole manner of issues and topics. Having broadly scoped out the ethics of care here, I turn to the next question that opened this concluding chapter: what are the possibilities of care (and care ethics) for expanding the contemporary social role of the museum? I address this by first looking at how care might be positioned as the basis for organisational change, and next, as the basis for a more fundamental shift in our approach to the museum.

Care as the basis for organisational change

Applying care and care thinking to the museum does not necessarily require wholesale structural change in organisations, though it does require significant shifts. I have already argued for a contingent politics of practice that take places within the institutional arrangements of the museum, in acknowledgement of how these are shaped by the political rationality of the museum (Chapter 2). It should be noted that this is not an argument to return care as a 'programme of the same type' as described by Bennett (1998: 212), as yet another variant of the contemporary re-ordering of the relations of governmentality in the museum. I make this clear in the next section: care and care ethics open up other avenues for understanding the museum that merit to be approached and indeed assessed through other theoretical lenses. Neither is it the same as suggesting that care can simply be taken on board the existing power structures of the museum and comfortably accommodated. There is much institutional work to be done to ensure that practical arrangements are in place to support caring practice in organisations – above I have described some of the key actions that museum leaders can take to support practices of care in the museum. We must also recognise that care is a 'loaded' term in bureaucratic contexts, and there will likely be resistance to its use. So, we need to be precise about our ways of understanding care as I have advocated throughout this book, and this will depend on the circumstances of different museums (since care itself is specific). Most importantly, care thinking for organisational change requires a sophisticated, emotional and embodied understanding of the ideas and practices that underpin care and the wider ethics that shape care. To talk about care across different professional roles in the museum as I have done might seem to imply a focus on individuals, since caring practice and values imply caring persons. However, this is not the exact point I am striving for. Indeed, this would reproduce the tendencies already observed in the museum, where community engagement is considered as either so specialised that only certain persons with distinct dispositions can do it, or it is seen as so simplistic that it requires little skill, experience or talent, and anyone can do it. Both have for effect the devaluing of this work and its practice. A focus on caring relations and practices of care within an ethics of care leads us to think through recommendations and evaluations of care based on engaging in a caring relational practice, rather than only thinking of individual talent.

Judgements about relations are very different to judgements about individuals (Held, 2006: 53). While some people will probably have more talent for it than others, attentiveness and sensitivity (understanding the feelings of others) towards caring relations can be learned, and this is the key point. As Held makes clear, 'one person might intuitively know when another person is in distress, say, whereas another might have to elicit verbal responses to figure it out. But both would be trying to exercise sensitivity' (Held, 2006: 54). Care is both a skill and a disposition, a practice and a value and can be improved by greater knowledge and understanding: 'one becomes a better participant in a better practice of caring, the more the practice employs the most knowledgeable insights available and the better the participants understands these' (Held, 2006: 54). If we recognise the contexts of our interdependencies over thinking of care largely in terms of independent individuals and needs, then the strong focus on relations and practices of care cuts through the description of community engagement practice as an either/or. Community engagement work is work that requires talent, but its focus on caring relations can be learned and nurtured. At the same time, merely going through the motions, without any appropriate intentions of seeking another's wellbeing or responding to their feelings, would not fulfil the requirements of this practice. Across the museum, then, there is a potential for organisational learning to take place towards becoming a more care-ful institution, if we first recognise the value and skill of this work.

I do however want to bring forward two notes of caution. If we do acknowledge the dispositions of caring persons as important in the dynamics of caring (and in community engagement work in the museum, as I have argued here), we are faced with a problem: as feminist scholars make clear, care is unfairly distributed along the lines of class, gender and race, and it is still disproportionally the work of minority groups (Sevenhuijsen, 1998; Tronto, 1993). It is essentialised as 'women's work' and often devalued and underpaid, reflecting care work's lower status in society (England and Folbre, 1999; Halford and Leonard, 2006; Rose, 1993). Munro's (2013, 2014) research on museums alerts us to these concerns by highlighting the feminisation of community engagement work in her field site (a large civic museum in Scotland). Munro is clear on this point: 'ideas about women's innate ability to care can serve to devalue the hard work that goes into cultivating and maintaining relationships within community engagement settings' (2013: 56). There were other dynamics at play at my research site which I have argued had the effect of devaluing community engagement work and its practices along other lines (though I should note a 6/1 ratio of women to men in the team at the time of the research). However, we must take seriously this analysis: the museum workforce in the UK, and elsewhere in the cultural sector globally, is markedly gendered (Schwarzer, 2010). There are clearly important questions here: about the value of care/community engagement work in the museum, its association with femininity and its potential to be viewed as having intrinsic rewards that are set apart from the wider codes of professional museum work. Indeed, staff at TWAM often spoke about their work being rewarding because of its impact on participants. However, problems arise when the caring relations that enable that impact are not recognised as such, and when they are not recognised as a form of work. In Eilean Hooper-Greenhill's often-cited vision of the post-museum, she remarks that 'the post-museum will represent the feminisation of the museum. Rather than upholding the values of objectivity, rationality, order and distance, the post-museum will negotiate responsiveness, encourage mutually beneficial partnerships and celebrate diversity' (Hooper-Greenhill, 2000: 153). Hooper-Greenhill does not develop this description further, using this instead to highlight a more relational and collaborative future for museums. Placing care, as I do, as a central value and practice in the museum demands that we concern ourselves deeply with *all* the effects of the 'feminisation' of the museum, in particular its effects on those staff (mostly women, and often BAME staff in the context of 'diversity' posts) who take forward these responsibilities.

Another implication of placing care in the museum is the need to recognise emotions as pivotal to caring relationships. In this book, I have been concerned with the emotional life of community engagement workers. In Chapter 5, I spoke of the difficult emotions they experience in the context of sessions with care service-users and patients. There are further pressing questions here that are of relevance to scholars in this field as much as museum professionals. In particular, around the management of emotions and its potentially exploitative value to organisations (Hochschild, 1983; James, 1989); about the possible burden of this work on professionals and the mechanisms to prevent emotional burn-out (Munro, 2014); and about self-care in museum practice, particularly around work in health and wellbeing contexts. I have only begun this work here and hope that further research may follow responding to ideas in this book to explore how museum workers deal with emotions and emotional management. To embrace the potential of care and emotions as the basis for organisational change, we must also seriously engage with their problems as much as their potential.

The museum as a space of social care

The notion of the caring museum outlined in this book and further detailed across these final pages captures the essence of the practices and values of such an institution, and those working within it. In this final section, I want to outline a wider theory of *social care* and what it can offer global contemporary museum practice. I use the concept of 'social care' to connect and extend the discrete caring practices of community engagement workers with vulnerable adults and their work in the community to the wider social role of the museum. Social care is a collective term that includes a broad range of activities linked to our everyday lives and how we live together. In general policy terms, social care refers to the services and provision that are available from the health and social care sector, both private and public, and other support services. In national policy terms (in England for instance where this study is set), adult social care provides support to adults with physical and learning impairments or physical and mental illnesses. Social care is different to healthcare's focus on treatment and aftercare, as it centres on providing support for people to live with independence and dignity, enabling them to participate fully in society and protecting them in vulnerable situations (c.f. Department for Health and Social Care, 2012). Social care is delivered by a wide range of organisations and professionals, including social workers, occupational therapists, nurses and care workers and within families and communities.[2] Because it covers such a wide range of activities, social care is difficult to define precisely. My use of social care here is twofold. On a *practical level*, social care is best understood as a system of related services and informal support, including welfare, health, housing, benefits and leisure. On a more *collective level*, social care is society's work, in the sense of the ethics of care.[3] My understanding of the museum as a space of social care emerges across both levels.

The work of the Outreach team at TWAM developed from a longer history of community engagement work in the service, which I presented in Chapters 3 and 4. The strategic approach of the team (at the time of writing) was born out of a particular set of influences, specifically external opportunities for working in closer collaboration with health and social care partners, and internal ambitions to reconfigure the team along local public health priorities and more sustained partnerships to reinvigorate the civic function of the museum. As the team manager put it, this was about positioning the museum as 'a link in a chain' of social care provision (Chapter 5): using culture and museum objects to support other organisations and their clients in their goals of supporting wellbeing and independence. The work that began in 2012 is, at the time of writing, secured through core funding and additional investment in staff training that has ensured that the team is supported and further specialised in this area of work. The management of this community engagement work has moved away from the systemic 'bolt on', 'scatter-gun' and 'conveyor belt' nature of projects (see Chapter 4) to more sustained, long-term programmes. These include:

- **The Wellbeing Programme** – supporting people living with mental ill health and in recovery as well as activities for everyone's general wellbeing.
- **The Recovery Programme** – supporting people in recovery from addiction and those who are involved in the criminal justice system across Tyneside.
- **The Platinum Programme** – for people aged over 55 across Tyneside.
- **The Network Programme** – working with groups of people from across Tyneside to build new and develop existing community heritage and archive collections, exhibitions and events.

Developing from these programmes, the team is looking to establish referral pathways for external care organisations in a social prescribing model whereby General Practitioners, nurses, link workers and other primary care workers can refer people to local, non-clinical services. They are also looking towards supporting commissioning bids led by social care partners where the museum provides the cultural interventions that support an established service-user need (see Camic and Chatterjee, 2013; O'Neill, 2010).[4] In essence, the practices of Outreach are about transforming the museum into a community asset and a community-support system. The new programmes actively position the museum into new partnerships for delivering cultural activities with a range of services in the community, including mental health and wellbeing, older people services, place-based health commissioning and community support centres more generally. They situate the museum as a link in a chain of organisations with social use and value, with activities free for participants at the point of delivery. Through these sustained programmes of activity, the museum becomes a space of social care in the community: a cultural space in a system of related services and informal support in the local area. As a cultural space, 'support' is configured uniquely based on the museum's practices of care and their particular relational, material and affective registers. This puts the museum at the heart of the community; not necessarily at the centre, but as an important link in chain of community organisations. The museum as a space of social care becomes a vital institution in the landscapes of care in the community. At TWAM, this is a developing but not yet complete project, currently led by the Outreach team.

In reflecting on the potential transformation of the museum, I am talking about 'social care' rather than 'social work' and I do so explicitly to move this away from comparisons with social work as a registered profession (as per Silverman, 2010). This reflects a key concern of community engagement workers expressed during my research.[5] My aim in talking about social care is to articulate both the specific and wider areas of support in which a cultural institution like the museum can play a role. Social care describes a new form of museum practice within a wider system of support for people that is underpinned by cultural work. As key respondents in this research made clear, community engagement work in museums is not social work; it is specialised in its use of collections and culture, *and* in the caring practices and relations developed with service-users, patients and the professionals they are working alongside. It is intertwined in the wider area of social care, where its contribution is both complementary and unique. This work is also designed for reciprocal learning. At the same time as the museum teams learn from social care professionals how best to support their clients in the context of a museum session, the aim of the Outreach team is to explain to social care professionals how they can use museums and their resources to support their own activities independently. In this way, the ambition of the team at TWAM is to support a wider shift in the health and social care profession so that they more routinely consider how cultural spaces such as museums and the collections they hold can be used in their own formal care settings; how to care creatively. For instance, developing staff confidence to use object handling boxes to spark conversations in a care home or on a hospital ward, or developing the skills to lead a guided tour of an art gallery for a client group accessing a mental health service. As one member of the team surmised:

> It links us up, it makes it bigger. It's a much more generous way of working. It distributes power as well I think.

This short quote actually goes a long way in summarising how the museum as a space of social care is made in practice. First, it is about actively searching for links and opportunities to include the museum in the lives of communities and, in particular, linking into a wider system of community support organisations and the different spaces in which care takes place. Second, it makes the museum 'bigger' by locating it outside its walls and into the community, as a link in a chain of community organisations that are enjoyed by communities in all their diversity, and which supports mutuality and wellbeing. Third, it is a more 'generous' way of working, which pays attention to the aims and agendas of individuals and communities. It is more open and transparent about the museum's own objectives to find collaborative ways forward. Fourth, it addresses issues of power by focusing on bespoke programmes based on person-centred and collaborative approaches where the museum is more directly useful to communities and support organisations. In all these ways, the museum as a space of social care is underpinned by an ethics of care in practice.

The research with TWAM shows how small cohorts of museum professionals are redefining the social purpose of museums by looking at how museum objects, collections, buildings and their own professional skills can be re-oriented towards the practical and emotional support of their close communities. As a case study, it outlines the shape of the museum as a space of social care as a productive new framework for public museums that imagines their civil role in more expansive ways and constructs their community engagement activities within wider landscapes of care in their local communities. The work of the TWAM team is in many ways unique to the institution, its local contexts, the specific ambition of its Outreach team and current institutional support to ensure that this work is becoming embedded through core funding. Over the pages of this book, I have narrated the care-ful nature of this work at specific moments as well as highlighting practical and strategic approaches, marking out TWAM as a leading example of the museum as a space of social care in-the-making. At the same time, TWAM reflects a number of current trends in the UK museum sector over the last six or so years and further afield for example in Australia, Canada, Japan, New Zealand and Belgium, where the movement of 'museums in health' is growing, with regular programmes being developed for people with dementia and their carers, mental health service users, women with post-natal depression, stroke survivors and individuals living with chronic illness. Internationally, museums and galleries are beginning to play an active role in public health partnerships with hospitals and in other formal care settings, and in delivering activities with social care and third sector organisations. At the time of writing, some museums are beginning to explicitly reconfigure their organisational structures in a similar way to TWAM. The UK Culture, Health and Wellbeing Alliance website now offers a number of resources to support organisations interested in culture-led social prescribing.[6] Succesful examples include the Museums on Prescription project (Veall et al., 2017) and Cambridge Museums' Arts on Prescription initative.[7] Other organisations that are developing a social care model include the Whitworth Art Gallery in Manchester, which is working with other local cultural institutions to develop 'manifesto for care' for the city, bringing together care and creativity as central working values. The Royal Museum of Fine Arts of Belgium is thinking through an organisational approach to care across its different teams building on its public programme 'the healing power of art', which worked with palliative patients and their carers. Other museums such as Hull Museums are considering the issue of staff wellbeing as a key starting point to support wider wellbeing work with communities. The dedicated work around dementia friendly venues led by the Museum of Modern Art (MoMA) in New York and the National Museums Liverpool in the UK is supporting other organisations to develop their practices in this area. Through all these activities, museums are increasingly playing a part in strengthening their communities as new spaces of social care. The case study of TWAM is the first to explore this orientation of the museum in detail.

There is also a certain urgency to the museum as a space of social care. Across the world, we are faced with pressing and difficult policy challenges in relation to public health, changing demographics and deepening health inequalities. At the same time, these challenges are defined by the relentless extension of market relations into all arenas of public life, including social care, and the retrenchment of state-provided welfare. In the UK, local authorities are under pressure to continue to reduce expenditure after a decade of austerity measures, which have entailed cuts to social care services with impacts on the most vulnerable and marginalised groups (Levitas, 2012). While local health has been devolved, budget cuts have continued year by year. The ten-year review of the Marmot report on health equity in England was unequivocal about the adverse effects of the rolling back of the state on health:

> Britain has lost a decade. And it shows. Health, as measured by life expectancy, has stopped improving, and health inequalities are growing wider. Improvement in life expectancy, from the end of the 19th century on, started slowing dramatically in 2011. Now in parts of England,

particularly among women in deprived communities and the north, life expectancy has fallen, and the years people spend in poor health might even be increasing – a shocking development. (...) [In this report], we show that austerity has taken its toll in almost all of the areas identified by the Marmot review as important for health inequalities (...) There are more left-behind communities living in poor conditions with little reason for hope.

(Marmot, 2020: 1)

In relation to social care, central government has not had a national workforce strategy since 2009, so many of the key challenges are currently not being addressed (Department for Health and Social Care, 2018). For those in need of support, an added challenge with social care in the UK more generally is that services are not well integrated or coordinated, meaning that people often only get help when they reach a crisis point (Barker, 2014). An orientation to social care is befitting of the potential of museums to broaden and deepen their response to these challenges, in particular issues of health inequality. The work of the Outreach team at TWAM can be read as a direct response to these conditions, especially how they are unequally manifest in the north of England (Morse, 2020; Morse and Munro, 2015). As a wider response in the UK, the recent All Party Parliamentary Group for Arts, Health and Wellbeing report (2017) makes clear that arts and cultural organisations can develop responses within public health's current structures towards addressing some of these societal issues in partnership with formal care organisations. The key challenge they identify is one of leadership, and an essential need for culture change in conventional practice in both health/social care and the arts through cross-sector working and place-based solutions. Immediately, there are hard questions here, including whether museums are being called upon to step in with reduced funding to fill the gaps left by the active dismantling of the public infrastructures of care and welfare (Morse and Munro, 2015). I suggest that we need care ethics precisely to ask these questions over the allocations of public resources to respond to health inequalities and as an alternative way to assertively approach social policy issues, including the questions of welfare (c.f. Noddings, 2002). The notion of the museum as a space of social care outlines a proactive proposal that connects the civic role of the museum to the notion of welfare as a societal issue. The example of TWAM offers one set of concrete methods by which museums can play a part in responding to some of these challenges through collaboration, creativity and care.

Going back to Fisher and Tronto's early definition, care more broadly is 'a species activity that includes everything we do to maintain, continue, and repair our 'world' so that we can live in it as well as possible' (1990: 40). The museum as a space of social care is oriented towards this work of 're-pair' in localities and cities through productive collaborations with caring organisations. My example focused on a small number of health and social care support organisations, but there are many other possible types of caring collaborations, from food banks to citizen's advice bureaus and soup kitchens (Gurian, 2010). In Marrakech, Morocco, the Museum of African Contemporary Art Al Maaden (MACAAL) offers regular couscous dinners to local people, while across the world in Boston's Children's Museum, a series of family dinners were held in public housing estates. Death cafés, informal gathering where people can come and discuss death in order to help make sense of our finite lives, are now monthly events in Museums Sheffield, in the Wellcome Collection in London and in the National Museum Wales. Macmillan Cancer Support has a dedicated information space at the Gallery of Modern Art, Glasgow. The Queens Museum in New York has an established programme working directly to care and support immigrant communities, including language classes. In some ways, these ideas aren't entirely new, and this partnership practice exists in different ways across the world, though for many museums, it may still appear radical. From one perspective, it might be suggested that a definition for the museum that puts its community's interest first might simply be described as a 'community museum' or a 'community-centred museum' (as proposed, for example, by Gurian, 2002). However, such definitions would be imprecise. They miss out the heart of the matter and the heart of the practice. As I have argued throughout this book, there is a significant logic – the logic of care – that underpins how this 'type' of caring museum is made. This logic needs to be recognised and articulated as such to realise the capacities of the museum as a space of social care.

From another perspective, the suggestion might be that the museum as a space of social care is parochial, as it only focuses on small groups of individuals. Mark O'Neill has called into question investment in intense museum work with small groups of individuals without broader population-level approaches to engage 'mixed audiences in the core': 'if you don't have these strategic aims then small projects become ethically questionable' (O'Neill, 2010). I believe ideas of care and social care have much wider reach to help us think through questions of scale, sustainability and impact. As one way to establish this, in Chapter 6, I discussed how the longer-term practice of community engagement in the neighbourhood of the West End developed through a logic of care as an expression of a sense of 'caring about' the neighbourhood. This connects clearly to the unique potential of museums as community spaces. There are many examples globally of museums that are embedded in their local areas, with the Santa Cruz Museum of Art and History leading the way in terms of imagining museums as organisations of/for/by communities (Simon, 2016). Considering this vision through care thinking can consolidate this type of work. More broadly, the sense of 'caring about' broadens the orientations of the museum as a space of social care further to consider the everyday practices of taking care of place. Museums are memory institutions and therefore hold a distinct role in taking care of place and memory across time. To consider the role of the museum as a memory site explicitly through social care and care ethics opens up new areas for conversations, particularly in the contexts of those 'wounded cities' across the world (Till, 2012). In these contexts, the museum can play an important role in city-wide practices of care and repair. The inclusiveness of Tronto and Fisher's definition enables us to broaden our thinking about the museum's role and how it relates to the places in which we live. Thinking through care can reveal the many possibilities, all taking different directions, each specific to their localities, by which the museum might best be used to care for, maintain and repair our neighbourhoods, our cities, our environments and our worlds.

At its most basic and essential, social care is about a whole range of activity that supports people with a range of needs to live their fullest lives. Taken more broadly, social care is society's work. It is about how we live together. In placing the museum within a framework of social care, my hope is to expand its radical potential rather than to diminish it along what might be first taken as a more narrow set of concerns (health and wellbeing) that might on first appearance lie outside of the museum's purview. Crucial to this move, I believe, is the need to connect the intimate scales of caring relations and their felt qualities to a wider ethics of care as the foundation of a museum practice that seeks to engage communities and audiences. By foregrounding the public character of care, the ethics of care reframes the responsibilities of museums, their workers and those who research them. In talking about social care, what I want to offer is a concept for museum studies and practice that extends well beyond the particular arrangements described in this book (though to understand it and its potential, this specificity was where we needed to start); a concept that challenges us to care across wider circumstances and geographies to enable a theory of social care for the museum sector that has global pertinence.

Towards a care-ful museology

In these final pages, I want to sketch out a future direction for museological work informed by the idea of social care and the interdisciplinary literature on the ethics of care that we might, for now, call 'care-ful museology',[8] and which I leave in this book for future conversations.

Museums are caring places. Many of us who write and work in this field are excited about museums precisely because they take the notion of care so seriously. Care is already a feature of the museum, though primarily focused on objects and their stories. As I have argued throughout this book, the relational work of museums (such as community engagement in a UK context) is not fully discussed, it is largely hidden from published work, and it is often undervalued within professional settings. And yet, given the widespread importance of participation and more engaging modes of museum practice, it is a significant feature of contemporary museum practice. The aim of this book has been to show how care is unmistakable in the practices of museum professionals across a range of engagement work. The different contexts of care in the museum can, and should, be brought together through their mutual orientations, drawing together care for things, care for stories, care for heritage, care for the issue, care for people, care for the community, care for staff, care for the present and the past and care for the future, in an effort to build care-ful public museums.

Talking about care and social care is also an explicit critique of a careless society where the habit of caring for others is largely undervalued, where neoliberal ideologies present those in need of care as those who have failed in their responsibility (Tronto, 2013), where there is little solidarity between individuals in a land of strangers (Amin, 2012) and where the environment is discarded rather than looked after (Puig de la Bellacasa, 2017). The ethics of care is a counterpoint to an uncaring world as well as a proposal for a better society. It outlines how practice and people co-operate to repair our communities, our neighbourhoods and our world. A care-ful museology would develop through the application of care ethics to a range of museological questions and practice. It would fit within broader museum ethics as a discourse and area of practice, connecting to how museums are approaching questions of social responsibility (Marstine, 2011; Marstine et al., 2012). One argument put forward in this final chapter is the need to consider how care can be imagined through the notions of 'caring for' and 'caring about', where a common purpose might be shaped in a shared awareness and active performance of both modes – care for close communities and care for those at a distance. As is made clear in the literature, the ethics of care is not opposed to justice ethics, and neither is it parochial: it accounts for distant and unknown others and is oriented towards solidarity – 'caring with' – which 'requires that caring needs and the ways in which they are met [are] consistent with democratic commitments to justice, equality and freedom for all' (Tronto, 2013: 23). In the museum, the discussions about justice and rights have focused many of the calls for more participatory practice. Participatory approaches present radical challenges to the museum, and, as I have shown throughout this book, care thinking provides new conceptual avenues.[9] There is also growing awareness and recognition in museums across the world of their latent social agency, and in some places, more clearly formulated aspirations to bring about political, social and environmental change (Janes, 2009, 2010; Janes and Sandell, 2019). Scholarship and practice continue to articulate a powerful potential for an active and activist role for the museum to respond to social inequalities, injustices and crises in nature.

Care ethics provides an anchor to these discussions as well as a rich and powerful guide for developing new forms of museum practices and institutions. A call for care-ful museology is not a departure from the politically engaged work of the participatory turn, but rather it is an effort to build forward with these initiatives and to recognise the political in a variety of contexts. The museum as a space of social care is one such proposal for developing a care-ful museology in research and practice. This book marks only the beginning of this work.

Notes

1 An obvious omission perhaps is how care might apply to thinking about audiences. James Thompson (2015) begins some of this work in describing the 'aesthetic of care' for performance theatre, a different but I would argue connected arena of cultural engagement. There is also a well-developed field in Visitor Studies that attends to this topic more widely in terms of audience needs, motivations and meaning-making that could be reappraised through the idea of care.

2 This last group provides unpaid care to family members. It is estimated that there are nearly six million carers in England alone, more than the health and social care workforce put together (Beesley, 2006).

3 Here, I am referring to geographer Victoria Lawson who draws on the ethics of care to position care as society's work: 'care is society's work in the sense that care is absolutely central to our individual and collective survival' (Lawson, 2007: 5).

4 A recent study at TWAM evidences this role for the museum in terms of the psychological wellbeing impacts and other health-related outcomes for participants (Not So Grim Up North Research Team, 2018).

5 In the UK, the key difference is that social work is a qualified, registered profession with a protected title, which is distinct from social care, which is a largely unqualified and unregistered workforce. Social work exits mostly in the statutory sector and operates within legal frameworks.

6 https://www.culturehealthandwellbeing.org.uk/

7 https://www.museums.cam.ac.uk/blog/2018/10/15/arts-on-prescription/

8 I take the idea of care-ful museology from geography's engagement with the ethics of care and geographers' involvement in debates about rights and responsibilities to care, an area of research that is broadly referred to as 'care-ful geographies' (DeLyser, 2016; Lawson, 2007; McEwan and Goodman, 2010; Popke, 2006; Staeheli and Brown, 2003). Care-ful geographies focus on the questions of who gives care, where and why, as well as using care thinking more broadly to call attention to our collective responsibility towards unseen and distant others, for instance, in areas such as ethical consumption or climate change (McEwan and Goodman, 2010).

9 There is also potential in applying an ethics of care to the whole range of other museum questions, for instance, the display of human remains, unprovenanced material and engagements with painful heritage. These are questions I have not engaged with in the book, and since care ethics are always developed within grounded particularities and in practice, it requires specific cases to explore this further, which I hope other scholars and practitioners may see fit to develop.

References

Ahmed S (2012) *On Being Included: Racism and Diversity in Institutional Life.* Durham, NC and London: Duke University Press.

All-Party Parliamentary Group on Arts, Health and Wellbeing (2017) *Creative Health: The Arts for Health and Wellbeing.* Available at: http://www.artshealthandwellbeing.org.uk/appg-inquiry/ (accessed 31 July 2017).

Amin A (2012) *Land of Strangers.* Cambridge, MA: John Wiley & Sons.

Barker K (2014) *Commission on the Future of Health and Social care in England: A New Settlement for Health and Social Care.* London: King's Fund.

Barnes M (2006) *Caring and Social Justice.* Basingstoke: Palgrave MacMillan.

Barnett C (2005) Ways of relating: Hospitality and the acknowledgement of otherness. *Progress in Human Geography* 29(1): 5–21. doi: 10.1191/0309132505ph535oa.

Beesley L (2006) *Informal Care in England: Wanless Social Care Review.* London: King's Fund.

Bennett T (1995) *The Birth of the Museum: History, Theory, Politics.* London: Routledge.

Bennett T (1998) *Culture: A Reformer's Science.* London and Thousand Oaks, CA: Sage Publications.

Bondi L (2008) On the relational dynamics of caring: A psychotherapeutic approach to emotional and power dimensions of women's care work. *Gender, Place & Culture* 15(3): 249–265. doi: 10.1080/09663690801996262.

Camic PM and Chatterjee HJ (2013) Museums and art galleries as partners for public health interventions. *Perspectives in Public Health* 133(1): 66–71. doi: 10.1177/1757913912468523.

DeLyser D (2016) Careful work: Building public cultural geographies. *Social & Cultural Geography* 17(6): 808–812. doi: 10.1080/14649365.2016.1147061.

Department for Health and Social Care (2012) *National Framework for NHS Continuing Healthcare and NHS-funded Nursing Care.* Available at: https://www.gov.uk/government/publications/national-framework-for-nhs-continuing-healthcare-and-nhs-funded-nursing-care (accessed 15 July 2019)

Department for Health and Social Care (2018) *The Adult Social Care Workforce in England: Report by the Comptroller and Auditor General.* London: Department for Health and Social Care.

England P and Folbre N (1999) The cost of caring. *The ANNALS of the American Academy of Political and Social Science* 561(1): 39–51. doi: 10.1177/000271629956100103.

Falk JH and Dierking LD (1992) *The Museum Experience.* Washington, DC: Whalesback Books.

Fine M and Glendinning C (2005) Dependence, independence or inter-dependence? Revisiting the concepts of 'care' and 'dependency'. *Ageing and Society* 25(4): 601–621. doi: 10.1017/S0144686X05003600.

Fisher B and Tronto JC (1990) Toward a feminist theory of caring. In: Abel E and Nelson M (eds) *Circles of Care.* Albany, NY: SUNY Press, pp. 36–54.

Gilligan C (1982) *In a Different Voice: Psychological Theory and Women's Development.* Cambridge, MA and London: Harvard University Press.

Graham H (2012) Scaling governmentality. *Cultural Studies* 26(4): 565–592. doi: 10.1080/09502386.2012.679285.

Graham H, Mason R and Nayling N (2013) The personal is still political: Museums, participation and copyright. *Museum and Society* 11(1): 105–121.

Gurian EH (2002) Choosing among the options: An opinion about museum definitions. *Curator: The Museum Journal* 45(2): 75–88. doi: 10.1111/j.2151–6952.2002.tb01182.x.

Gurian EH (2010) Museum as soup kitchen. *Curator: The Museum Journal* 53(1): 71–85. doi: 10.1111/j.2151–6952.2009.00009.x.

Halford S and Leonard P (2006) *Negotiating Gendered Identities at Work : Place, Space and Time.* Basingstoke: Palgrave Macmillan.

Haylett C (2003) Class, care, and welfare reform: Reading meanings, talking feelings. *Environment and Planning A* 35(5): 799–814.

Held V (2006) *The Ethics of Care: Personal, Political, and Global.* New York: Oxford University Press.

Hochschild AR (1983) *The Managed Heart: Commercialization of Human Feeling.* 2nd edition. Berkeley: University of California Press.

Hooper-Greenhill E (2000) *Museums and the Interpretation of Visual Culture.* London: Routledge.

James N (1989) Emotional labour: Skill and work in the social regulation of feelings. *The Sociological Review* 37(1): 15–42. doi: 10.1111/j.1467–954X.1989.tb00019.x.

Janes RR (2009) *Museums in a Troubled World: Renewal, Irrelevance, or Collapse?* Abingdon and New York: Routledge.

Janes RR (2010) The mindful museum. *Curator: The Museum Journal* 53(3): 325–338. doi: 10.1111/j.2151–6952.2010.00032.x.

Janes RR and Sandell R (2007) Complexity and creativity in contemporary museum management. In: Sandell R and Janes RR (eds) *Museum Management and Marketing.* London and New York: Routledge, pp. 1–15.

Janes RR and Sandell R (eds) (2019) *Museum Activism.* 1st edition. Abingdon and New York: Routledge.

Kittay EF (1999) *Love's Labor: Essays on Women, Equality and Dependency.* New York: Routledge.

Kreps C (2003) Curatorship as social practice. *Curator: The Museum Journal* 46(3): 311–323. doi: 10.1111/j.2151–6952.2003.tb00097.x.

Kröger T (2009) Care research and disability studies: Nothing in common? *Critical Social Policy* 29(3): 398–420. doi: 10.1177/0261018309105177.

Lawson V (2007) Geographies of care and responsibility. *Annals of the Association of American Geographers* 97(1): 1–11. doi: 10.1111/j.1467–8306.2007.00520.x.

Levitas R (2012) The Just's Umbrella : Austerity and the Big Society in Coalition policy and beyond. *Critical Social Policy* 32(3): 320–342. doi: 10.1177/0261018312444408.

Lynch BT (2011a) Collaboration, contestation and creative conflict: On the efficacy of museum/community partnerships. In: Marstine J (ed.) *The Routledge Companion to Museum Ethics: Redefining Ethics for the Twenty-First Century Museum.* London: Routledge, pp. 146–164.

Lynch BT (2011b) '*Whose Cake Is It Anyway?' A Collaborative Investigation Into Engagement and Participation in 12 Museums and Galleries in the UK.* London: Paul Hamlyn Foundation.

Marmot M (2020) Health equity in England: The Marmot review 10 years on. *BMJ* 368: 1–4.

Marstine J (ed.) (2011) *The Routledge Companion to Museum Ethics: Redefining Ethics for the Twenty-First Century Museum.* London: Routledge.

Marstine J, Bauer AA and Haines C (eds) (2012) *New Directions in Museum Ethics.* London: Routledge.

McEwan C and Goodman MK (2010) Place geography and the ethics of care: Introductory remarks on the geographies of ethics, responsibility and care. *Ethics, Place & Environment* 13(2): 103–112. doi: 10.1080/13668791003778602.

Milligan C and Wiles J (2010) Landscapes of care. *Progress in Human Geography* 34(6): 736–754. doi: 10.1177/0309132510364556.

Mol A (2010) *The Logic of Care: Health and the Problem of Patient Choice.* Abingdon: Routledge.

Mol A, Moser I and Pols J (eds) (2010) *Care in Practice: On Tinkering in Clinics, Homes and Farms.* Bielefeld: Transcript.

Morse N (2020) The social role of the museum: From social inclusion to health and wellbeing. In: Glenn H and O'Neill M (eds) *Connecting Museums.* London: Routledge, pp. 48–65.

Morse N and Munro E (2015) Museums' community engagement schemes, austerity and practices of care in two local museum services. *Social & Cultural Geography* 19(3): 357–378. Online First. doi: 10.1080/14649365.2015.1089583.

Munro E (2013) 'People just need to feel important, like someone is listening': Recognising museums' community engagement programmes as spaces of care. *Geoforum* 48: 54–62. doi: 10.1016/j.geoforum.2013.04.008.

Munro E (2014) Doing emotion work in museums: Reconceptualising the role of community engagement practitioners. *Museum and Society* 12(1): 44–60.

Noddings N (1984) *Caring, a Feminine Approach to Ethics & Moral Education.* Berkeley: University of California Press.

Noddings N (2002) *Starting at Home: Caring and Social Policy.* Berkeley: University of California Press.

Not So Grim Up North Research Team (2018) *Not So Grim Up North: Investigating the Health and Wellbeing Impacts of Museum and Gallery Activites for People Living with Dementia, Stroke Survivors, and Mental Health Service-Users.* Available at: http://www.healthandculture.org.uk/not-so-grim-up-north/research-publications/ (accessed 1 August 2019).

O'Neill M (2010) Cultural attendance and public mental health - From research to practice. *Journal of Public Mental Health* 9(4): 22–29. doi: 10.5042/jpmh.2010.0700.

Parr H, Philo C and Burns N (2004) Social geographies of rural mental health: experiencing inclusions and exclusions. *Transactions of the Institute of British Geographers* 29(4): 401–419. doi: 10.1111/j.0020-2754.2004.00138.x.

Parry R, Page R and Moseley A (2018) On a new threshold. In: Parry R, Page R and Moseley A (eds) *Museum Thresholds: The Design and Media of Arrival.* Florence: Routledge, pp. 1–10.

Popke J (2006) Geography and ethics: Everyday mediations through care and consumption. *Progress in Human Geography* 30(4): 504–512. doi: 10.1191/0309132506ph622pr

Puig de la Bellacasa M (2017) *Matters of Care: Speculative Ethics in More Than Human Worlds.* Minneapolis: University of Minnesota Press.

Rose G (1993) *Feminism and Geography: The Limits of Geographical Knowledge.* Cambridge, MA: Polity Press.

Ruddick S (1998) Care as labor and relationship. In: Haber JG and Halfon MS (eds) *Norms and Values: Essays on the Work of Virginia Held.* Lanham, MD: Rowman & Littlefield, pp. 3–14.

Schwarzer M (2010) Women in the temple: Gender and leadership in museums. In: Levin AK (ed.) *Gender, Sexuality, and Museums: A Routledge Reader.* London: Routledge, pp. 16–28.

Sevenhuijsen S (1998) *Citizenship and the Ethics of Care: Feminist Considerations on Justice, Morality and Politics.* London: Routledge.

Sevenhuijsen S (2000) Caring in the third way: The relation between obligation, responsibility and care in Third Way discourse. *Critical Social Policy* 20(1): 5–37. doi: 10.1177/026101830002000102.

Sevenhuijsen S (2003) The place of care: The relevance of the feminist ethic of care for social policy. *Feminist Theory* 4: 179–197. doi: 10.1177/14647001030042006.

Silverman LH (2010) *The Social Work of Museums.* New York: Routledge.

Simon N (2016) *The Art of Relevance.* Museum 2.0.

Slote M (2007) *The Ethics of Care and Empathy.* Abingdon: Routledge.

Smith DM (1998) How far should we care? On the spatial scope of beneficence. *Progress in Human Geography* 22: 15–38. doi: 10.1191/030913298670636601.

Staeheli LA and Brown M (2003) Guest editorial: Where has welfare gone? Introductory remarks on the geographies of care and welfare. *Environment and Planning A* 35(5): 771–777. doi: 10.1068/a35132.

Thompson J (2015) Towards an aesthetics of care. *Research in Drama Education: The Journal of Applied Theatre and Performance* 20(4): 430–441.

Till KE (2012) Wounded cities: Memory-work and a place-based ethics of care. *Political Geography* 1(31): 3–14. doi: 10.1016/j.polgeo.2011.10.008.

Tronto JC (1993) *Moral Boundaries: A Political Argument for an Ethic of Care.* New York and London: Routledge.

Tronto JC (1995) Care as a basis for radical political judgments. *Hypatia* 10(2): 141–149. doi: 10.1111/j.1527–2001.1995.tb01376.x.

Tronto JC (2010) Creating caring institutions: Politics, plurality, and purpose. *Ethics and Social Welfare* 4(2): 158–171. doi: 10.1080/17496535.2010.484259.

Tronto JC (2013) *Caring Democracy: Markets, Equality, and Justice.* New York: NYU Press.

von Krogh G (1998) Care in knowledge creation. *California Management Review* 40(3): 133–153.

Veall, D et al. (2017). *Museums on Prescription: a guide to working with older people.* London: Arts and Humanities Research Council.

Watson N, McKie L, Hughes B, et al. (2004) (Inter)dependence, needs and care: The potential for disability and feminist theorists to develop an emancipatory model. *Sociology* 38: 331–350.

Index

Printed in the United States
By Bookmasters